D1370730

# GRIEF COUNSELING AND
# SUDDEN DEATH

# GRIEF COUNSELING AND SUDDEN DEATH

## A Manual and Guide

*By*

**POLLY DOYLE, M.A.**
*Coordinator, Grief Counseling Program,*
*Contra Costa County Crisis and Sucide Intervention Center*

*1980*

**CHARLES C THOMAS • PUBLISHER**
*Springfield • Illinois • U.S.A.*

*Published and Distributed Throughout the World by*
CHARLES C THOMAS • PUBLISHER
BANNERSTONE HOUSE
301-327 East Lawrence Avenue, Springfield, Illinois, U.S.A.

© *1980 by* CHARLES C THOMAS • PUBLISHER
ISBN 0-398-04060-5
Library of Congress Catalog Card Number: 80-245

*With* THOMAS BOOKS *careful attention is given to all details of manufacturing and design. It is the Publisher's desire to present books that are satisfactory as to their physical qualities and artistic possibilities and appropriate for their particular use.* THOMAS BOOKS *will be true to those laws of quality that assure a good name and good will.*

*Printed in the United States of America*
*N-11*

**Library of Congress Cataloging in Publication Data**

Doyle, Polly
    Grief counseling and sudden death.

    Bibliography: p.
    Includes index.
    1. Sudden death—Psychological aspects. 2. Bereavement—Psychological aspects. 3. Counseling—Study and teaching. 4. Mental health services—California. I. Title. [DNLM: 1. Attitudes to death. 2. Counseling. 3. Grief. 4. Death, Sudden. BF575.G7 D754g]
BF789.D4D7                          155.9'37                          80-245
ISBN 0-398-04060-5

# CONTRIBUTORS

**WILLIAM M. BOGART, M.D.**, *Chief Medical Examiner, Coroner's Unit, Contra Costa County, Martinez, California*

**NORMAN L. CARDEN, M.D.**, *Psychiatrist and Jungian Analyst, Walnut Creek, California*

**HOWARD B. LIEBGOLD, M.D.**, *Medical Director, Kaiser Foundation Rehabilitation Center, Vallejo, California*

**ALAN LUNDBERG, M.D.**, *Department of Pediatrics, Kaiser-Permanente Medical Center, Sacramento, California*

**LIEUTENANT AL MOORE**, *Unit Commander, Coroner's Unit, Contra Costa County, Martinez, California*

**ERNEST F. PECCI, M.D.**, *Psychiatrist and Director, Institute of Integrative Therapy, Orinda, California*

**JOHN W. SCHIEFFELIN, M.D.**, *Pediatrics Department, Kaiser-Permanente Medical Center, Walnut Creek, California*

**TONY 1277**, *Samaritans, Professional writer and broadcaster, Independent Broadcasting Authority, London, England*

# PREFACE

SINCE THE beginning of time mankind has died from natural causes or perished in environmental accidents or at the hand of another. *Mandi musti mati*—mankind must die—has been recognized, always reluctantly, as man's fate. Early artifacts, drawings, and later writings have portrayed the fallen hunter, the fallen warrior, and how his survivors prepared his burial. How the survivors felt about these events has also received varied treatment across the world. Whether in the Egyptian Book of the Dead, biblical literature portraying the grief of Job, the psalms and liturgies of death, or the ceremonies of different tribes and clans, the lamentations of the bereft throughout the world have been the object of considerable attention by artists, writers, and especially their medicine men, shamans, priests, clergy.

For centuries this is how the Takwena tribe in Africa has introduced news of death among themselves, saying with the rich instinctive symbolism of their speech: "Get ready to weep tears of sorrow as bright as the brightest beads, and like the bright beads you string to wear round your throat at the burial, gather your tears and string them on a thread of your memory to wear round your heart, or its shattered fragments will never come whole again." (Van der Post, *Flamingo Feather,* 1955) .

This book is an effort to describe how a group of nonprofessionals—unpaid volunteers—banded together in order to bring help and comfort to the survivors of sudden death in an entire county in California. This grief work has been not only a challenge but a rewarding experience both for the persons they served and for the volunteers themselves. It is hoped that you readers will be encouraged and motivated by the account of this project to do something similar in your communities.

Although this book may be of primary interest to health and

medical professionals, social scientists and clergy, an effort has been made to eliminate as much professional terminology as possible. It is my hope that the book will be of interest to many general readers. In a period of social activism, I believe it will be.

In counseling the bereaved, it is not enough to know *how* to do it. It is also of primary importance to know *why* we do it. For us the original *why* was bound up in the traditional commitment of our Crisis Center to the idea of prevention and intervention in cases of suicide. The extension of these concepts of prevention and intervention into the realm of postvention led us into mental health concepts that helped "flesh out" what had previously been an incomplete, unfinished process involving persons in a suicidal crisis. The new dimension of postvention led to far-reaching aspects of dealing with crisis that seemed to augment and round out the limited work we had originally set out to do on a Hot Line service.

These new mental health aspects forced us to raise our sights to consider the problem of a cooperative arrangement between our agency and the County Coroner's Unit as a source for providing the clients for our work and the information and community support essential for effective counseling. This cooperative arrangement was a prime factor in the development and success of the program.

This book presents the basic material that needs to be known in order to have a broad understanding of the essential information available in the area of grief and bereavement. In addition, it deals with the specifics of how to select persons to do grief work, how to train them, and how to counsel the bereaved.

The book is divided into four parts. Section I is concerned with providing theoretical material concerning grief and bereavement. Presentations in the areas of stress and depression are singled out from a number of negative emotions that beset the bereaved. These two topics are given special attention since they are the two conditions that are most commonly encountered by anyone recently bereaved.

Section II is concerned with cardiovascular fatalities, the sudden infant death syndrome, accidental deaths, industrial accidents, and the dynamics of suicide—its epidemiology, how to assess suicide potentiality and lethality, and suicide among the young and the elderly.

Section III is concerned with how to counsel the bereaved survivors of sudden death, the anniversary interview, the Coroner's Unit, the autopsy, and funerals. Illustrations of actual cases drawn from our files are included throughout the entire text.

Section IV describes how this first-of-its-kind program was started by the Contra Costa County Crisis and Suicide Intervention Service, located in Walnut Creek, California. Included in this section are the specifics of how these grief counselors are selected and trained, and how counselors can take care of themselves in order to be available for long periods of time for this arduous and time-consuming task.

This book does not include any discussion of the general topics of either death and dying or of religion. These subjects have been very thoroughly covered by persons well and eminently qualified in their fields. I have listed these writers and their books by including them in the partially annotated bibliography and selected readings. The Appendices contain materials used in the training classes and samples of report forms used in grief counseling.

Throughout this book there is ample evidence that grief and bereavement in suicide or other forms of sudden death are not phenomena of the male only. Both sexes are affected. In order to eliminate the repetitive he/she, him/her in these circumstances I have chosen to use the pronoun "he," which must also be understood to include the pronoun "she." The same caveat applies to other groups referred to, such as counselors, next-of-kin, etc.

POLLY DOYLE
*Walnut Creek, California*

# ACKNOWLEDGMENTS

GRIEF COUNSELING by a public or private agency, for maximum effectiveness, involves a delicate relationship between the agency and the office and personnel of the Coroner's Office. The establishment and maintenance of an effective interagency relationship is no less important and no less difficult than the counseling work itself. In addition to the need for personal flexibility in attitudes and tangible expressions of caring and compassion for the grieving clients, there must also be a thorough understanding of the laws, regulations, and related administrative practices of the cooperating agency. The counseling agency must adapt its own practices and its own records to those of the Coroner's Office. Access to the records of the Coroner's Office is not sufficient for a systematic and effective grief counseling program. Such a program depends on mutual trust and respect between the cooperating agencies. Each party to the arrangement must find tangible and demonstrable benefits from the arrangement.

Sheriff-Coroner Harry D. Ramsey endorsed the idea of our program. We have had the privilege and pleasure of working with two Unit Commanders of the Coroner's Office. Lt. Will Cullison was in charge when the program was inaugurated and served on the Board of Trustees of the Crisis Center. Lt. Al Moore, who succeeded Lt. Cullison, endorsed the expansion of the counseling service to include the survivors of all traumatic deaths in the county that are coroner's cases; he also helped initiate and prepare counselors for their role in grief counseling in the event of any disaster in our county. Lt. Moore has also served on our Board of Trustees.

The distillation of our experience cannot be limited to the development of the material used in the formal training classes.

Our volunteer counselors talk to hundreds more grieving persons than are ordinarily seen in any kind of individual professional setting. In order to do such work week in and week out requires that volunteers must develop *within themselves* qualities that surpass a knowledge of the theory and practice of counseling the bereaved. The grief counselors of our Crisis Center who have sought out this work and trained for it have developed these qualities. Without their dedication, our program, our clients, and this book could not have progressed. There is no praise sufficient to express my appreciation and gratitude to this stalwart group. It is their strengths, their vicissitudes, trials, and experiences that must be understood as being the essential basis for any "distillation process" attempted here.

The persons who received our assistance have also shaped our experience. These bereaved persons who have shared with us their innermost thoughts and feelings have taught us many things not encountered in books, tapes, or classes. Delving into the depths of our clients' losses, sharing their grief, being privy to their most intimate selves have not been shadowy occupations or morbid experiences. They have provided a new growth for us also, and for this I am grateful.

All of these relationships have come together to produce what I believe is a unique, challenging, and tremendously effective program for bringing mental health techniques to bear on an age-old concern for those who survive a sudden death.

A program of this kind and an explanation of the details of its operation cannot be undertaken without a sense of great indebtedness to many persons. A succession of Boards of Trustees for our agency encouraged the initiation of the program and then the alteration of its format and scope as experience and confidence were gained. Their support, encouragement, and formal approval were important factors in the on-going health of this project.

Professor Richard Seiden of the School of Public Health, University of California, Berkeley, was the first to encourage me to put it all down on paper in order to let other persons and agencies know "what it is you are doing." Thanks to his encouragement, I have written and presented papers at several annual meetings of the American Association of Suicidology; a meeting of the International Congress of Crisis and Suicide Prevention in Jerusalem; and to the Samaritans of England, Scotland, Wales, and Ireland meeting at York University, England.

My indebtedness to Ernest F. Pecci, M.D., Director of the Institute for Integrative Therapy, Orinda, is one that can never be adequately acknowledged. As a friend, teacher, and mentor he has encouraged me to expand my own self-awareness and to apply what I have learned to helping others expand theirs. I have adapted many aspects of his teaching to the area of grief counseling; those who know his work will recognize this effort. I hope he will be pleased with the uses to which I have put some of his teaching materials.

I am indebted to Jerome A. Motto, M.D., of Langley Porter Neurological Institute, University of California Medical School, San Francisco, and to Thomas C. Welu, Ph.D., M.P.H., of the University of Texas Medical School, Houston, for the generosity of their time and effort in reading the first draft of this book. Their criticism and advice were timely and valuable. Any errors of fact or omission are mine, not theirs.

I am grateful to the persons who have made contributions to this book: Drs. William M. Bogart, Norman L. Carden, Howard B. Liebgold, Alan Lundberg, Ernest F. Pecci, and John W. Schieffelin; Lt. Al Moore and Tony 1277.

I am indebted to the L. J. and Mary C. Skaggs Foundation for the financial support given our agency which enabled me to prepare the first version of this work.

And last, but not least, I wish to thank my husband, Len, for his help and support.

# CONTENTS

## SECTION IV
## ORGANIZATION AND TRAINING

# GRIEF COUNSELING AND
# SUDDEN DEATH

## Section I

# UNDERSTANDING GRIEF

### Introduction

THE PURPOSE of Section I is to provide the theoretical background for an understanding of grief among adults and children. Opinions and treatment of this topic by various writers are discussed and cited in the references. Summaries of actual cases illustrate this presentation of material. The combination of theory and case summaries provides the general reader with (1) an awareness of mental health, social and personal problems that arise during grief, (2) an understanding of the theoretical material dealing with grief, and (3) actual cases that illustrate the material being presented.

The first two chapters of this section deal with an understanding of grief in adults and children. Two topics, stress and depression, are singled out in Chapters 3 and 4 because of the frequency with which they arise in grief following most deaths, whether sudden or not. By giving special emphasis to these common components of grief it is hoped that the reader will become especially competent in recognizing stress and depression; in acknowledging that they occur often and are normal, to-be-expected reactions to a death; and will learn how to help the bereaved cope with these problems.

*Chapter 1*

# UNDERSTANDING GRIEF

## WHAT IS GRIEF?

IT IS NOT at all uncommon to learn from a roomful of adults that only a few understand what grief is. They have read and observed that some people "are real sad" when there is a death in the family, but they seem to have little idea of what is "going on" with them. Moreover, there is a sense of considerable discomfort among those in the room. What is causing this restlessness: the avoidance of another's gaze, the eagerness to get on to another topic? A bit more probing and the secret is out. It is death that is being avoided as a topic of discussion. At the time of the death of another we are drawn inevitably to an awareness of our own mortality, our own vulnerability, Often one's first confrontation with this vulnerability leads only to confusion and bewilderment. When this occurs it helps to have someone to talk to.

We can all benefit personally by learning something about what happens at the time of death of one close to us. At the very least we can learn how to promote our own well-being at that time. We should also anticipate and plan for our own regrowth and our own potential for growth during this time of crisis.

Our culture encourages preparation for marriage, parenthood, entrance to school, jobs and professions, retirement, and even for hospital experiences. But there is uncertainty and some uneasiness when we explore the emotions that arise from a death and a strong tendency to avoid the subject. It is important to dispel our ignorance and fear connected with death and grief. But ignorance and fear are not easily affected by rational learning, for their roots lie in our subconsciousness and are often expressed

5

with some degree of irrationality. Some of these irrational responses tie in with early childhood reactions to loss and abandonment, which are revived whenever we experience loss in later
life. The insights of psychology have helped us bridge the link
between emotional processes in infancy and later life situations in
which we feel helpless and dependent, such as illness, old age,
and dying (Erikson, 1963, Bowlby, 1961, and Parkes, 1965).

What do we mean when we speak of grief and bereavement?
Do these words mean the same thing? What is the difference? It
is confusing, for one author speaks of bereavement and another
speaks of grief. In our society we hear of a family "being in
mourning," of a family being "bereaved," of a person being
"grief-stricken." According to Switzer (1970), bereavement is the
"actual state of deprivation or loss and grief . . . is the response
of emotional pain to the deprivation." Since pain and anguish
are both present—sometimes subtly, sometimes obviously—the
word *grief* will be used in most instances in this book. In the
context of grief counseling, our attention is focused on helping
the bereaved person become aware of his pain, to experience it,
and by working through the pain to pass ultimately through the
grief. This process will be discussed fully in Chapter 11 on How
to Counsel the Bereaved.

We think of grief as an abiding and pervasive sense of sadness
that overwhelms us when we are separated from a person, place,
or object important to our emotional life. Such a definition
serves well in our counseling whether the grief is caused by the
death of a loved one or by the loss or separation from a place or
object.

## LOSS AND SEPARATION

We shall in most instances be referring to grief that is the
result of a death of a loved one. But it is well to begin first by
speaking of other kinds and forms of grief. In the process of growing up, of maturing, we are all subject to innumerable losses and
separations. This begins when we are separated first from the
womb, then from the breast, then subject to longer and longer
periods of time away from our mother. Erikson (1963) points to
the time we learn to tolerate separation from our mother as a

critical step in the entire process of learning to develop basic trust. It is this basic trust that we have to rely upon to carry us through the despair of loss and abandonment, which are revived whenever loss is experienced in later life.

From infancy on we are all involved in the process of learning how to cope with our separations. The infant can only cry when he needs food, a change, or experiences dis-ease of any kind. He associates mother with the comforts that follow his cries of distress and identifies with that mother because it is her presence that becomes meaningful and satisfying to him. When these cries do not bring her, the infant becomes more and more distressed, feeling abandoned, and may cry until exhausted at this failure of the mother to appear. When she does appear, he looks earnestly at her, watching her facial expression, listening intently to her sounds, aware of her body language. By imitating sounds similar to those made by the mother, the infant even begins the process that ultimately ends in the miraculous use of language. In this early stage the infant is learning *basic trust* of the parent— the trust that says, "she will return to comfort me." This basic trust has to be stretched and stretched to accommodate longer and longer intervals between the first expression of a need for comfort and the appearance of the parent. His survival depends upon her return, so the child must learn that she will, indeed, appear.

Anyone who has ever played peek-a-boo with a baby knows how the game goes. The infant shows distress and anxiety when the parent covers his face with his hands. When the hands are removed, the child bursts into an enchanting smile of relief that the parent who had "disappeared" has now "appeared" once more. Such a game underscores this basic need of the infant for the parent and helps him handle a short-term separation. As basic trust is established, long– and short-term separations are less anxiety-ridden. The child moves gradually into acceptance and can move on to the next stage of infancy. In later life, however, some of these same anxiety patterns are felt and relived when other separations are experienced. The fear that a person or object of his emotional attention may not appear in time to "save" him can recreate the panic felt earlier as a child.

We are continually subjected to unplanned or unwanted

losses and separations. Each person can draw up a list of such experiences, but no two persons will draw up the same list. *We have all experienced many different kinds of losses and will continue to experience them throughout our lifetime.*

When we undergo a violent loss that does not result in a death, we seldom identify such experiences as an appropriate time for grief. That such a need does exist is apparent from the writings on grief by Parkes, 1965; Pincus, 1974; Switzer, 1970; Bowlby, 1969, and Schoenberg, 1970. What are some of these losses and separations that result in grieving? Pincus gives us a list of a few obvious ones; you will think of many more. The illustrations are from our files.

**1. Little children who feel rejected in their family circle.** There are little children who feel apart from the rest of the family. Sometimes this is because of the separation in years from the other children; more often it is because of their belief that they are not loved or not loved as much as other children in the family. Some children become scapegoats for the entire family —the butt of every joke, the object of derision, and generally the one who is most severely punished. Such children feel themselves to be different—outsiders, unloved, unjustly punished. They are filled with distrust, fear, or envy. They often withdraw more and more into seclusion in order to deflect some of the blows, real or imagined.

> Kerwin was the youngest in a family of seven children. As a child he was frail and sickly and unable to participate in the rough-and-tumble of the rest of the children. He was alone a great deal, and no one seemed to pay much attention to him except to punish him. He was a chronic bedwetter. For this he was punished at home and rebuked by his brothers. When he started to school, he was set apart there also. His teacher complained that he was dirty and smelly at school; she gave him a seat in the rear of the classroom that further removed him from his classmates. Of course, neither the teacher's nor the parents' scoldings, rebukes, or punishments had any effect on Kerwin. He did poorly in school, and cruel comparisons were drawn between him and his brothers. Life became very grim for him. He was alone at home, ostracized at school; without friends, family, playmates. Both Kerwin and his family muddled along this way until he was nine. At nine Kerwin hanged himself.

**2. Sudden, unwanted divorces, military separations, imprisonment, and placement of children in foster homes.** If I single out divorce for discussion, it is because it and the loss of a pet are the two most frequent causes of grief in children, according to our experience. The grief that accompanies the dissolution of a marriage is often called the result of "a death without a body." It is not uncommon for dissolutions to take a long time to heal. The parties to the dissolution may well benefit in both *self-actualization* and *regrowth,* but those benefits come sometimes after long and cruel months of despair. Moreover, the children are often the innocent victims of divorce. While the parents are seeking growth and self-actualization, the children are feeling loss, abandonment, and pain. Consequently, all the old feelings of insecurity during infancy rise up again.

Phillip was an illegitimate child who was placed in an orphanage soon after birth. There he never received the cuddling, comfort or attention given the newborn in a family. By the time he was seven months old, he was sick, underweight, unresponsive, and withdrawn. Fearing that he might die in the institution, the administration placed him in a foster home where he soon regained his weight and began to pick up muscle tone. He took an interest in the things around him and began to identify with his new "mother."

Because of some administrative foul-up, the child was removed from this home where the parents wished to adopt him and he was placed in a series of other foster homes until the age of seven. During this time Phillip reverted to the depressed, unsure child he had been at the age of seven months. Because of his physical weaknesses he was the object of derision in home after home and became the scapegoat for the other sturdier children. He lost confidence in himself and was in doubt about how far he could trust those around him. He failed again and again in school but never became quarrelsome or aggressive.

When Phillip was seven years old, the original foster family took legal action to regain and adopt him. When they succeeded, he responded to their love, affection, and patience. They gave him room to develop his talents and skills which became bulwarks for his self-image. He excelled in a number of crafts, did well in school and college, and embarked upon a satisfying and rewarding job. He married and had children. But he became dependent upon his wife and children for things he could do for himself. They began to view him as a burden to them. After many physical examinations that showed him to be in excellent health, the family embarked on family counseling. Phillip was always agreeable to suggestions, but he could never follow through with them. When the marriage broke up and he realized that his support system had failed, Phillip suicided.

**3. Sudden changes in location when friends and relatives are left behind.** This is a very common source of family crisis. The average length of residential occupancy in our county is three years. We are all aware of the numerous arrivings and departings that occur wherever we live because of job transfers, retirement, and relocation when the "opportunity" seems to beckon us to move on. These persons leave behind relatives and friends, schools, churches, and the climate and geography they have become accustomed to.

When Grace's husband died suddenly, neither she nor her grown children felt any grief. Indeed, the fact that they felt they "weren't feeling the way we ought to" caused them considerable bewilderment. They also sensed that to be without the feelings of grief expected by their neighbors somehow set them apart. Grace said she and her children did not have any friends; they just "knew" a large number of people. Later on, Grace mentioned that she never seemed to "get acquainted with people and the children are the same way." Little by little the story unfolded.

The family had moved every two years during twenty-five years of marriage. They never lived anywhere long enough for them to get settled and feel a sense of belonging. Her husband had been transferred time after time, from one area of the country to another. Since she never felt comfortable or at home anywhere, she sought the sense of "home" among her children and kept them close to her. Both she and the children never felt very close to her husband for he was never home except on weekends. When he died he was hardly missed.

Grace seemed to want to find out why she felt no sadness at his death, but she felt she had no time for counseling. She was already packing for a move across the country to where she thought she might like to live.

**4. Homesickness.** The immigrant grieves in his new land, hungry for the sights, sounds, and smells of his familiar home far away. This same sense of incompleteness affects children in their first visit away from home or at summer camp, students in dormitories, young men in boot camp, and unwed mothers who have released their babies for adoption. These persons experience yearning for what they have left behind, a sadness for the old familiar faces, places, and food. They long to be once again in the warm circle of family and loved ones.

Robbie came from a middle-class family that was warm and loving. His parents encouraged self-confidence and the development of individual talents. Robbie left for boot camp with a feeling of confidence and a sense of high adventure for an undertaking that had elements of both compliance with society's requirements and a sense of developing responsibilities. Little by little Robbie seemed to lose his sense of self. In boot camp his head was almost shaved, he had little time to himself, and he was continually exhausted from the numerous efforts to "get him in condition." He became homesick. The family was concerned about the numerous telephone calls and letters indicating an apparent inability to cope with the new surroundings. Being a church related family, they encouraged him to seek the counsel of the chaplain. They felt this suggestion had been fruitful because his calls and letters diminished in number and length.

Several weeks later he called from a location away from the base. He was crying and said he must come home, that he could not talk openly to them by phone. His efforts to seek help from the chaplain had led to a homosexual encounter. Robbie did not want to see the chaplain again but was fearful to state his reasons for fear it would affect his record at camp. In short, he was desperate, anxious, and fearful about the outcome of his efforts to seek comfort for his homesickness.

At this point his parents called for help. A long session with them encouraged them to counsel their son to drop his appointment with the chaplain. In addition, they gave their son help and knowledge that they were supporting him in these efforts. They planted the seeds of hope that this kind of harrassment would end when the boot camp term was over. They encouraged him to hang on until the end of training when he had home leave. He returned home during this leave and found his family awaiting him with love and caring. They had an appointment for him to see a professional who could help him think through and get into perspective what had happened to him.

**5. Lost jobs, lost pets, and lost reputations.** Such losses engulf one in feelings of inadequacy and regrets. Vague statements such as, "If I had only . . ." crowd in on feelings of guilt, anxiety, and shame until the bereaved is completely cast down by the weight of these burdens.

Agnes came from a family where divorce occurred early in her childhood. Her mother become a "figure" in the career world and also in social life. Agnes grew up in a fashionable hotel without much supervision. She was put into many extracurricular classes in order to keep her time occupied. She grew to hate these cultural expectations of her mother's, even though she did excel in some of the lessons. At an early age Agnes married a considerably older man who already had fame and fortune. She delighted in becoming the talented hostess, traveling companion, and social butterfly.

She was shocked by her husband's sudden death and immediately became incapable of making decisions for herself, postponing everything because she "had never had to do that." Her dependency upon a husband for intellectual stimulation, social life, security, and prestige left her an abandoned widow who felt she could not survive without him. Later she fell in love and hoped to marry only to discover that her new love was in no position to marry. This sudden end to her efforts to find someone to "care for me" left her feeling shame and gave her a sense of complete loss of her reputation. She felt she could never trust any one again, and even an offer of friendship to another made her too vulnerable to losses. She experienced a sense of guilt that she never wished to repeat.

We saw her twenty years later—alone, bitter, without friends or relatives. Now she is facing old age and another kind of dependency without any support system. She has never budged from her early belief that "people aren't nice; they are untrustworthy, they always leave you." She is completely negative; she is completely alone.

## 6. Abortions.

In the process of our work we receive many requests to be guest speakers in local high schools and colleges on topics of suicide, sudden death, and grief. Recently, while talking to students about these losses, two students in the room began to weep when abortion was mentioned. Their weeping was noticeable to the entire class. The class indicated that this was an example of a kind of loss and separation that is not generally recognized and for which no ritual is provided to help work through the emotional feelings that build up at such a time. It was suggested that we all join hands and send these two classmates our sympathy, our empathy, and our support in this time of sadness. The class responded and we all joined hands. I said we would continue the work we had to do, but our thoughts and our energy in this area would still be going to the couple who need our help now. We did go ahead with our discussion, and the two young people wept silently for about twenty minutes.

At the conclusion of the class period, the bereaved couple came up to me and said they felt as though a load of bricks had been removed from their chests.

It is well to keep in mind the grief that accompanies the losses and separations that have been mentioned. We need to be aware that these smaller griefs precede and run concurrently with grief of any kind. Life does not stand still while one is grieving. Problems still arise concerning family members and one's own self: babies are born; new responsibilities occur with changes in employment; there are failures or successes in school; illnesses develop among family members; minor traffic accidents take place; children leave home; others return. Moreover, how one has coped with earlier griefs often determines how one will react to grief associated with death.

## STAGES OF GRIEF

There are three stages of grief that I shall describe. One should keep in mind that these three stages often overlap or that there can be long gaps or arrests at one stage or another. Allowance must be made for flexibility, unreadiness, and for individual differences.

### Stage One

The first stage of grief consists of shock, protest, anger, and disbelief. The person cannot comprehend what has happened. He experiences disbelief, anger, and protest. This period of grief is given social recognition for it is at this time that friends, relatives, and neighbors rally around the family, bringing food, running errands, and performing domestic tasks that are commonly needed in a household in mourning. This support and the emotions of shock, anger, etc., usually last from the occurrence of death until the disposal of the body.

Where there is sudden death and nonrecovery of the body, such as in drownings, military deaths, industrial accidents, fires, floods, or earthquakes, the bereaved can be stuck at the first level for a long time (Grim et al., 1970). The fact that the bereaved has not seen the concrete evidence of the dead body allows him to fantasize that the person is not really dead, that this event did not happen. When the death occurs outside the milieu of the family, far from home or in a region either unknown or unexplored by the family—especially if the body is not found or found only after a protracted length of time—the family finds it increasingly diffi-cult to envisage the place or the reality of the death.

A sudden death by drowning in a locale far removed from the family's knowledge or experience is often followed by a time of unrelieved anxiety and bewilderment. The family has to under-go the terrible ordeal of the search for the body. This is a time fraught with great anxiety as well as the wildest flights of imagina-tive denials. The deceased, they say, was an excellent swimmer, a superb outdoorsman, in fine physical condition. He knew well the conditions of the current, tides, or contours of the land. Even though he is missing and search parties have explored for hours (days or weeks), the family may fantasize that he has been struck on the head and is now dazed and wandering somewhere in the wilderness, a victim of amnesia.

It is not at all uncommon during this first stage of grief for a survivor to indicate he has no need to grieve. Following is an example of a person who was not yet ready to grieve.

> When George's wife suicided he declined to see a counselor be-cause he said he was doing okay. A bit of conversation was sufficient for the counselor to realize that the husband did not have other help, that he had not experienced anticipatory grief or relief. He said he would call any time he felt the need to talk about what had happened.
>
> Almost a half-year later George called, greatly distressed, crying, and suicidal. He and the counselor talked for over an hour. Every-thing had been going well until that morning when he awakened with a tremendous sense of sadness. He began to cry and had been crying most of the day before he telephoned. During that time he ex-perienced such despair that he felt all he wanted to do was to kill him-self and join his wife.
>
> When this first outpouring subsided, George was asked if he would like the counselor to visit him at once. When he hesitated, he was asked if he had any friend or relative with whom he would feel com-fortable talking. He had no one except a relative several hundred miles away. Was that relative available? He did not know. Could he telephone him? Yes. This he did. His relative would start at once, but it would be ten hours before he would arrive. During these ten hours George and the counselor spoke frequently by phone.
>
> At one point George said, "You know, I do feel better already. It helps to talk to someone." When his relative arrived the counselor was able to speak with him and give suggestions for support and help in knowing what things would be expected of him as a listener.

These two men spent an entire weekend in a marathon session: talking, reminiscing, weeping, speaking of the deceased, sharing each other's life experiences and, much later talking and *laughing* about some of the things they had *all three* shared.

This weekend together "let the water go over the dam." Later, George called to speak at length about what had been said and how they had shared each other's feelings. George now recognized that his grief process was well under way and that he could now proceed with his grief work alone. This work was discussed and he said he felt he could manage it, but he was encouraged to telephone us if and when he felt any need for more support.

During the first stage of grief, whether one is in the care of friends, relatives, or a doctor, the bereaved is often offered tranquilizers or depressants "to get him over the hump." Upon psychiatric advice we recommend, wherever possible, that these kinds of pills not be given to anyone experiencing the shock of a traumatic death unless his physician feels that person presents a clear danger either to himself or to others. The reason for this advice is that grief is a new emotion. It needs to be felt in all its ramifications. To be sedated means to be limited in one's awareness of the hurt, the pain, the anger, and the anguish. A person denied this awareness of his pain can be arrested at this level and never move on or move on to the next stage only after great tribulation. In other instances, what is a normal reactive depression can be plummeted into a chronic depression as a result of this early "papering over" by tranquilizers of the expression of perfectly normal emotions (Crary and Crary, 1973).

### Stage Two

The second stage is one of intense emotion. There is no norm for its duration. The time limit for this stage varies with the closeness of the relationship and its quality, the attitude toward the deceased, as well as the circumstances of the death (sudden, long search, or unrecovered body). The way previous losses and separations were met are often indicators of how the bereaved will meet this new grief. The inner resources of the bereaved play a significant role. Long-established support systems, lack of dependency on the deceased, and a strong belief system are invaluable assets at this time.

This is a period of intense separation anxiety. We have already discussed how one has learned very early to experience the anxiety of separation in the entire process of progressing from infancy to adulthood. Some of these old anxieties are reactivated in subsequent fears arising from the loss of a person with whom a deep attachment exists. *This is a natural process and the basis for grieving.*

If a child has not experienced separation anxiety, this indicates that he has not been able to develop a true attachment, and his ability to cope with loss through grieving will be crippled. Crippled also will be his chances to internalize the lost person as a part of the grieving process. This internalization is accomplished by making the deceased an integral part of himself through his memory of the loved one. The bereaved's own identity is then strengthened by the support of the memory of the deceased. In short, *to tolerate separation anxiety and to grieve are signs of a healthy personality that is capable of deep attachment.* Without real attachments, there is no grief to work through, and there is no need to attempt closure for a nonexistent grief. (See Anticipatory Grief at the end of this chapter for exceptions.)

Loss through death strikes at the deepest roots of human existence, recalls the experience of previous attachments and losses, and reactivates the pain of earlier losses, physical as well as psychological in nature. All of these adjustments produce a time of intense grieving. The bereaved has disturbed and restless sleep, often with vivid dreams or nightmares; he has a loss of appetite and of weight. Depression, disorientation, helplessness, and fear of mental illness are present. Some of the simplest tasks that were normally performed are now difficult to begin or impossible to complete properly. Even the bereaved's sense of perception has changed; people and objects now seem smaller to him. These symptoms are accompanied by much weeping, sighing, hand wringing, brushing the hand across the brow, exhaustion, and a lump in the throat that often makes speech difficult.

*More social support and assistance are needed during the second stage of grief than at any other time since that person was a child.* But this is when the bereaved gets less social support and assistance because most of the people who were helpful during the week of the funeral have now returned home. Their duties and responsibilities call them homeward and they leave, feeling that they have been helpful and given generously of their time. Consequently, the bereaved is left alone. Intense separation anxiety causes him to feel abandoned by his friends. This abandonment, on the heels of the abandonment by death, seems more than can be tolerated. Those friends and neighbors who have returned to their homes are not callous or insensitive to the bereaved's needs, but rather they do not know what to say or do.

### Stage Three

Stage three is the period of final adaptation. Sleep and weight are stabilized and interest is again directed outward. The bereaved can now speak of the deceased without bursting into tears. He has resumed his daily routine and can perform ordinary responsibilities satisfactorily. The bereaved expands his activities, seeks new situations with increased ease, and is optimistic and full of hope for the future.

### What Happens When Grief Is Not Worked Through

What if stages one and two are not worked through by persons who do have a genuine and strong attachment for the deceased? If these adjustments toward adaptation and completion are not made, the outcome is likely to be long-term despair of depression or melancholia, an impairment of the capacity to love again, or various irrational attitudes toward death and destruction.

The British anthropologist, Geoffrey Gorer (1965), has an interesting theory regarding the lack of adaptation in these two stages. His theory is based on his observations of the senseless violence and vandalism that have occurred throughout the Western world and that is largely committed by young people. His observations lead him to the belief that such violence and vandalism are evidence that these young persons were never able to work through griefs that occurred during their childhood. He speculates that these young adults have developed irrational attitudes toward destruction because of an unsatisfactory working through of early losses.

## STYLES OF GRIEVING

In addition to broad cultural differences that exist in styles of grieving, there are several individual reactions that are likely to be encountered by those who spend much time with grieving persons (Gorer, 1965). Listed are some of the more common reactions:

1. There is a *complete denial of death,* not in the psychological sense but as a religious statement of belief by the followers of Spiritualism and Christian Science.

2. *Absence of grief* may occur with a parent, brother, or sister who has been separated for a long time by either geographical distance or by alienation. Absence of grief is rare in the case of a spouse or a child who lived with the deceased. Still being in shock or being unready to move into the next stage may also account for an absence of grief. Relief that the deceased has passed through his long ordeal of pain and suffering also lessens one's need to grieve. A repression of one's emotions can greatly impede the progress of grief.

3. There are *people who hide their grief by keeping busy.* This appears to help, for it often wards off any overt symptoms of depression. But it can lead in many cases to a life filled with trivia (the unimportant, insignificant matters of daily living).

4. The Orthodox Jews have a system of *time limited grief.* During the seven days following a death the relatives and friends gather about the bereaved family to talk and review the life of the deceased. The good times, the bad times, the funny times are recalled and recounted. In the course of recollecting and sharing these events of the past, the bereaved come, in the end, to a readiness to pick up life again without the deceased. The memory of that person has now been internalized in their minds.

Irish wakes do much the same thing in a briefer length of time—generally one long evening of reminiscing. This night of recollection is accompanied by liberal amounts of alcohol which may or may not remove the emotional inhibitions and provide for a full recall of the deceased's life.

5. There can be several kinds of *time unlimited grief,* in the sense that the grief never seems to be adequately terminated. The

person who says, "I'll never get over it," is generally making a demonstration of how dutiful and loving he is. Others, more fortunate, acknowledge that they will never forget the person once his death has been worked into their own internal system.

6. There is *time unlimited grief* in a situation called *mummification*. Here the bereaved preserves his grief by keeping the house and every object in it precisely as the deceased left it. The bereaved gives the impression that the house (or room, etc.) is a shrine likely to be reanimated by the deceased at any moment.

7. There is the *time unlimited grief of depression and despair*. This needs professional attention as soon as it can be identified.

8. And, finally, there is *time unlimited grief that enthrones* and elevates the deceased to a role of honor, infallibility, and unwarranted virtue unknown to the deceased's other friends and relatives.

### Anticipatory Grief

There can be grieving before death in cases of incurable illness, invalidism, war, or imprisonment. This is known as anticipatory grief. Nurses are especially familiar with anticipatory grief because they have patients whose diagnosis and prognosis are known to them long before the patient knows. Nurses know the trajectory of the disease and they know what lies ahead. They have also developed an attachment for the patient, and they begin to grieve for what he must go through and for his death. Families of invalids and persons with a long illness experience anticipatory grief; so does the patient.

The patient may begin to grieve when he learns that the loss of a leg or some other part of his body is imminent. Grief of this kind can be especially acute when it is known that the prognosis is not a good one. When the prognosis is poor, the patient knows that ultimately there will not only be the loss of a part of his body, but his job, his interests, his wife and family—everything he holds dear. The patient grieves for himself; he also grieves for the loss of all these other attachments.

It is exceedingly difficult for a family to grieve for the anticipated death of a loved one and at the same time have the responsibility for daily care and communication with that loved one. This painful experience may be repeated several times if the invalid passes from remission to relapse. The length of time needed for grief *after* a death may be greatly foreshortened following repeated episodes of remission and relapse. Indeed, the need for grief can be entirely eliminated when the bereaved is greatly relieved that the time of anguish, suffering, and dependency are over at last.

When anticipatory grief occurs, it is accompanied by the same symptoms of despair, anguish, depression, loss of appetite and sleep that accompany any grief. The person experiencing it must also progress through stages one and two. *Anticipatory grief also requires the same social support and assistance as any other grief* in order for the bereaved to pass successfully through stage three.

### Abnormal Grief

How can one tell when grief has passed beyond what is normal and expected into a condition that needs special assistance? One way is to be aware of *any one* symptom of grief or *any combination* of symptoms that has become *persistent, prolonged,* and is causing *perturbation* (agitation), *or a grief that is long delayed in its expression.*

Lindemann (1944) points out that these symptoms can show themselves in a number of ways. There can be excessive crying or an inability to cry, suicidal thoughts or fantasies, unusual dependency, cover-up, insomnia, inappropriate behavior or responses, hysteria and panic, or angry outbursts. There can be a persistent hostility that shows itself in intense guilt, self-blame, and anger. Some persons may develop low back pains, chest pains, breathless attacks, recurrent vomiting, choking, strokes, or a replication of symptoms of the deceased. There can be expressions of fear, withdrawal into social isolation and loneliness, intense separation anxiety, or attempts to avoid grieving.

All of these symptoms, if allowed to persist, not only affect normal living and working conditions but also the health of the bereaved. Other members of the family can be affected also. They may develop some manifestation of illness or self-blame and anger that can lead to a rupture in the marital relationship. Older children find excuses to leave home; younger ones may run away.

If the main cause of delayed or prolonged grief has been a denial of the cause of death (suicide, drugs, alcohol, etc.), such a cover-up can lead to either a complete breakdown of trust in the family or a blind acceptance of the new mythology of the family. In the latter instance, disturbances may develop that can lead later to unexpected mental health problems.

There are wide differences in individual responses to the need for grief. Even though one may be alert to the possibilities of prolonged or delayed grief, what is a normal expression of grief for one individual may be difficult to determine for another. While the grief process seldom needs therapeutic intervention, professional help should be offered to persons whose symptoms are unusually prolonged or whose depression has deepened greatly.

### Factors in Outcome of Grief

Many factors that may influence the outcome of a grief reaction have already been mentioned—the previous losses and separations that have occurred and how they were coped with and the whole area of determining how emotionally significant to the bereaved the loss has been. Parkes (1972) has made a list of what he calls "Determinants of the Outcome of Bereavement" which is helpful in identifying some of these *preexisting conditions:*

Antecedent
  Childhood experiences (especially losses of significant persons)
  Later experiences (especially losses of significant persons)
  Previous mental illness (especially depressive illness)
  Life crises prior to the bereavement
  Relationship with the deceased
    Kinship (spouse, child, parent, etc.)
    Strength of the attachment
    Security of the attachment

Degree of reliance
Intensity of ambivalence (love/hate)
Concurrent
    Sex
    Age
    Personality
        Grief proneness
        Inhibition of feelings
    Socioeconomic status (social class)
    Nationality
    Religion (faith and rituals)
    Cultural and familial factors
Subsequent
    Social support or isolation
    Secondary stresses
    Emergent life opportunities (options open)

### Importance of Listening

The bereaved spends a good amount of time telling and re-telling the events that led to the sudden death that is now causing him much pain and anguish. A good counselor allows this to occur and listens carefully to the details. When in doubt about some part of the account, the counselor should feel free to ask for clarification and allow a more complete account to be related. The counselor needs to 1) listen for the previous losses and separations of early childhood and later life. These losses can explain a great deal about that person's previous ability to cope with such a problem, and 2) listen for indications that either the bereaved or someone close to him has a history of depressive illness.

There is scarcely an item on Parkes' list that will not be revealed by the bereaved while making an early effort to sort out his feeling about the death. At this time the bereaved is attempting to organize his thoughts about how the death occurred, under what circumstances, its similarities or dissimilarities to other losses, and what the bereaved said, did, and felt at that time. Not infrequently, the bereaved may indicate having a previous, unresolved death, loss, or separation that may need to be resolved *before* the present grief can be dealt with comfortably. For these reasons, it is important for the counselor to take plenty of time for the first sessions. Our counselors seldom take less than two hours for the first session. This allows the bereaved to delve into his grief and to express thoughts and feelings without regard to an arbitrary limitation on the length of the visit. Taking time at the beginning of the sessions "saves a lot of grief." By this is meant that kind of grief that may become prolonged and troublesome if allowed to progress without attention to these important antecedents.

It is assumed in normal losses, separations, and death that the bereaved has an abundance of social support. Social support means friends, relatives, and others who rally around the bereaved, helping in any way they can but still allowing the bereaved plenty of privacy. This support can mean just being with the bereaved, listening to the account of what happened, allowing the tears and protests to happen, helping make arrangements for the funeral, running the grieving household, providing transportation for members of the family, preparing meals, answering the phone, or tidying up the house. Most friends and relatives know how to do these things in a normal, anticipated death, but they are at a loss to know what to do when a sudden or violent death occurs. They have rarely had any experience with these kinds of death, so how can they know what to say or do when it happens to their friend, neighbor, or relative?

In such cases of traumatic death, it is likely that the bereaved does not get the kind of social support he needs, for no one around him can fathom the kind of thoughts that are obsessing him. The bereaved may be overwhelmed by thoughts of guilt, blame, shame, horror, anger, rage, or a desire for vengence. He may be unable to speak of these frightening thoughts because they are so terrible he feels like a monster for having them.

## CONDITIONS THAT INTERFERE WITH GRIEF

Often grief cannot be expressed or felt because the terrible thoughts just mentioned interfere with both the expression of grief and the voicing of these terrible thoughts. Excessive guilt or blame prevents the bereaved from *feeling bereaved*. The bereaved is alone with his unspeakable guilt and blame, etc., and cannot feel any sadness, any great loss, or shed any tears. He becomes sunk in a morass of anger, depression, guilt, anxiety, or perturbation. Sometimes this situation results in withdrawal or depression, over talkativeness, excessive crying, or sadness. But these expressions are for *one's self* and not for the loss that has to be experienced. Crying and sadness under these conditions are often accepted by the family and friends as grief, but they are not; they are substitutions for grief. Such grief reactions can become excessive. Then it is important for the counselor, friend, or clergy to know that professional help and assistance are needed.

The fact that a death is a sudden one complicates nearly all grief. Sudden death *is* sudden; there has been no adequate preparation for its occurrence. Sudden death is often a violent, traumatic death that leaves the deceased's body in a shattered, mutilated, or ugly condition. The kinds of sudden death give the reader an opportunity to imagine the condition of the body of the deceased: suicide; homicide; auto, motorcycle, and plane accidents; drownings, industrial accidents; accidents by choking; hemorrhaging; overdose; falling from great heights; or cardiovascular episodes. None of these deaths are timely; they are all premature, unanticipated. The next-of-kin and friends are distraught when the body is left in a broken or ugly condition. Moreover, some of the modes of death are less socially acceptable than others. Suicide survivors know that the death was *intentional,* whereas the other modes are accidental.

It is not uncommon for grief to be arrested or delayed following a homicide. This is especially evident when the homicide seems to be without any apparent reason, committed by someone who has not yet been apprehended or who has committed other violent acts, such as rape. Under these circumstances, there can often be so much anger and rage that the bereaved cannot feel his grief. This situation can be aggravated because of the police investigation, which extends over a long period of time. The reality of the anger is reopened with every recurrent check with the family about new events and suspects. These reopenings of old wounds of the family are often unbearable. The family becomes frozen at the level of conjuring up the violence with which their relative died. There seems to be no space left for the family to deal with the death *in terms of their own loss and sadness.*

To deal with such anger, to allow it to proceed for a necessary length of time, and to recognize when that time is past requires a counselor who has great amounts of compassion, restraint, and diplomacy. At first empathy is important. Almost anyone in similar circumstances would feel the same way. But there comes a time when this statement of outrage is no longer appropriate, and the bereaved needs to be led along other paths more conducive to working through grief. Such a change is generally unwelcome to the bereaved. His interest in bringing the perpetrator of the homicide to accountability through the efforts of the police and the court system has become a way of life, a means to deny grief. Where the perpetrator is never apprehended, the bereaved often never completely works through his grief unaided. Counselors who cannot perform this kind of service must recognize their limitations and make proper referrals to professionals.

Some bereaved persons approach homicide in a different way. They speak from the very first of their desire for the perpetrator to be found *in order that he may be helped.* They voice forgiveness and wish only that society *help* this person so that he may never be tempted to perform such an act again. They speak of love and forgiveness and not of vengence or punishment. This attitude may last for several months and then, usually, it bursts like a bubble. Anger and outrage occupy their thoughts and actions now. However, they are embarrassed by their previous protestations of love and forgiveness. They feel a need now to conceal their *real* feelings. This conflict makes it more difficult for such clients to do justice to their feelings and at the same time work through their grief.

Where there is this conflict between love and justice or forgiveness and anger, it is sometimes helpful to remind the bereaved that love can still exist in the midst of angry feelings. It is possible to say, "I love myself for finding this act so despicable." In later periods of grieving we suggest ways the bereaved may use this terrible experience in helping himself and others by some activity, project, course of study or self-awareness. During these later periods we often bring together groups of persons who are bereaved by similar modes of death. These group meetings provide an opportunity to discuss how they felt at the time and what they found helped them most. In helping each other in this way, they help themselves consolidate many of the advances they have been striving for in their grief.

## REFERENCES

Bowlby, J., "Processes of Mourning," *Int J Psychoanal, 44*:317, 1961a.

———, *Attachment and Loss,* Vol. 1, *Attachment.* London: Hogarth; New York: Basic, 1969.

Brim, Orville (Ed.), *The Dying Patient.* New York: Russell Sage, 1970.

Crary, William G. and Gerald G. Crary, "Depression," *J Nurs,* March, 1963, p. 475.

Erikson, Erik H., *Childhood and Society,* Revised ed. New York: Norton, 1963.

Gorer, Geoffrey, *Death, Grief, and Mourning.* New York: Doubleday, 1965.

Lindemann, E., "The Symptomatology and Management of Acute Grief," *Am J Psychiatry, 101*:141, 1944.

Parkes, Colin Murray, *Bereavement, Studies of Grief in Adult Life.* New York: Intl Univs Pr, 1972.

Pincus, Lily, *Death and the Family, the Importance of Mourning.* New York: Pantheon, 1974.

Schoenberg, B., A. C. Carr, D. Peretz, and A. H. Kutscher, *Loss and Grief: Psychological Management in Medical Practice.* New York: Columbia U Pr, 1970.

Switzer, David, *Dynamics of Grief.* Nashville: Abingdon, 1970.

*Chapter 2*

# CHILDREN AND GRIEF

## Introduction

R EADERS MAY be surprised to learn that the majority of the survivors of death are children. Children, like adults, experience grief, but the books written on the subject of grief show that
a large number of authors write as though grief is an adult
experience only.

Experts say children are often and wrongly discouraged from
grieving. The surviving parent is so perplexed and overwhelmed
with grief he cannot explain the death to the children. If a child
never resolves his grief, he may become unable or afraid ever to
love again because he may be unable to form close relationships
in later life.

In his book *Facing Death,* psychologist Robert E. Kavanaugh
(1974) says, "I wonder if our efforts to spare little people a harsh
reality are not our own badly disguised struggle to avoid the
trauma in telling [them about death]? Meanwhile, our hesitation
allows time and opportunity for them to concoct weird fantasies
that may affect their lifelong attitudes toward mortality."

Such problems can be avoided if death is explained to the
child when a parent dies. In her book *Death, the Final Stage of
Growth,* psychiatrist Elisabeth Kubler-Ross (1975) says, "We
routinely shelter children from death and dying, thinking we are
protecting them from harm. But it is clear that we do them a
disservice by depriving them of the experience."

Parents must remember to be honest with their children.
They must confront death, and we can help by answering their
questions. It is not necessary to burden children with more than
they can ask about.

## CHILDREN'S REACTIONS TO DEATH

Children react to a death the same as adults do in stage one. They cannot believe the person is dead, and they try angrily to regain the loved one. They undergo the same pain, despair, and disorganization as adults until they begin to accept the fact that the loved one is really gone. Children can also achieve the same hope and stage of rebuilding as adults when they begin to organize their lives without the presence of the lost person. But children take *longer to pass from one stage to another and the entire grief process lasts longer than it does for adults.* If children do not pass completely through their grief and come soundly out on the other side, there is grave danger that some kind of mental illness will complicate their lives 5, 13, even 40, years later (Cain, 1972). As we have seen, new losses and separations reactivate the old ones, and until the old ones are resolved there is an impasse.

Children's reactions take many forms and are often misleading for parents who do not know what to look for. Following are a few important facts (Nagy, 1959; Grollman, 1967; Cain, 1972):

1. Children usually take longer than adults in going through the phases of grief. While an adult normally requires a year or two, a child may grieve for many years.

2. A child over six months of age is deeply affected by the death of anyone close to him, especially parents, brothers, and sisters.

3. Children under six years cannot conceive of the finality of death. They expect the loved one to return. Every separation, even though temporary, is somewhat disturbing.

4. Children often express their feelings about a death in indirect, delayed, and disguised ways. Often a bereaved young child seems neither to know nor to care about his loss, but such appearances are deceiving.

5. Between six and nine years of age the permanency of death is generally accepted, but the inevitability of death for the child and his loved ones is likely to be too difficult for him to face.

6. In many cases, children cannot move out of the first phase of reaction to a death. They continue the protest, the anger at separation, and refuse to face the finality of the loss. The phase

of despair and disorientation may come only after several years, with hope and reorganization coming even later.

7. Whether dealing with bereavement or simply facing the existence of death, children are helped in expressing their thoughts and feelings by sympathetic discussion with a trusted and loved person.

We began to rework our files and records to include the numerical count of the children involved and to make an inquiry about them an integral part of our conversation with the adult client. This led us directly into the problem of helping the parent meet the child's overwhelming need at the same time that the parent struggles with his own inability to cope with the psychological stress and burdens typical of such a loss.

It is not uncommon for parents to build a barrier around the children in order to keep them from hearing their own grief. Children are kept from hearing the conversation about the deceased, plans for the funeral, and many other of the normal activities of a bereaved household. It is apparent that many parents do not know what to say about death, especially suicide. Their discomfort with the subject and the suddenness of the event combine to create a situation that can seriously threaten the mental health of the child.

If it is important to allay the guilt, fears, and blame at the time of grief among adults, it is equally important to help children in these same situations. To delay or impede this process may mean that the present scenario will be acted out again with other children in the family. Professor Cain (1972) writes, "Such preventive interventions with the survivors of suicide might reduce what we elsewhere called the 'senseless arithmetic' of adding newly warped lives to the one already tragically ended." We found ourselves catapulted into the broader aspects as stated by Shneidman (1969 and 1972), "It may be said that of the three approaches to mental health—prevention, intervention, and postvention—that in suicide, postvention contributes to the largest aspect of the total problem." How do we perform this postvention work?

We begin by asking about the children and making the parent

aware of the reason for our inquiry. Gently, but firmly, we lead the parents to accept grief as a fact for children, to share their own grief, and to learn some of the basic points in discussing death with children. We have included this special attention to children and their grief in all aspects of our work with the next-of-kin of all traumatic and sudden deaths.

Early on we prepared a radio and television script for a two-part program on "Explaining Death to Children," which was based on Grollman's books (1967, 1970). In addition to these media efforts, our counselors now speak in the community about grief and how to explain death to children. We accept guest teaching engagements at local intermediate and high schools, community colleges, and nearby state universities. We also speak to adult clubs and organizations (Council of Churches groups, clergy meetings) and to groups of professional workers, such as nurses, social workers, chaplains, probation officers, teachers, and counselors. From time to time presentations are given to national and state organizations in psychology and psychiatry.

Out of our experience has grown a conviction that the mental health of us all—child and parent—is not the denial of tragedy but the frank acknowledgement of it. Children need to be helped to see death as an inevitable part of human experience. *Not to assist a child of any age through his grief denies him something of his basic birthright as a human being.*

### Advice for Parents

One cannot improve on Grollman's suggestions (1967) for parents. The numbered suggestions are his, the cases illustrating these suggestions come from our files:

**1. Do not tell children what they will later need to relearn.** Avoid fairy tales and half-truths; do not give the illusion that some day the loved one will return. Imaginative fancy gets in the child's way at a time when he is having trouble enough distinguishing the real from the make-believe.

> Eddie was the only child of Bertie and Wilda. He was four when
> we first became acquainted with the family. They had recently moved
> to our county in order to get away from a family situation that had

involved the entire family in six violent deaths. In addition, Bertie's friends were largely made up of drug users, and he had become one also. He was also drinking heavily. Both parents were followers of a religious group that was intolerant of Bertie's drug and alcohol abuse and his suicide attempts. They were put out of this church shortly after we met them.

Eddie had been included in all family conversations regarding the numerous deaths. He was also present and attentive to all the family situations that involved his parents and their progressive disagreements with the larger family—the church and the law. A good part of his experience centered on the ambulance service that removed his father after repeated suicide attempts.

Wilda was depressed. As the periods of Bertie's absences during treatment increased, Eddie became depressed also. Our help extended to plans for getting Bertie into treatment and motivating him to remain there and to help Wilda maintain the family on insufficient funds by teaching her better ways of making purchases. She was open and responsive to these ideas, and we began to work with her on ways of improving the family diet for less money than she was presently spending. We assisted her in getting treatment for her depression and for her diet for weight loss. An entire regimen of diet, exercise, and recreation were worked out for her and Eddie. This also included Bertie when he was home.

Bertie and his family made great progress in the year-and-a-half we worked with them. Bertie completed his treatment, earned a high school diploma, and was considered ready for the job market. Wilda lost weight, helped clean up and paint her house, and was enjoying Eddie more than ever. He was no longer depressed.

When Bertie broke his pattern of drug and alcohol addiction, he and Wilda were invited back into the church. They were so delighted to be reunited with the church that they became very zealous members, striving to extend their religious commitment and their faith.

Bertie suicided almost a year after we stopped seeing the family. We got in touch with Wilda again and saw her and Eddie until they moved away. Wilda felt very confident of her renewed faith in the church and explained to Eddie over and over again that he would see his father. The child was open about speaking of meeting his "daddy, any day now." Wilda was cautioned about putting so much emphasis on this point, but she felt that was one of the beliefs of her church and she must uphold it because of all it had done for her.

We never saw how Eddie coped with this situation, but it is likely to cause him difficulty at some time during childhood or later.

## 2. Allow the child to give vent to his emotions. Allow him to

share yours. Invite your child to cry with you. Expressions of grief can provide a healthy outlet in minimizing guilt feelings. Assume that guilt exists and talk about it. Children feel more guilty than adults since, in their experience, bad things happen to them when they are naughty.

> Fred, 10, was the youngest of the family. When his father suicided, the family displayed tight control and very little emotion at this death, which was not unexpected. The surviving parent gave assurance that "everything is all right; we have the finest help in the world." Nevertheless, she kept calling us, and we kept responding to her requests.
>
> It was some time later that she mentioned, after we had inquired about Freddie again, that there was something unusual about him. After his father's death he had soaped all the mirrors in the house. His mother found this an exasperation when there were so many other things to attend to. We talked about this for a while and suggested that perhaps he felt he had something to do with that death and, consequently, was unable to face his own image in the mirror.
>
> After considerable discussion and questions, she accepted our recommendation that she and Freddie visit the family psychiatrist and give Freddie a chance to work through his guilt feelings with a professional.

**3. Suffering and death should not be linked with sin and punishment.** The death of a loved one is not a retribution for his wrongdoing.

> Eddie, in the earlier example, was also subjected to a great deal of talk about death being a punishment for the sins of drug and alcohol abuse. The various misdemeanors and felonies in which the family had been involved were also viewed in the same context. With the increased enthusiasm Wilda felt for her religion, there was no doubt that this explanation, from that time on throughout his childhood, would be repeated over and over again to Eddie.

**4. Do not close the door to doubt, questioning and difference of opinion.** Respect the child's personality. If he is to find an answer he must struggle with the problem for himself. Remember language has different meanings for adults and children.

**5. Do not teach the child as if you have the final answers that he must accept.** Children must learn that adults do not have all the answers posed by life and death. Do not be afraid to say, "I don't know."

**6. From age seven funerals may be attended by a child if he chooses.** Children under the age of three are too young to know what is happening. Their presence may also detract from the beneficial effects that the adults need to experience. Whether a child chooses to attend or not, prepare him for who will be there, what will be said and done, why people have come, and what is expected in the way of behavior and deportment. Explain about cemetaries or crematoria.

Items 4, 5 and 6 are difficult for parents to feel comfortable with unless the counselor spends considerable time explaining how these suggestions can be followed, as the following case illustrates.

> When Jim died he left an extended family of his own, children of his wife's by a previous marriage, and several foster children. His wife, Madeline, felt she did not know how to cope with children of such varying ages and closeness to Jim. She asked the grief counselor to come and talk with all of them in their home.
>
> Madeline stated frankly in the children's presence that she felt they all needed help. She asked the counselor to talk to them about Jim's death and to help them get started talking about him. She urged each child to speak up about his own feelings and doubts.
>
> In the security of their own living room, Madeline and the nine children, ranging in age from six to eighteen years, began to speak of Jim and some of the questions that were uppermost in their minds. At first the children were shy and bewildered. As soon as they saw that their mother also felt she could ask anything, they joined in.
>
> The topics ranged from where Jim is now to plans for the funeral. Would the family be kept together or would they be separated? By her openness and frankness Madeline helped her children begin to think through some of life's most important questions. More importantly, she created a situation in which the children realized they were free to inquire about their doubts and feelings. No child or Madeline would feel a question unimportant. Madeline built a very solid foundation that evening for future confidences from her children in an atmosphere of sharing, caring, and honesty.

**7. Help the child to unburden his feelings through remembrance and release.** He needs to talk, not just to be talked to.

Give the child permission to express hostility as well as affection for the deceased. A necessary part of grieving at any age is the gradual working over of such old thoughts and feelings—a prelude to acceptance of the death as a fact.

When Dick died at the age of sixteen as the result of an accidental fall, a group of his friends indicated that they would like to have a "rap" session in order to talk about Dick's death and their feelings about it. Four young people and the parents of one gathered together. It was slow getting started because no one felt very comfortable about talking, but once Dick's closest friend began the others joined in.

There was a good deal of anger and impatience with Dick because he had started on his climb without letting anyone know about his plans. They felt if they had known more, he would at least have been accompanied. Perhaps there would not have been the long delay in finding his body.

One or two spoke highly of his competence in hiking and climbing. There was no doubt about Dick's enjoyment of remote areas. They all shared a sense of being independent and having a feeling of release in the solitude of such locations.

One youth produced pictures of Dick and his friends on such a trip. The conversation turned towards incidents that had occurred on other such trips. They recalled how they trained for trips and funny things that happened because they had forgotten some items of equipment. Others recalled small arguments about routes, etc. Soon everyone was contributing remarks, asides, and humorous accounts. Each recollection led to an appraisal of Dick as a friend, a companion, a nature lover, a person.

One friend was disturbed because they would never do these things again with Dick. Even worse, Dick would never do these things again because he was dead and confined to a coffin buried on a hillside. This remark led to a discussion of the funeral. The group felt that the funeral could have been arranged so that there was more emphasis placed on Dick's love of nature and the outdoors. They wished more effort had been spent on trying to comfort his friends by encouraging them to think of Dick now as *being a part of natural landscape* of the world.

That night as these teenagers relived many of their experiences with Dick, their own thoughts and philosophies began to take shape. Amid some laughter and many tears they began to work Dick and his life into the fabric of their own lives. This evening's session was just the beginning of a gradual reworking of their thoughts and memories. This process would require more time and effort, but *they had begun the process.*

**8. Avoid focusing on morbid details.** Recall also the beauty of the deceased's life and love.

At the time we were talking with Myron and Isabel about the death of both his parents in a traffic accident, they were concerned with their own grief. It came as a surprise when we inquired about the grief of their two children, Amy and Jeff, ages four and six. They dismissed their children's involvement in this death by saying, "They're too young; they don't really understand what has happened."

Gently, we reminded them that Amy and Jeff *know* something has happened because their parents look sad. They sense many details are being kept from them. Their parents' behavior indicates to the children that they *are upset about somethng*. Myron and Isabel stated that they had not intended telling Amy and Jeff what had happened.

Conversation about the relationship between the children and the grandparents led Myron and Isabel to see that the children had been close to the grandparents and would certainly wonder "where they are and why we don't see them any more." It was apparent that Myron and Isabel were uncomfortable with the knowledge that they probably needed to inform their children of this death. Questions were asked about how to do this. There was a discussion of whether the children should attend the funeral. The pros and cons were discussed for some time. Finally they reached the conclusion that they could tell the children and that they could talk to them about the funeral. They felt they could leave themselves open to the spontaneous questions of Amy and Jeff. And they did.

Later, when they called to express their appreciation for our help, they said the whole experience had been a blessing to them all. The children's questions had led them to begin a scrapbook of family pictures of the grandparents with their children and Amy and Jeff. Some of the recorded incidents were ones Amy and Jeff were too young to remember. The scrapbook had fostered the growth of the idea of the continuity of life, its cycles, and the place each of us has in the life span of another.

**9. Help the child not only by the tone of your voice but by the nonverbal response of the warmth of your body.** Love contributes to a child's security and gives a feeling of being valued. When a child feels valued, he is then able to love in return. (See Chapter 7 for a case illustrating how the counselor and parent focus on the young children affected by an industrial accident.)

## Grief and Adolescents

By the time children approach puberty a whole new set of factors has entered the picture. Adolescents normally follow a course that swings between feeling they are invincible and feeling that they are going to be annihilated by some cataclysmic force or disaster. At one moment the adolescent is an adult, the next he is a child, confused in his identification between mother and father, between male and female. The death of a parent inevitably disrupts working through this stage of an adolescent's life, and unless he is helped by a supportive environment, he may suffer badly. Early adolescence is a particularly vulnerable time for the death of a parent to occur.

When a person is unable to complete a grief task in childhood, he has to surrender his emotions in order that they do not suddenly overwhelm him or else he may be haunted throughout his life by a sadness for which he can never find an appropriate explanation. Most of us have had some experience with these two instances of incomplete resolution of childhood grief. We have observed adults whose control of their emotions is so tight that they do not seem to register emotion at all. Whatever happens, they show little or no emotion—they may marry but show little or no affection or demonstrativeness as a spouse, parent, colleague, or friend. The restraint they display is a holding back of the ordinary expressions of joy, happiness, love, or anger. They fear that if they do allow any such expression, they may find themselves unaccountably unable to stop the flow of emotion. What awful thing might happen then? Their emotion is unalterably tied into a terror, a fear of losing control of themselves, which might lead to some kind of new horror.

Another example of incomplete grief resolution is the person who looks sad. His face is full of sorrow, his demeanor is that of a person heavily weighted down by a burden from which he will never be free. These expressions become so much a part of this person's existence that he cannot remember a time when he was free of the feeling. He goes through life with a stony countenance, never knowing what has produced such sadness but knowing that he will never be free of its burden.

Children of the same sex as the parent who died often fear to identify with the parent. This can be because a boy who loses his father does not want to think that he, too, can die. Or the boy may also fear reaching the age at which his father died.

### Grief and Young Adults

Lily Pincus (1974), who came to grief counseling by way of marriage counseling at the Tavistok Institute, London, says that young married adults will respond to a parent's death in a way that will depend largely on how far they have resolved in their own marriage and conflicting feelings and childhood fantasies about the parent. These old fantasies are reactivated following a parent's death. Pincus' work clearly indicates that the marriage difficulties of these clients were easier to deal with *after* the clients were assisted in working through their grief.

### Explaining Death to Children

It is still difficult to explain death to a child, even when one has all of the information regarding children and grief presented in this chapter. We have come to believe that there is no news so terrible that it cannot be told. Even very young children can be told of a death, how it happened, and what is happening in a family that is grieving. Any news, however sudden, traumatic, or shocking, can be told if a person gives the information in simple, direct language and with love and affection.

In deciding how to explain death to a child, prospective counselors may be helped by giving some thought to their own deaths. Simply by making this statement, prospective counselors begin to feel upset, anxious, and uncomfortable (Doyle, 1977). It is important to give counselors assurance that it is all right to feel this way. Eventually one can think of his own death without becoming upset. Encourage the counselors to spend a brief time each day thinking of the kind of death they would like to have. Suggest that they include here the standards set for meeting death, some of the difficulties that will be encountered, and how these difficulties can be dealt with. By becoming aware of these matters regarding our own death, we find that it does help our thinking about how we would explain a death to a child. Here are some pointers and thoughts we discuss while exploring this situation with ourselves:

There are three big questions that confront all of us. Sometime during our lives we have to come to grips with these questions and settle them. These questions are—Who am I? Am I safe? and Will I survive? We are not very sure about the first question in regard to small children because their limited use of language impairs their ability to talk about it. We do know, though, that from preadolescence all through the rest of our lives we are often hounded by this question, and we give it a great deal of thought. We are at first enmeshed in questions about the roles we think we are expected to assume. Since these roles have a way of blending into each other, we begin to get anxious about them, upset, and fearful of the outcome. One of the first roles that upsets us is that of our sexuality. Are we male or female? As we develop, this question of sexuality undergirds much of our thinking about ourselves and our succeeding roles. Our sexuality may create barriers that affect our roles as students and searchers for occupational selection; our loveableness; and our potentiality for becoming attracted to and by persons suitable for life companionship. We express concern for our role as a parent, a nonparent, or as a single person, with or without a family. The role we find ourself in affects us in our job, profession, or outside interests, and all of these roles sometimes come into conflict with each other. At some time we are concerned with the philosophical, religious, or cosmic question. We search and search for an answer that is satisfactory to us.

We know the second question, Am I safe? from childhood on. We ask ourselves, What will happen to me? This question arises again and again: when I finish school, leave home, get married, change jobs, get a divorce, move far away, retire, get old and ill. It also arises when a parent dies. A child inevitably wonders then if the other parent will also die. What will I do, he asks, if I have neither father nor mother? Am I safe?

The third question is Will I survive? Human beings have a prolonged period of dependency before being able to be self-sufficient. This dependency is an acute problem. A child has very specific requirements. He needs food, constant body temperature (here I would add not only warmth but love), fresh air, sunlight, and water. Without these basic requirements a child either dies or has some kind of crippling or arresting development. When a death occurs, a child also wonders whether he will be able to survive; we also think of this as adults.

It is important to keep these three questions in mind when telling a child about death. Our experience has been that the important questions a child asks can be met in a simple statement. We suggest that you draw the child to you and put your arms around him. Look directly into the child's eyes and say, "Your father (or other relative) has died (suicided, and I don't know why), and we all feel sad. I'm crying and you are crying. Right now we wonder how we can go on, but we will because we are going to work together, and we're going to do things pretty much the way we did when Daddy was with us. (Or, we are going to work together and we're going to build a new life together.) We're going to make it, and we're going to live together for a long time."

This provides the immediate answers to the three questions mentioned previously. After making this short statement, allow the child to cry with you, to share your grief, and to ask anything he wishes. Questions may not occur at this time, but give every assurance that you will always be open to talk about his thoughts, fears, and feelings.

With a few adjustments, the foregoing statement can also be adapted to breaking the news of a death to a person of any age. The same kind of support and openness needs to be extended to adults and to children.

It is important that all of us—counselors, parents, or helpers—acknowledge that we have to search for the answers to the three questions discussed sometime before *we* die.

## REFERENCES

Cain, Albert C. (Ed.), *Survivors of Suicide.* Springfield: Thomas, 1972.

Doyle, Polly, "Grief Counseling for Children," in Danto, Bruce and A. H. Kutscher, (Eds.), *Suicide and Bereavement.* New York: Arno, 1977.

Grollman, Earl (Ed.), *Explaining Death to Children.* Boston: Beacon Pr, 1967.

Grollman, Earl, *Talking About Death, A Dialogue Between Parent and Child.* Boston: Beacon Pr, 1970.

Kavanaugh, Robert E., *Facing Death*. New York: Penguin, 1974.

Kübler-Ross, Elisabeth, *Death, the Final Stage of Growth*. Englewood Cliffs, New Jersey: P-H, 1975.

Nagy, Maria, "The Child's Theories Concerning Death," *J Genet Psychol*, *73:* 3, 4, 27, 1948.

——, "The Child's View of Death," in Feifel, Herman, *The Meaning of Death*. New York: McGraw, 1959.

Pincus, Lily, *Death and the Family, the Importance of Mourning*. New York: Pantheon, 1974.

Shneidman, Edwin S. (Ed.), *On the Nature of Suicide*. San Francisco: Jossey-Bass, 1969.

Shneidman, Edwin S., "Postvention and the Survivor-Victim," *Proceedings*, 6th International Conference on Suicide Prevention, Mexico City. Ann Arbor, Michigan: Edward Brothers, Inc., 1972, pp. 31–39.

*Chapter 3*

# STRESS

## Introduction

IT HAS BEEN stated in the preceding chapters that grief may be a new emotion, in the sense that this may be the first time one has been bereaved. Yet the components of the "new" emotion are the same negative feelings that have been encountered in other situations. The negative components of grief include anger, anxiety, depression, fear, guilt and blame—all of which can add up to a stressful situation. The writer has selected two of these components of grief for separate comment: stress and depression. Both states are nearly always present in grief. Depression needs to be understood thoroughly in order to assess whether it is still the normal, uncomplicated kind of depression found in grief or whether it is growing into a more serious kind. Stress needs careful attention because it manifests itself as a kind of environmental catchall of the stressful emotions listed earlier. The two following chapters will be devoted to a discussion of stress and depression.

## Signs of Stress

It is a common experience to seem to have more worries, problems, and stress at some times than at others. Sometimes this experience extends over a long period, and we become nervous and irritable to the point of considerable discomfort, anxiety, and depression. When tuned into our stressful state, a condition develops that makes us aware of an increased amount of body movement and an increased heart rate. We even become aware of our skin and that we are breathing and swallowing. In addition,

41

there may be insomnia. Prolonged symptoms such as these can bring on ulcers, high blood pressure, heart disease, even itching or tremors.

Any kind of change in life involves stress and the need to adapt to it. How we adapt or cope effectively with change can mean the difference between dealing satisfactorily with stressors and being overwhelmed by them. Signs of stress are a warning that something is amiss; they are not an indication of weakness. Becoming aware of the signs is a first step in recognition that stress exists. The next step is to determine the cause of the stress or the stressors.

Much later comes the discovery that somehow we managed to come through all right. This is a period of feeling more like ourselves and ready, even eager, to get on with life, the job, and family relationships. It is a relief to arrive at a point where we feel good about ourselves, relationships, and daily tasks. Often the relief is so great that we fail to look back at what preceded this malaise. But we do need to look back in order to discover what brought it about.

The advantage of the backward look is that it helps determine what happened. What was the constellation of conditions that gathered together to create the particular set of circumstances that led us to become tense, anxious, irritable, perturbed? By examining this constellation of events, it is possible to recognize how much effect preceding events have upon us—often for periods of time long removed from the actual happenings. One way of coming to this realization is to rate our own selves.

### The Life Events Rating Scale

Holmes and Masuda (1972) drew up a rating scale that covers the changes occurring in our lives. They selected forty-one life events, both good and bad, that are likely to create a stressful situation. They gave each event a value in relation to the amount of stress that event produces. They tested this rating by using it with large groups of people, especially doctors, medical students, army personnel, and athletes. As a result, they learned that the amount of stress one incurs can have an effect upon one's health, even to the extent of predicting some kind of physical symptoms within two years. The rating scale is intended to be an indicator of the kinds of changes that have taken place *in the past year*. By jotting down the point values for these events and adding them up, one arrives at the "stress level" for the past year. They found that if the total for the year is under 150, the person probably will not have any adverse reaction. A score of 150 to 199 indicates a "mild" problem, with a 37 percent chance the impact of stress will result in some physical symptoms. A score of 200 to 299 indicates a "moderate" problem, with a 51 percent chance of experiencing a change in health. A score of over 300 is one that may threaten one's health. The Holmes-Masuda rating scale is found in Appendix C.

In the process of filling out the rating scale, one is aware that some items are ignored. For example, the rating scale makes no reference to events in present-day life that are fairly common: use of drugs, alcohol, acting out suicide attempts, being burglarized, vandalized, mugged, raped, or a violent, sudden death. Even the figures for mortgages are highly unrealistic during this time of rapid inflation. Even with these omissions, their evaluations still hold, and we must take into account that our score is probably much higher than the rating scale indicates.

A common fault of most rating scales for stress is that they do not take individual differences into account. If it is difficult to adjust for individual differences, it is also difficult to adjust for regional ones. Some areas are more prone to cyclones, tornadoes, earthquakes, and floods than others. The same applies to urban and rural life; even areas of the same city present more hazardous life events than do other areas.

The score each person receives by this rating reveals some of the events and changes in each life that are likely indicators of the stress one is presently feeling. The higher the score, the more likely it is that there will be some physical symptoms of illness or disease within two years. There is no reason to become alarmed, however. There are things that can be done to relieve this stress, *right now*. Some items on the list relate to events over which there is no control, but there are many events over which there is control: changing jobs, living conditions, recreation, social conditions, even going on a diet.

## Ways to Avoid Stress

In addition to identifying the cause of the stress and avoiding those situations over which there is control, one may also lessen the stress by taking three deep breaths, by exercise, by meditation, by being realistic about what can be accomplished, and by learning to pace oneself.

Let us take, for example, the housewife whose husband is frequently transferred. Moving away is a stressful situation; one leaves old friends, relatives, and neighbors, as well as familiar places, recreations, sights, sounds, regional climate, and foods. By becoming uprooted because of frequent moving, one can develop many stressors. These stressors, in turn, make adaptation in the new locality fraught with discomfort, unease, even fears. There are aspects of the moving situation that *can be controlled.* If one makes the effort, he can greatly speed up the process of adaptation and make the new location a pleasurable experience. A nationwide network of real estate firms, the InterCity Relocation Service, gives the following advice on how to lessen some of the stressors of moving by following the route to learning more about the new location:

1. Subscribe to the local newspaper.
2. Look through the city's Yellow Pages for ideas about the community's shops and services.
3. A local street guide or road map will help orient the family to its new surroundings.
4. A copy of the high school yearbook will help teenagers "meet" some of their new friends.
5. Talk with the librarian at the public library. Here is an excellent source for information about schools, transportation, and community services.
6. Make a list of all the services you take for granted in your present community—from shoe repairs to doctors. Make a habit of asking people you meet in the new community about resources for services you can check out later for yourself.
7. Once you have selected your new home, plan a relaxed, fun weekend for the whole family to become orientated to your new hometown.

If you are interested in an effort to avoid some of the changes occurring in your life, you want to know other ways that can affect the stress in one's life. If that is your situation, do get acquainted with what Hans Selye (1974) has written on the subject of stress. He suggests that we must become more aware of ourselves. We need to know the type of person we are—do we push ourselves, or do we want to function in a quiet, tranquil environment? Do we relish an active, full, crowded life, or do we prefer a life that is less hurried, less crowded with events and decisions? Finally, he suggests that we revise our attitude towards various events in our lives. "Attitude," he says, "determines whether we perceive any experience as pleasant or unpleasant, and adopting the right one can convert a negative stress into a positive one—something I call 'eustress'."

Any negative kind of stress that produces anxiety, irritability, bodily discomfort, or displeasure produces "distress." "Eustress" is a positive response that is the opposite of distress. Both negative and positive kinds of stress place demands on the body. In fact, any stress is "the body's nonspecific response to *any* demand placed on it, whether that demand is pleasant or not." What we need to do is accentuate the eustress situations in our lives because eustress does not place as high demands on the body as does distress.

In accentuating the pleasant, the eustress, Selye places great emphasis upon each person finding *for himself*—without pressure from either parent or teacher—the kind of work one wants to do. He expresses his concern that we, and especially the young, are overwhelmed by a loss of motivation. Without the stabilizing support that comes from finding constructive goals in our lives, we subject ourselves to a "purposelessly drifting" behavior, unsure of ourselves and our lives. Such behavior, he says, leads to "one of the most stressful situations imaginable." Too frequently we feel that either alcohol or tranquilizers can be used to cope with our stress, but both have undesirable side effects, and neither method really works.

Instead, Selye suggests that after we have found what we want to do vocationally, we need to expend our energies in becoming competent in that area. *Pleasure* is found by approaching work in the spirit of both being kind to ourselves and using our work as a means of making an altruistic contribution to our fellow men. Indeed, Selye's comments on altruism color much of his thinking about the kinds of attitudes that lead to a less stressful life. Rather than concentrating on a ruthless and exclusive pursuit of one's own vocation, he suggests we devote our attention "to looking out for oneself by being necessary to others, and thus earning their good will. . . . Striving to make yourself ever more useful and necessary is an aim you can safely pursue throughout your life, and one that will protect you from the worst of all modern social stresses, purposelessness."

This, of course, does not mean that we shall be completely free from stress or that being entirely free of stress is a good thing in itself. Levine (1971) says, "It may be that effective behavior depends upon some optimum level of stress." It is generally considered that some degree of stress is always present. Certainly stress occurred in the past. Historically, stress was just as apparent and unbearable because of the plague, and later tuberculosis, as it was more recently for poliomyelitis and now for cancer. It was important for our ancestors to learn how to change attitudes and to develop a philosophy of life in order to cope with their traumatic events. It is no less important for us to do likewise.

In a recent book, Vaillant (1977) underscores the points that Selye makes. Vaillant made a study of the lives of young men in several successive classes of liberal arts colleges from 1937 until the present. In this study, he attempted to determine by tests, questionnaires, and interviews how such potentially successful young men coped with the problems they faced. Through precise accounts and life histories, he concludes that the difference between emotional health and some degree of emotional unhealthiness is found in the way these men reacted to challenges, defeats, and sorrows.

### Stressors

In addition to the challenges, defeats, and sorrows that arise in our lives, there may also be built-in stressors in the jobs we choose. While men and women are equally prone to stress, some women are susceptible to new kinds of it when they move into areas where women have never worked before, such as prison guards or corporation executives. Such work related stress can effect one's sexual life, family relationships, or social life and can even lead to excessive use of alcohol or drugs. Recently, a local public television station, KQED, in its program "Turnabout" dealt with job situations that produce such reactions as a knotting stomach, headaches, sweating hands. The program emphasized that some of the most stressful jobs are those held by health technicians, waiters and waitresses, practical nurses, inspectors, musicians, public relations persons, clinical lab technicians, dishwashers, warehousemen, and nurses aides. Omitted by this program were other leading contenders for the stress list, such as firemen, policemen, doctors for the terminally ill, psychiatrists, dentists, airport traffic controllers, and teachers in urban high schools.

## BURNOUT

Stressful occupations can lead to an emotional state that has been made the object of study by Dr. Christina Maslach at the University of California, Berkeley. She has been making a study of the problem of "burnout" which, she says, takes an incalculable toll in the form of alcoholism, divorce, mental illness, low productivity, and high absenteeism.

"When you burn out," Maslach (1977) explains, "your emotional center goes. There is nothing that you really care about. You do not have any optimistic feelings, only negative ones. You do not like the people you work with and wish they would go away. You treat them in institutional, routinized, dehumanizing ways." She sees burnout as a modern malady, the other side of alienation. What she has uncovered in her studies is that it makes no difference whether people suffering from burnout have cared too much or too little, ultimately they simply become incapable of caring. While this dreadful state may happen to anyone, it happens most frequently to those for whom caring is an integral part of their occupation. It happens to those for whom caring is the very core of their being.

Burnout is not a new situation. Modern literature, the theater, and films have been dealing with the topic for a long time. Graham Greene, the novelist, gave a name to the malady when he wrote his book *A Burnt-Out Case.* Camus wrote *The Stranger* in which he described a man so empty of emotion that he could no longer remember on what day his mother died, so how could he grieve for her? We have viewed M* A* S* H* in book, film, TV, and its numerous reruns until we are well acquainted with its characters who act and reenact their burned out lives where only their black humor keeps them functioning. These instances of burnout give us an idea of its variety and intensity; they cannot give any surcease to those who are either experiencing a lack of emotion or to those who are the victims of persons with burnout.

### Examples of Burnout

Let us look, now, at some examples of burnout and what can be done to lead its victim back to health and emotional well-being. We have read a great deal lately of the stressful hazards of being a law enforcement officer. Infrequently, in the course of his duties, a policeman kills someone. Our society has conditioned that officer through movies and police training to expect that he would feel that he had been successful in his duty or that he had done what was required or what was necessary. But after the event, he finds himself feeling cold, dehumanized, and very nonheroic. No amount of preemployment testing can determine how a person who is considered "within normal limits" of stress will react once he has taken another's life. Minderman (1975) has said that "the genesis of the post-killing reaction is the emotionally perceived discontinuity between the officer's expectations about the shooting and reality." Such a postkilling syndrome affects not only the officer but his subordinates, his superiors, and especially his family. Perhaps the officer has had only a "heartbeat" in which to make his decision. This decision will be investigated, explored, and deliberated upon for days, weeks, even months, if necessary. Depending upon whether the shooting was an acceptable one or a controversial or "bad" one (but often in either case) the officer is likely to fall prey to frequent reactions such as Lindsey (1977) suggests.

1. Sensory deterioration or a slowing down of time.

2. Flashbacks.
3. Fear of insanity.
4. Sorrow over depriving a person of life.
5. Crying that usually occurs outside the police environment.
6. Grasping for life.
7. Paranoia about someone evening the score.

Minderman also points out that there are other effects of burnout, such as apathy, alcoholism, marriage problems, bizarre activity, lashing out, and suicide. Whatever the aftermath, the officer needs help. But neither his peers nor his superiors are the answer. They cannot see the whole picture, for they are already programmed by preconceived feelings and guilt reactions that lead them to classify or label their colleague. Police departments should provide counseling for their officers. To be truly effective, this counseling needs to be voluntary and confidential. Moreover, the entire police training program needs to deal more realistically with the demands placed on officers by their jobs. Both the recruitment and in-service levels can be used as vehicles for utilizing techniques that identify stress and prepare officers for dealing with these stressors.

Another person who is prey to burnout in our society is the single parent. This parent is often desperate, driven, and barely able to hang on to sanity. He/she is continually faced with the fact of sole responsibility for the children and their myriad problems. In addition, there are job and employment insecurities and separation anxieties. A kind of social ostracism, real or imagined, seems to deny them ever again the felicities of the world of couples.

The Contra Costa County Health Department (1978) suggests that the best way to refill the cup that has been drained by the kind of burnout experienced by the single parent is to think first of oneself. This is not a selfish action but one that is healthy and positive. Do whatever makes you feel good, positive, and well taken care of. Here are additional suggestions:

1. Consciously seek out and spend time with people who make you feel good, who give you assurance and support. Avoid people, including family, who criticize, offer un-

wanted advice, drain you, and make you feel worse.

2. When someone tells you something that makes you feel good, remember it, savor it, and mentally replay it for yourself when you need a boost.

3. Spend more for a while on babysitters than on toys. Fix some of your favorite foods, and set the table attractively. Plan and then DO something you really enjoy. Go somewhere you would like to go. Join a supportive group, making new friends with people who share your life-style.

4. Your children do not want or ask for a parent who "gives it all up for them." They want you to be happy and enjoy yourself. They will respond to your winning behavior, for it gives them permission to be winners too. The emotional well-being of the parent the child lives with is one of the most crucial aspects of the child's well-being.

5. Remember you are not alone. There are other single parents with the same problem. There are other people making decisions every day in an effort to put positive forces into their lives and their special situations. Help yourself become a healthy single parent.

A psychologist named Karpmah said it well:

DECIDE TO BE HEARD
NOT HURT
DECIDE TO MATE
INSTEAD OF HATE
DECIDE TO BE SMARTER
NOT MARTYR

There are many ways of dealing with or preventing burnout. Here is what Tony, a Samaritan who serves his organization in London, did about it (1977). Samaritans are about 18,500 men and women in England, Scotland, Wales, Ireland, and the United States who dedicate a generous part of their leisure time to the prevention of suicide by alleviating human loneliness, misery, and despair. They spend countless hours in patient, undramatic "befriending" of persons who often have no one else to turn to.

## TAKE A BREAK
### TONY 1277, LONDON

A lot of us, especially if we are young and enthusiastic, fail to recognize the signs that tell us it is time to "give it a rest," to give ourselves a break from Samaritan duties, and get away from the problems and clients.

I say this because I have just returned to duty after giving myself leave of absence for almost a year, and I am finding that I have a totally new view of my work and an incredible feeling of freshness.

Besides being a Samaritan, my job was a contributory factor; I work in broadcasting. I was then engaged in launching a program of radio counseling so that it seemed I was never free of other people's troubles. There was no doubt that my approach to clients was becoming stale and tired. Frankly, I was more of a liability than an asset to my branch.

It is essential that volunteers learn to recognize the "danger signals" and not let themselves continue to do duties when they are close to emotional or even physical exhaustion. Most of us Samaritans face difficult times over and over again. We are the better because we know well how it feels to be in a state of crisis or tension. But we are of no help to the clients if our own troubles or our own weariness gets in the way of our helping.

I wrote asking for a leave of absence. After the specified six months were up and I still did not feel ready to go back, I stayed away a few more months. Finally I was able to sort things out for myself. When I returned to the Samaritans I could see things in a different perspective. I knew that I was ready to "befriend" again. The clients, after all, are the only reason for our existence, and they deserve the very best we can give them at all times. We cannot give of our best if we are tired or restless!

### REFERENCES

Levine, S., "Stress and Behavior," *Sci Am, 224*:21–31, 1971.

Lindsey, Robert, "Police Stress: Cause, Effect and Solution," *Vita* (International Association for Suicide Prevention), December, 1977.

Maslach, Christina, "Burnout," *Shanti Symposium*, Second Annual Conference for Physicians on Death and Dying, Berkeley, California, 1977.

Minderman, John, "Traumatic Incident Reaction in Law Enforcement Officers," *Behavioral Science Unit,* Quantico, Virginia:   FBI National Academy, 1977.

Seyle, Hans, *Stress Without Distress.*   Philadephia:   Lippincott, 1974.

Tony, 1277, London, "Take A Break," *Vita* (International Association for Suicide Prevention), December, 1977.

Vaillant, George E., *Adaptation to Life.*   Boston:   Little, 1977.

## Chapter 4

# DEPRESSION

THERE ARE times when nearly all of us have experienced a kind of malaise that affects the way we feel, the way we react toward others, and the way we behave. During these periods, our comments often express a sense of feeling "down," "fed up," or "blue." By these phrases we acknowledge that we are unaccountably low in spirit and energy. We feel useless and pessimistic. The word "unaccountably" creeps into this evaluation of our feelings because we do not usually feel this way. Our ordinary experience is one of enthusiasm, joy, hopefulness, and optimism about the present and relationships with others. Why, out of the blue, is this feeling uppermost in our minds? What is happening to us?

If you and I can look at events that have occurred some time before "down" periods appear, we can often see that slight depressive moods come upon us after we experienced a disappointment over some loss. Sometimes there is no awareness that there has been a preceding cause for our sudden change in mood. Often this depressive feeling passes away just as quickly as it occurred and is explained away by saying that it was "just one of those things," "just one of my moods," or "I just had an off day."

But sometimes depressive periods arise from actual experiences that leave us feeling bereft of appreciation and love. Somewhere we have picked up a sense of feeling devalued, denigrated, that someone has demeaned or humiliated us so that we lose faith in ourselves and our self-image. Nursing these feelings of frustration and resentment encourages an attack in order to hurt the object of our resentment. Suddenly, there are feelings of frustration, resentment, and anxiety.

A depressive state may be observed in a friend and labelled as "That's the way he responds to everything." By this observation we acknowledge that there are different types of people who have quite different attitudes toward life. There are people of varying temperaments: Some are habitually happy and jolly or unhappy and sad; stable or unstable; confident or lacking confidence; optimistic or pessimistic. These temperaments reflect a person's attitude toward life. We recognize that there are some people who cope with things, others who do not; some seldom need help or encouragement, and others rely heavily on outside strength and support. Most of us know persons who seem always to be pessimistic. Careful observation can sort out whether this temperament is marked by a *transient* pessimism, a response to a stimulus, or a *persistent* pessimism, not a response to anything but rather an attitude toward life.

It is important to recognize that these depressive states can be the result of either temporary moods, of an experience, or of an attitude toward life. This knowledge helps us decide not only what may be causing our depressive feeling but also what can be done about it. Any one of the three kinds of depression mentioned can be brought about by some disappointment, some loss, some specific kind of experience, or just our own temperament as reflected by our attitude toward life. Let us take a look at what happens and how experiences change and affect us.

We are continually passing through crises as we grow and mature, and it is not hard to select a few that have persisted in our memory as "trying" times. From birth onward we have been subjected to a developmental history that has provided an opportunity for us either to progress and go ahead or to get stuck at some particular place.

## DEVELOPMENTAL CHANGES

The birth experience itself is a real shock to most babies. The Lebouyer method of childbirth points out how even our modern, highly technological medical methods subject the newborn to unnecessary shock and trauma. This trauma is produced, Lebouyer says, by allowing the umbilical cord to be severed too soon; by slapping the baby immediately after birth; by subjecting it to bright lights, complete baths, and isolation from its mother. He points out in his speeches and film that babies born in this fashion do not smile for two or three months, whereas the Lebouyer method produces a smiling newborn baby.

We pass through many stages where a good deal of change is occurring in our lives: the first day at school, a move away from home, the newly emotion laden situation of the first boy-girl affection, completing school, getting a job, getting married, having a baby. At the same time, these stages create changes in the amount of our dependency on others. In fact, they force us into new roles: we are no longer a baby but starting school; we are no longer a child but an adolescent; no longer a student but an employed person.

At certain stages of our development, we are vulnerable to external stress. In childhood, for example, a child may never have described himself as "feeling depressed," but he may have a strong recollection of those childhood days when he felt that "they seemed to forget that I was there." This experience of being shut out or even absent comes into his consciousness as a denial of his own personal worth. The result is depression. Such a child may not cry, but becomes silent and withdraws into himself. Again, he may become overactive or even violent, breaking up toys, furniture, or family belongings because he feels broken up inside. The loss of a parent in the critical years of childhood, particularly around the ages of four to six and eleven to fourteen, predisposes a child to depression in later adult life.

The adolescent years are especially turbulent times. During these years a teenager swings between opposite poles: at one pole he is invincible because of good reflexes, good health, eyesight, strong muscles, and acute hearing; at the opposite pole he feels he is going to be annihilated by some cataclysmic force or disaster such as war, the bomb, an earthquake, etc. One moment the adolescent is an adult, the next a child, confused in his identification between father and mother, between male and female. He is characteristically moody, bad tempered, and depressed; then he swings into a state of wild, unpredictable enthusiasm. He feeds on a diet of high adventure tales in literature, television films, and romantic fantasies where the reality is never as enjoyable as the anticipation. His romantic idealism is destined for disillusionment. These swings in moods and roles fill him with doubts, guilt, disappointment and, ultimately, depression. Sometimes these depressions are severe enough to lead to suicide.

At a later period of development when a young adult becomes engaged, married, or experiences the birth of a child, he is pulled up short from his earlier fantasies. Here new restrictions are laid upon him by his relationship to his spouse or his child. Either young parent can fret to the point of grief for the lost freedom, the funpacked, carefree days of the single person, even for the time when there were just the two of them. A young couple can also be upset, agitated and moody about their ability to keep up the competition in the race for retaining their jobs, youthfulness, beauty, or sexual advantage. Close relationships undergo a special strain at this stage of development. There is a good deal of worry, introspection, doubt, and guilt as to whether they "can make it."

The ones who know they are beginning to slip are the middle-aged and the elderly. Both these groups experience real or imagined loss of function and status. The middle-aged suffer the slings and arrows of the male and female menopause. This is a time for a new appraisal of themselves and their sexuality and their ability to maintain their power or earning capacity. The elderly see a loss of status and function at the time of retirement. Too often they feel there is "nowhere to go, except down." Depression may increase with advancing years, but then the causes of depression are internal rather than external.

If you are beginning to feel depressed by reading this, take heart. Mitchell (1975) says, "Depression is not inevitable at these critical stages of life. But clinicians show that it is those who have been through an early sense of loss in infancy, or have not had their needs met to some extent at that stage, who are more likely in later life to become depressed when change . . . exposes them to stress. There is then a re-experience of the early loss and a reenactment of the early depression."

## Accidental Crises

While the foregoing developmental changes are taking place, we are also subjected to a number of accidental crises. These crises spring out of our relationship to outside events that may be threatening to us and our emotional safety. Such accidental crises are another way of describing losses and separations that beset us from birth to death. Many of these separations have already been noted in the section on Loss and Separation (Chapter 1). Mitchell (1975) mentions some of these losses:

1. Failures, either of our own making or of others, but failures which we regard as such. These may include loss of material wealth, security, examinations, promotions, retirement, or being fired from a job.
2. Acute losses which leave us in a painful space. These losses include the death of a loved one, abortion, infidelity, loss of a boy- or girl-friend, divorce, loss of sexuality, loss of function or efficiency during a severe illness, or a failure of power in an occupational situation.
3. There are also cultural transitions where we move from one role to another or from one way of life to another. In the process of changing roles we lose the comforting guidelines we previously relied upon. These situations are experienced when we go away to college; shift to different ideals, morals, customs; move from one country to another, or even from one time zone to another.

Many of these accidental crises involving loss, bereavement, and grief will produce depression in individuals who cannot cope with change. There are also those who will ultimately cope but in whom the depression appears before the adaptive mechanism can be brought into play.

## Life Cycles

It is timely here to review the recurring and changing episodes that mark the cyclical nature of our lives. The cyclical view of life is a very old one. Most of us are aware of the frequency with which this view of life occurs in both biblical literature and our own national literature. Humanists today talk anew of a life cycle, but in the recent past we have usually meant a lifeline. This linear view of life has encouraged us to think of birth as though it were a form of extraction; child development as though it were life's only formative period; adulthood as though it were a long, even plateau; old age as though its main characteristic were deterioration; and death as though it were a medical failure. So long as we are influenced by this linear approach to the developmental side of our natures, we are likely to get "stuck" at some place along this developmental line, pull in our coping mechanism, withdraw, become depressed and say, "I've had it."

The cyclical view, on the other hand, stresses a continuous process of unfolding; a series of passage points at which outgrown self-images, values, and roles are relinquished and renewal is possible. This cyclical perspective enables us to emphasize development as a lifelong pattern. Viewed in this way, many problems may be seen not as pathological conditions but as the signals of turning points in life. At those turning points, one may seek to facilitate the natural but difficult process of passage between one life phase and another. At such turning points, one may rediscover the age-old sense of the individual's lifetime as a symbolic journey where even dying itself may be a stage of growth.

### Depression and Bodily Reactions

Whether the depressive state is due to a mood, an experience, or an attitude toward life, it can lead to a difference in our bodily reaction to daily life. There is at first an acute change that produces a loss of effectiveness in our bodily and mental functions. The most apparent effect of this distress is that we are no longer able to absorb stress and deal with it. There is not enough energy to cope with the problems we have. In this regard, a depressive state may be an effective way of providing protection, for it temporarily switches the person off until he can cope later.

A mild depressive state is a commonplace experience, and one needs to know that a majority of people experience it. Our reaction to it is to want to be by ourselves, to think things over. How better or more appropriate when we have lost a job, or a friend, or are trying to think through a difficult relationship? In such situations a depressive state is customary, appropriate, even desirable. We recognize that we are either passing through a developmental stage or one of life's accidental but recurring misadventures. In the process, we have come upon something that gives us trouble with our coping mechanisms.

## CAUSES OF DEPRESSION

There is little doubt that at certain stages of our development we are more vulnerable to external stress. But this vulnerability is largely dependent upon genetic factors, individual weaknesses, and biochemical and psychological changes. Mitchell (1975) lists the causes of depression as being due to physical, psychological, and social causes:

1. Organic (physical)
   a. Traumatic—head injury, concussion; certain operations; loss of valued parts, such as head, hands, eyes, ears, genitals, etc.
   b. Infective—following influenza but also infections such as encephalitis and hepatitis.
   c. Vascular—following nonfatal stroke or thrombosis, resulting in paralysis of limb or loss of clear speech.
   d. Hormonal—biochemical changes in body (after childbirth, menopause) and in certain glands in the body that fail, such as thyroid.
   e. Epileptic—seizures can result in unpredictable mood changes or violent alterations of behavior (psychomotor epilepsy).
   f. Degenerative—when the brain ages, it loses its efficiency. Being aware of this can become depressive. Premature aging of the brain (presenile) or irreversible loss of brain function in the elderly (dementia) leads to depression.
   g. Pharmacological—certain drugs can lead to depression: drugs to control high blood pressure and certain types of contraceptive pills. The result is not inevitable, but in some susceptible individuals it is likely.
2. Psychological
   a. Childhood experiences of separation and loss.
   b. In adult life nearly all psychological causes for depression contain some re-creation of early childhood experience of loss. People who have not been able to deal adequately with some early loss by death, separation, etc., may be more prone to depression from psycho-

logical causes in later life.

c. Certain body build (somatotype). Persons with a heavy build, especially around the shoulders and abdomen, tend to depression more than others. It is uncertain whether this is due to psychological or physical causes.

d. Compensation neurosis—after an injury, a patient may be depressed or anxious to an extent quite out of keeping with the degree of the accident, and this may clear up completely after there has been a judicial settlement.

3. Social

a. Poverty, bad weather, minority group membership do not of themselves cause depression. The key lies in considering separation and loss. If poverty means a loss of status, if bad weather means the loss of a cherished plan, if being a minority group member cuts one off from others and leads to persecution or loss of privilege, depression can result.

b. Critical periods of life can lead to depression.

c. Social isolation, such as women isolated in the home, no matter what the economic class. Often there are self-destructive acts where people are cut off from one another. These situations are not associated with income or social class. Examples of social isolation are the spinster, widow, widower, or divorced person living alone or without adequate social communication with others.

## GRIEF AND DEPRESSION

The loss of a loved one who is important to one's emotional well-being is the most wrenching of the losses and separations experienced. It is commonplace that such a loss will produce a depression. The depression that follows death and accompanies the bereaved throughout much of his grieving period is different from other kinds of depression in many ways. A grief depression comes on suddenly and is specifically related to the loss by death. It bears no relationship to a history of depression in the family.

Grief depression is generally mild to moderate in intensity, but it can occasionally be severe. It may last from three months to a year and generally improves with time, although it may become chronic. The main characteristic of grief depression is that there is a constant feeling of sadness that varies very little in its intensity. There may be difficulty in falling asleep, but once asleep, the bereaved generally sleeps through the night and awakens with some feeling of repose and refreshment. While the bereaved's appetite is not good, food is not usually rejected. There is some weight loss.

Sadness expresses itself by a steady tearfulness and quiet sobbing when thoughts wander again and again over the extent of the loss. Emotional control is sufficient for the person to manage his daily life, but he often has reservations about his ability to do so. This is largely because at this time memory is poor, and the bereaved frequently feels disorientated, disorganized, and unable to concentrate. Sometimes this feeling is so strong that the bereaved may feel he is losing his mind. Even though self-esteem remains, the bereaved often feels a terrible sense of emptiness. Through all these vicissitudes, the bereaved is still able to retain a sense of the reality of his environment and surroundings.

Paramount is a sense of fatigue. In spite of this, the bereaved can often perform for considerable periods of time before the fatigue bears down again. The concern about this fatigue leads to complaints about stomach, chest, and lower back aches and pains. There may be suicidal thoughts that are usually attempts to relate to the loss of hope. Fortunately, the depression that accompanies grief does not recur unless there is another loss by death or another form of separation.

Proper diet and exercise do wonders to relieve grief depression. Several light meals a day seem to be a better arrangement for most persons than one or two heavy meals. Particular attention needs to be paid to the nutritional value of the food consumed. It is important to choose fresh fruits and vegetables, easily digested proteins, etc., instead of the frequent diet of cookies, pies, and cakes that friends and neighbors usually bring to a household in mourning. Light exercises before an open window, walks in the fresh air, or other moderate forms of exercise (swimming or bicycling) help get oxygen into the bloodstream and to the brain. Such exercise and walks can be first step toward the resocialization of the bereaved by getting him out of the house and into his environment again.

Prospective counselors are encouraged to familiarize themselves with Crammer's chart, Comparison of Different Types of Depression (1971). It is important to be acquainted with this excellent chart (see appendix) in order to assess when, or if, the bereaved needs professional assistance.

## REFERENCES

Crammer, Leonard, *Up From Depression.* New York: S&S, 1971.
Mitchell, Ross, *Depression.* Harmondsworth, Middlesex, England: Penguin, 1975.

## Section II

# SUDDEN DEATH

### Introduction

I HAVE TRIED to impress upon the reader that grief is a normal expression of a healthy personality; that it is the response to the loss of a person who is important to one's emotional well-being; that it seldom requires therapeutic intervention. All the symptoms of grief—the steady crying or sobbing, the depression, anger and guilt, loss of weight, insomnia, and distressing disorientation—are to be expected. Grief symptoms such as these are welcome indicators that grief is being expressed and, if allowed its full expression, healing will eventually occur.

While the majority of us hope that our lives will go on and on, we realize that we are mortal and that death will come to us all. Death is a part of life; there is no life without death. We live with the hope that our life will be a long and gratifying one and that "it will be rounded off at the end" by a peaceful, pain-free death. This is a comforting thought and devoutly to be wished for, but the probabilities are against it. The probabilities are that the majority of us will die in a sudden, unexpected way, often traumatically.

A *sudden* death complicates nearly all grief. Unlike a prolonged illness or invalidism, there is no opportunity for "a long good-bye." There has not been enough time to anticipate its happening. Sudden death is frequently violent and traumatic and can leave the deceased's body in a battered, mutilated, or ugly condition. Sudden death may be caused by suicide; homicide; auto, motorcycle, and plane accidents; drownings; industrial accidents; accidents by choking, hemorrhaging, overdoses; falling

63

from great heights; and cardiovascular episodes. Friends and relatives are especially upset when the body is disfigured. Moreover, some types of death aren't as socially acceptable as others. Suicides are intentional; the other modes are accidental.

The chapters in this section will discuss aspects of sudden death as they relate to cardiovascular fatalities and the sudden infant death syndrome, accidental deaths, and to the violent deaths of industrial accidents, homicide, and suicide. Where relevant, these chapters will also discuss ways of preventing some of these kinds of sudden death.

Again and again a grief counselor sees, listens to, and shares the grief of persons whose sadness strikes at the heart and wrenches the mind. One who does grief counseling for the bereaved of a sudden death is too frequently haunted by the thought, "This death need not have occurred." Realizing that a death need not have occurred is as difficult for the counselor to handle as it is for the one bereaved. All the grief, the family disruptions, the economic, physical, and human sufferings could have been avoided, if. ... Clients recognize this aspect of sudden death and want to talk about it. Indeed, some of them direct their own healing by later becoming involved in such matters as gun control, abuse of prescription drugs, alcohol abuse, or traffic safety measures. Just as families that have had a loved one die from cancer, multiple sclerosis, cystic fibrosis, or sudden infant death syndrome later become active in organizations that work toward a better understanding of the disease or syndrome, its research or medical aspects, so survivors of sudden deaths also interest themselves in preventive or educative aspects of such deaths and, in the process, help heal their own grief and despair.

It is important for the reader to know how different kinds of sudden deaths are usually classified. In order to make this differentiation clear, to understand what varieties of death must be dealt with in a counseling setting, I have prepared the following list that should be helpful:

## COMMON TYPES OF SUDDEN DEATH, LISTED ACCORDING TO MODES

| *Kind of Sudden Death* | *Usual Classification* |
|---|---|
| 1. Traffic fatalities by auto, motorcycle, plane, train, bicycle (passengers, pedestrians, and drivers) , and horse. | Accidental |
| 2. Fatal cardiovascular episodes that are unattended by a physician. | Sudden Death—CV |
| 3. Homicide, violence against another person. | Homicide |
| 4. Suicide, violence by the self. | Suicide |
| 5. Falls from high places while hiking, skiing, children climbing trees, rocks, etc. | Accidental |
| 6. Falls from beds (usually the elderly), doorsteps, faulty pavement, over unusual objects left on the path. These falls usually cause concussions or fractures of hip, leg, or rib bones which cause complication from which the victim dies. | Accidental |
| 7. Aspiration or choking. Most common among babies, children, the elderly, alcoholics. Portions of food or a foreign object gets caught in the throat and cannot be dislodged or vomitus is aspirated, causing death. | Accidental |
| 8. Drowning. Falling into pool, stream, ocean, or lake; boating mishaps; or hyperventilation (holding one's breath) by teenagers while playing in a pool. | Accidental |
| 9. House fires. Death results from smoke inhalation. | Accidental |

| *Kind of Sudden Death* | *Usual Classification* |
|---|---|
| 10. Inhalation of toxic substances caused by faulty heaters, faulty ventilation. Can occur during sleep either at home or in a recreation vehicle during a trip. | Accidental |
| 11. Ingesting toxic substances, such as an overdose of prescription drugs, poisons. | Accidental |
| 12. Falling objects, such as falling rocks or boulders and work equipment around the house or garage. | Accidental |
| 13. Falling objects or overturned tractors or heavy equipment at work. | Industrial Accident |
| 14. Gunshot. Improper use or storage of guns which endanger both adults and children who play with them. Occurs most frequently while cleaning or storing a gun "that isn't loaded." | Accidental |
| 15. Electrocution. Occurs any place where faulty electric power connections and water come together or where fallen electric lines are touched. | |
| If it occurs in the home it is | Accidental |
| If it occurs at work it is an | Industrial Accident |
| 16. Scalding. May occur in the home or elsewhere if water tanks with exceptionally hot water are not protected against accidental use. May occur in the home and endanger the elderly or children. Known to occur in sauna baths where user falls asleep. | |
| If it occurs in the home it is | Accidental |
| If it occurs at work it is an | Industrial Accident |
| 17. An explosion in the home is | Accidental |
| An explosion at work is an | Industrial Accident |
| 18. Inhalation of toxic fumes at home is | Accidental |
| Inhalation of toxic fumes at work is an | Industrial Accident |

| *Kind of Sudden Death* | *Usual Classification* |
|---|---|
| 19. Unexpected deaths during or following surgery or a surgical misadventure. | Accidental or Sudden Death |
| 20. Fatal at term births. | Sudden Death |
| 21. In California, any death in which the deceased has not been attended by a physician in the 20 days before death or where the physician cannot sign the death certificate because he cannot certify the cause of death.* | Sudden Death |

All of these modes of death, whether they be classified as accidental, homicide, industrial accident, suicide, or sudden death, have many problems in common that must be discussed and worked through by the counselor and the client. Over and above the effect of the suddenness of the death that affects bereavement in *all* sudden deaths, all of these modes of death have many factors in common that touch the bereaved and can be looked upon as seedbeds for future difficulties if left unattended. Following are some of the factors that must be considered.

---

*In order that the reader may know the kinds of death requiring inquiry by a coroner in California and the broad scope of the cases grief counselors deal with, the following may be helpful:

California Government Code 27491 — DEATHS REQUIRING INQUIRY BY THE CORONER: It shall be the duty of the coroner to inquire into and determine the circumstances, manner, and cause of all violent, sudden or unusual deaths; unattended deaths; deaths wherein the deceased has not been attended by a physician in the 20 days before death; deaths related to or following known or suspected self-induced or criminal abortion; known or suspected homicide, suicide, or accidental poisoning; deaths known or suspected as resulting in whole or in part from or related to accident or injury either old or recent; deaths due to drowning, fire, hanging, gunshot, stabbing, cutting, exposure, starvation, alcoholism, drug addiction, strangulation, or aspiration; death in whole or in part occasioned by criminal means; deaths associated with a known or alleged rape or crime against nature; deaths in prison or while under sentence; deaths known or suspected as due to contagious disease and constituting a public hazard; deaths from occupational diseases or occupational hazards; deaths under such circumstances as to afford a reasonable ground to suspect that the death was caused by the criminal act of another, or any deaths reported by physicians or other persons having knowledge of death for inquiry by coroner. Inquiry in this section does not include those investigative functions usually performed by other law enforcement agencies. In any case in which the coroner conducts an inquiry pursuant to this section he shall personally sign the certificate of death.

I. Preexisting conditions, such as
   1. Lack of communication between the deceased and the bereaved.
   2. Unfinished emotional and personal business, such as expectations of either separation or divorce.
   3. Financial, employment, or legal complications in the family, such as the lack of a will, lengthy unemployment of either spouse, problems with the children (school difficulties, delinquency, leaving home for school, job, marriage, or incompatibility).
   4. Physical or mental health problems of a member of the family.
   5. Recent arrivals in the community (without supportive systems of relatives, friends, or institutions).
   6. Depression.
   7. Several previous deaths.

II. Death related problems of an immediate nature, such as
   1. Plans for or reactions to the funeral.
   2. Questions regarding how the accident occurred; what happened; police, coroner, and autopsy matters.
   3. Decisions regarding disposition of the damaged vehicle, apparel, gun used, etc.
   4. How to clean up after the accident (if it occured in the home). It almost never occurs to people that this can be a traumatic problem. Many janitorial firms will not undertake this job. Until the job is done, however, it may be impossible for the family to inhabit the home. Under the circumstances it is a job that no family member should have to perform. Inquire at the Coroner's Office for suggestions; some coroners have aides who can do this on their own time.
   5. Disposition or care of pets dependent upon deceased.

III. Interaction with family/friends/relatives, such as
   1. Closed family situations where help or assistance is never sought.
   2. Take-charge friends/relatives who shut out rest of family.

3. What to tell the children; how much, when, where.
4. Decision to allow children to remain at home or to farm them out to friends/relatives.
5. Family that feeds on anger, resentment, old grudges.
6. Dependence upon drugs, alcohol, overeating, silence.
7. Family believes death is a punishment for wrongdoing.
8. Indecisiveness.
9. Hysteria.

IV. Death related problems that must ultimately be decided, such as
   1. Financial arrangements—insurance, pensions, welfare, seeking employment/changing jobs, seeking alternative housing.
   2. Disposal of deceased's belongings.
   3. Visits to the cemetery; who goes, how often, when do they end?
   4. Learning to talk about the deceased with family/friends.

*Chapter 5*

# CARDIOVASCULAR FATALITIES
# AND
# SUDDEN INFANT DEATH SYNDROME

## CARDIOVASCULAR FATALITIES

HEART ATTACK is the number one killer among diseases. While the incidence generally increases with age, a greater number of younger people are now experiencing heart attacks and accompanying fatalities. High blood pressure affects over 24 million Americans, and more than 7 million of those are unaware they have the disease. High blood pressure is almost twice as prevalent among blacks as among whites. Blacks also have a higher rate of hypertensive heart disease and have a higher mortality rate. Hypertension (high blood pressure) is a major contributing factor to heart attack. Stroke also often results from high blood pressure. It is estimated that close to two million Americans are afflicted by stroke.

An epidemiological study of the United States Public Health Service has documented the significance of the major risk factors in heart attack and stroke. It also shows that the danger increases with the number and severity of risk factors. Some of these risk factors cannot be changed, such as heredity, sex, race, and age. Others, such as high cholesterol level, high blood pressure, diabetes, smoking, high saturated fat diet, stress, and lack of exercise can be changed by medical supervision and by the person at risk.

Risk factors that can be changed by medical supervision center largely on three medical procedures:

71

1. Cholesterol is a fatty substance that is necessary for good health. There are times when the cholesterol level in the blood is too high, due either to improper diet or to an unusual amount being manufactured by the body. A physician can measure the amount of cholesterol in the blood by a simple blood test and prescribe diet regimens for most to maintain it within a normal range. Drugs are also available for highly resistant individuals.
2. High blood pressure is an insidious factor in both heart attack and stroke because it has no characteristic symptoms and must be diagnosed by a doctor. It is important to have this simple test made. There are a wide variety of drugs that can control it.
3. Diabetes, or a familial tendency toward the disease, is associated with an increased risk of heart attack or stroke. A physician can detect diabetes and prescribe drugs, diet regimens, and weight control and exercise programs to keep it in check.

There are other risk factors that can be changed by the person himself who is at risk. These do-it-yourself changes can result in a tremendous reduction in risk of heart attack and stroke.

1. Cigarette smoking increases the risk of heart attack and stroke. The death rate from cardiovascular disease of cigarette smokers who stop is nearly as low as that of people who have never smoked.
2. A nutritious diet low in saturated fat and cholesterol, consumed at a low calorie level to maintain the proper body weight will help reduce the risk of heart attack and stroke.
3. Stress is a common environmental factor that may contribute to cardiovascular disease. Sometimes stressful situations can be identified and changes can be made. (See Chapter 3 on Stress.)
4. Some studies show that men who lead sedentary lives run a higher risk of heart attack than those who get regular exercise. However, exercise programs should be undertaken only on the advice of a physician. The doctor should test to determine the capacity of the system for exercise

and then prescribe the appropriate kind and amount of exercise.

The American Heart Association believes that risk factor modification by the individual will produce the greatest reduction of risk if an attempt is made simultaneously to lower *all* the possible factors. The Association also urges the development of a pattern in early childhood that tends to prevent controllable risk factors from developing in the first place. A great deal can be done by the individual to avoid these two disabilities if he does not smoke cigarettes, controls high blood pressure, eats foods low in saturated fat and cholesterol, controls weight, gets regular daily exercise, and has regular medical checkups.

Libby's case, which follows, is an example of the patience and restraint required of a counselor. It is not easy to spend a great deal of time with someone who is unresponsive. This counselor offered suggestions but never fell into the trap of forcing the client to accept them. The client was permitted to take her time, to learn to assess her own situation, and to decide what priorities to set for herself.

Libby's husband died suddenly of a heart attack, leaving her helpless and dependent. He had been responsible for all decisions in the family. There seemed to be few things Libby could do by herself. She did not drive a car, never went unaccompanied to shop, never had friends or relatives in for meals, never had planned her own wardrobe or daily activities. When she found herself completely alone, unable to do the simplest domestic chores without supervision and guidance, her despair and loneliness became intolerable.

She regularly saw a therapist who kept her heavily sedated. This allowed her to be even more remote from the reality of her situation. She made numerous suicide attempts and hated herself for being unable even to end her own life. She wandered aimlessly about the house, unkempt, dressed in her husband's dressing gown with his picture always in one pocket. She did not eat, slept badly, and had frequent chest pains.

Family and friends welcomed the visits of the counselor, for they had given up trying to pull her out of her depressed state. Nothing much happened for a long time. Efforts toward a better diet and a little exercise fell on deaf ears. A medical checkup showed she had nothing physically wrong. She was encouraged to be taken to the market and to shop while the counselor waited in the car. Several times Libby fled from a store for the safety of the car. Little by little she made progress. As freedom of movement improved she also gained freedom of mind.

Then it came out. She had always resented being trapped in a marriage that kept her helpless and dependent. She could not grieve for her husband but felt the social necessity to do so. Anger with herself for feeling this way plus the helplessness that had been built into her were the  motivations for her suicide attempts. When she become free enough to talk about her condition, her suicidal thoughts, fears, and inhibitions began to fall away.

Little by little she recognized some of the patterns of her life. Alternatives were talked about and, painfully, she learned to make choices and efforts to live. It took over a year to learn to do some of the simplest tasks. The process of resocialization gained each time another fear got cast away. At the end of eighteen months, she was driving a car, doing her own shopping, walking to the library, even thinking "about doing something for someone else." When Libby learned that it was not the death of her husband that depressed her but the kind of marriage she had, she was free to acknowledge the loss of her husband. Then she showed some genuine grief. Only after she was able to grieve was she free to proceed with the pressing demands of rebuilding her life.

## SUDDEN INFANT DEATH SYNDROME

Approximately 8,000 to 10,000 babies die of sudden infant death syndrome in the United States (two or three per 100,000 live births). Such a death can be one of the most traumatic experiences for young parents. One minute the infant was sleeping quietly in its crib and the next time the parent took a look it was dead, struck by a syndrome commonly called "crib death," but medically called the sudden infant death syndrome (SIDS). It is defined as a sudden, unexpected death of an apparently healthy infant in which no lethal lesions are found at autopsy.

An SIDS death strikes quickly. It cannot be predicted or prevented, and its etiology is unknown. It is the number one cause of death in infants after the first week of life, with a peak incidence at three months of age. It occurs more frequently in the winter months, with a higher incidence in males, premature babies, low-birth-weight infants, and lower socioeconomic groups.

SIDS is as old as the Old Testament. In biblical times it was referred to as "overlaying." Then, as in some cultures today, mothers slept with their infants. When the mother awoke to find her child dead, she assumed she must have rolled over on him and caused the death. It seems to have been at least as frequent in the eighteenth and nineteenth centuries as it is now. SIDS deaths have occurred all over the world and have been investigated throughout the western world. Studies of this syndrome show similar rates of incidence in Europe, Australia, Canada, and the United States and that the incidence is not rising.

Parents whose child dies from this syndrome can take some comfort from the knowledge that SIDS has been present for a long time and cannot be the result of new environmental agents, such as birth control pills, fluoride in the water, or smoking.

Since there is no known way to prevent its occurrence, this situation creates a certain amount of mystery and leads to a great deal of anxiety among parents. Even when told that the autopsy ruled out smothering, strangulation, or infection as possible cause of death, many parents continue to believe that some member of the family had "done something" to the baby. Such thoughts lead to considerable guilt, self-doubt, incrimination, even psychosis. When left without help, such behavior can contribute to emotional breakdown or family dissolution. Blaming relatives, babysitters, even the physician who last saw the child and found it well is a common reaction to this kind of death.

There have been several theories advanced as possible causes of SIDS. None of these have yet been proven, and most of them have been discounted. Some of the causes thought responsible for this syndrome and discounted are allergy to cow's milk, an enlarged thymus gland, bacterial infection, radiation fallout, use of modern machines and drugs, smoking, adding bleach to the diaper wash, whiplash injury to the spinal cord, air pollution, and fluoridation.

It is sometimes assumed that the baby died of suffocation since a victim of SIDS is often found in the corner of his crib, sometimes with his face turned towards the pillow. The fatality occurs even when there are no articles of bedding, toys, or pets around or near the face. Autopsy records lead specialists to say with certainty that SIDS is not caused by external suffocation.

Another worry is that the child may have choked on his last feeding. Additional fear accompanies this assumption since often the baby is found with a ring of milk and blood froth around his mouth. Autopsies indicate that this ring usually occurs after death, and that the froth in no way blocked the infant's air passages. While the literature indicates that SIDS occurred in previous centuries when breast-fed babies were common, we now know that SIDS occurs to bottle-fed as well as to breast-fed infants.

Parents often ask the question, Am I to blame? While parents feel responsible for the death of a child, needless blame should not be put upon oneself or others who were around the baby. Since SIDS has no specific symptoms, it can and does happen to healthy, robust babies. It can occur in hospitals and can befall the children of doctors and nurses.

Parents also have apprehension about other children in the family. SIDS is not contagious. There is no need to be concerned about contamination from clothing, bedding, or furniture of an SIDS infant. Neither is SIDS hereditary. A future child runs very slight risk of this syndrome—less than one percent. Parental anxiety about SIDS can do a future child more harm than good.

Another question parents ask is, Did my baby suffer? An SIDS death can occur within five minutes and is almost instantaneous. It is assumed that there is some movement that occurs during the last few seconds, which would explain the rumpled blankets or unusual positions of the infant. SIDS infants do not cry out, neither do they show any trace of having been disturbed in their sleep. Authorities conclude from their investigations that SIDS does not cause suffering or pain to the baby.

### Where to Go for Help

The National Foundation for Sudden Infant Death, Inc., 1501 Broadway, New York, New York 10036 publishes brochures, articles, and films that are distributed to persons who request this information. This foundation also publishes a pamphlet, "The Subsequent Child" by Carolyn Szybist. Additional scientific information on SIDS is available from the following sources— Sudden Death in Infants: Proceedings of the Conference on

Causes of Sudden Death in Infants (1963), National Institute of Child Health and Human Development, Bethesda, Maryland 20014, and proceedings of the Second International Conference on Causes of Sudden Infant Death in Infants (1970), University of Washington Press, Seattle, Washington 98105.

There are SIDS associations in most counties. Your local Coroner's Office or the local public health department can tell you where these associations are located. Such associations are staffed by persons who themselves have had an SIDS death occur in the family. Association members give considerable comfort and assurance to recently bereaved SIDS families, for they can speak from personal experience about the death and its aftermath in a family. However, they generally do not do any grief counseling.

In our county, the coroner sends a letter to an SIDS family regarding the findings of the autopsy. The letter explains that a public health nurse is available to the family and contains the area health department telephone numbers and a copy of the "Sudden Death" information pamphlet.

When the Coroner's Office notifies the health department that an infant death has been found to be an SIDS death, the maternal-child health director contacts the infant's physician to (1) discuss the presumptive diagnosis of SIDS on the basis of gross autopsy findings, (2) determine whether the physician wishes the health department personnel to contact the family to provide information about SIDS.

At the request of the physician, a public health nurse calls the family and suggests an appropriate time for such a meeting; the maternal-child health director then telephones the public health nurse supervisor to request a follow-up. At this time the public health department forms are transmitted to this supervisor. The public health nurse telephones the family to arrange for a home visit. The nurse gives information about SIDS to the family and informs them about the local SIDS association. The public health department forms are filled out and returned to the maternal-child health office which, in turn, sends these forms along with the infant's birth and death certificates to the California State SIDS Program, Sacramento.

SIDS follow-up is a state mandated program in California.

## SIDS AND GRIEF

The grief following an SIDS death presents some unusual complications. In the first place, the death leaves two young parents, who may never have experienced any loss by death before, in a quandry about the death itself. The circumstances of the death—without warning and occurring quickly—lead the parents into blaming each other for the death of the baby. If other persons were in charge of the baby, such as relatives, friends, or babysitters, they also become the target for this blame. *All of the persons concerned* at the time of the baby's last feeding or last bedding down should be helped *at once* before such blaming can wreck the interpersonal relations of that group.

It is of utmost importance to inform all of these persons that SIDS is sudden, unpreventable, and *nothing they did* was responsible for the infant's death. It is most helpful for the family to be visited by a member of the local chapter of the SIDS Association, a person who has also been through this experience. If such a person is not available, then a public health nurse, physician, coroner, or clergyman needs to bring this information into focus for all the persons involved in the last care of the child. Generally, none of these persons, except the clergy, have much of an idea how to begin and help along the grieving process, so it is important that help with their grief also be provided. Where grief counseling is not available, it is to be hoped that any of the above persons will recommend some of the reading suggested in the accompanying bibliography under the heading of Sudden Death. Material suggested in previous chapters of this book on parental grief, grief in children, etc., is also applicable to SIDS deaths. It is important to spend considerable time and numerous visits with parents in order to make sure that the grief process is well begun for them and for other children in the family.

All of the symptoms of grief that were outlined in Chapter 1 apply to these parents. They will have the same symptoms, setbacks, and anxieties. Grief work cannot be done properly by the parents until anxiety about their responsibility for the infant's death has been thoroughly talked about and until they understand that neither they nor anyone else was to blame for the baby's death.

It is not at all uncommon for the husband and wife to approach bereavement in different ways. Generally, the wife wishes to talk about her grief, while the husband tends to want to return to work and try to bury his emotions in his job. The wife is vocal about her anxieties, fears, and worries; the husband is silent, uncommunicative, suffering alone. Both parents need to understand this divergent way of behaving. At the same time, they need to be brought together so that they can communicate *with each other* about their mutual fears, anxieties, and sadness. *A specially trained* grief counselor is often required to bring SIDS parents to the point of *sharing* their grief.

Such a grief counselor can also interpret to the parents the new anxieties created in them by friends and relatives who can be unkind in unintentional ways. Sometimes close associates of the parents make a remark they hope will be helpful but instead stirs up much new anxiety or anger. Parents can be devastated by their grief when their friends are unaware that it was "just a week ago today" or "three weeks ago today" that the baby died. Parents may even resent the help of friends and relatives, and this also creates a good deal of additional guilt.

Other children in the family need to be helped also. It is difficult, however, for the parents to meet the needs of other children when they are feeling so much guilt, anxiety, or shock themselves. When this occurs, the parents neglect the same feelings of guilt, anxiety, or shock in their own children. Very young children need to be given a good deal of attention, affection, and holding at this time. Remember that they have feelings they cannot express except through irritability, kicking or crying, doing naughty or unusual things, or clinging to their parents.

Older children can be filled with guilt by an SIDS death because they feel that something they said or did—their particular kind of magic—caused the death. Special attention should be given children of any age *to assure them* and *to tell them* that this particular death is not preventable and *happens only to babies.* Such assurances are needed to prevent them from thinking this sudden death may strike them. They may even feel that the death was due to their resentment of the baby's presence.

For more detailed information about how to deal with other children in the family, refer to Chapter 2 and select a few of the books listed under that heading in the bibliography.

*Chapter 6*

# ACCIDENTAL DEATH

## TRAFFIC ACCIDENTS

I N THE PAST YEAR, there were 1,129 cases of sudden death in our county. After determining those that had no relatives in our county or had sufficient help and support, etc., there were 436 cases that required our special help. The majority of these sudden deaths were caused by traffic accidents. Traffic accidents involving automobiles are the number one killer in our country and the sixth leading cause of death for persons of all ages.

The National Center for Health Statistics in Washington shows that auto accidents are the leading cause of death for the country's young people between the ages of 1 and 25. Nationally, the next leading cause of death among this age group were homicide, cancer, suicide, and birth defects. The Census Bureau report for 1976 shows that auto accidents accounted for 65 percent of all accidental deaths among youths aged 14 to 24; 48 percent among children 5 to 14; and 37 percent among children 1 to 4. These automobile deaths cover collisions, single car drivers, passengers and pedestrians.

Such carnage on our streets and highways may be acceptable to adults for adult traffic fatalities, but how can we live with the knowledge that such large numbers of our children are perishing as drivers, pedestrians, and passengers in this horrendous number of automobile crashes? More youngsters between the ages of 1 and 14 are injured and killed by auto accidents than by any disease or any other kind of mishap.

## Motorcycles

Both motorcycle injuries and deaths are increasing. Howard B. Liebgold (1977) reports that when the Kaiser Foundation Rehabilitation Center, for which he is medical director, first opened in the 1940s, most of the patients were victims of polio or mining accidents. Today, over 10 percent of the patients are victims of motorcycle accidents. Dr. Liebgold is unalterably opposed to the use of the motorcycle, but he has this advice for those who use them:

> Although providing only minimal protection, it is important to wear leather pants, jackets, boots and gloves, and a helmet with eye coverings. One must remember that when a rider is dislodged from the motorcycle, (s(he) continues at the same speed and direction. Sliding on asphalt without protective equipment frequently sandpapers off all skin and ligaments until the underlying bone is exposed . . . . If not wearing a helmet when hitting a solid object headfirst at a speed of 50–55 m.p.h., (s)he will either be killed or suffer permanent brain or spinal cord damage with resultant permanent paralysis or loss of intellectual functioning.

## Safety Devices for Children

One cause of the tragic toll among young children and babies is that many parents believe laps are safe. This is untrue. If a parent is holding a child in the front seat, that child becomes a projectile in a collision. The child is hurled through space or, more frequently, strikes the instrument panel or windshield before the parent's reflexes can be brought into play to save the child. Adults also rely too much on standard seat belts, which are not designed for children under fifty pounds. The use of such belts can, in fact, seriously injure them. It has been pointed out by safety experts that a lap belt puts too much pressure on a child's abdominal area in a forward crash. Also, his center of gravity is higher, and that results in a greater body mass above the belt. In this situation, a child tends to whip forward more suddenly than an adult. It has been suggested that if no other safety belt is available, one can use a small pillow between the belt and the child. There are, however, restraining devices designed especially for children. These are "an infant carrier" for babies under fifteen pounds and safety seats for youngsters whose weight is between fifteen and forty-eight pounds. The infant carrier should ride in the front passenger seat with the back to the windshield. The safety seat for toddlers should always be installed in the rear seat.

Additional car safety rules for children are:

1. Lock the doors and keep them locked *all the time* the car is in motion.
2. Forbid children to dangle heads or hands from windows while the car is moving.
3. Never leave a child or infant alone in a parked car.
4. Never leave a child unrestrained in the cargo section of a wagon or van.
5. Never allow a child to play with the controls, even in your presence. This can lead him to believe this is OK when, in fact, it can be dangerous.

### Children and Wheeled Toys

Other kinds of traffic fatalities involve the use of children's wheeled toys, such as bicycles, gasoline driven minibikes or mopeds, tricycles, skateboards, and roller skates. For these methods of children's transportation and fun, children need to be taught all traffic laws and signals, to ride in designated routes or avoid busy intersections or heavy traffic, to use retroreflective trim on clothing, fenders, handlebars, chainguards, and wheel sidewalls for night riding.

## ADDITIONAL VEHICULAR ACCIDENTS AND GRIEF COUNSELING

Adults and children are also victims of train, plane, or horse accidents. The following account of Lillian's case shows how shock, fear, and multiple losses can complicate the resolution of grief. It also demonstrates the steady, unhurried approach of a counselor whose patience helped Lillian to face and deal with her fears and losses in a way that led to new strength. This strength was the base upon which Lillian's hope and rebuilding were built.

Lillian received counseling when her husband suicided. At that time, she expressed her grief, anger, and sadness satisfactorily. She was left almost penniless following a series of expensive and harrowing malpractice suits. In addition to grief counseling, we were instrumental then in directing her toward financial assistance. Our ties with her and the family lasted almost two years.

Several years later she called for help again. She had met and was preparing to marry a man whom she and her children loved dearly. They had already purchased the house where they would live. On a weekend trip in his plane they crashed in a mountainous terrain. He was killed instantly. Even though she was injured and in heavy shock, Lillian walked an almost inaccessible route in order to reach help.

Following the funeral, she sought help from numerous sources but was still in too much shock to know where she had been or to whom she had talked. For three months prior to her call to us she had been in bed, crying. The sound of planes overhead sent her into hysteria. She was unable to care for herself or her children. There was no place she felt safe from her bad dreams at night or her panic during the day. She lay curled in a ball, red-eyed and pale.

At first she was encouraged to talk about the accident, if she could, or to express the fears she was experiencing. Much later, she was told with calmness and assurance that these fears need not continue. This statement captured her interest. Questions followed and an explanation of the fantasy of the sanctuary was given (see Chapter 18, Training Class). If she wished to make the investment of the time it would take, she could make the sanctuary a part of her own resources. She wanted to try.

The sanctuary process was run through, and at the conclusion she fell asleep. The counselor remained with her while she slept. At her request, this was repeated several times a week until she felt that she could do it herself. Concurrently, there was talk of better nutrition, exercise, and suggestions for meeting some of the needs of her children. She and the counselor spent many days outdoors or on her patio listening to the drone of planes overhead. There was some subsidence of her apprehension about them, although there were times when other, unrelated noises caused similar episodes. She was assured that there would be other lapses, but in time these too would be under her control.

The relationship inched along in this way for a long time, alternating between periods of considerable change and periods of lapses. Finally, the lapses became more infrequent. There was a celebration the day she received the counselor with her hair groomed and with some makeup. Talk of the accident and its aftermath slowly diminished. More and more interest was shown in simple plans for picnics for the children, household chores, maintenance, and finances. Both Lillian and the counselor worked hard to consolidate each gain and to celebrate each bit of progress.

Making social contacts was encouraged at this point. Plans were made to meet and talk first with persons who knew nothing about the ordeal she had passed through. This went better than she expected. It was harder to revive old friendships that had not survived the trials and tribulations of a difficult grief. Lillian cherished the old friends who did respond to her overtures.

When she was satisfied with her social successes, Lillian was encouraged to think about job preparation. She was eager and enthusiastic and did well in several vocational classes. There followed periods of ups and downs of reluctance to look for a job. She feared both a failure to obtain an interview and a fear of suddenly bursting into tears. She did get a job, and it led her into new areas of socialization and strength.

From that time on there were only occasional calls to report good things that were happening or to grumble about job related frustrations that at times beset us all. Support was always offered when she called. After a while even this need disappeared. After two years, there were no more calls; Lillian had completed the hard journey through her grief.

## DROWNING

John W. Schieffelin (1977), Chairman of the Northern California Accident Prevention Committee of the American Academy of Pediatrics and a member of the Academy's National Accident Prevention Committee, states that "nearly one-third of all drowning victims are children fifteen years of age or younger and another third are between the ages of fifteen and twenty-four. . . . Drowning constitutes a major health risk to our children and young adults. In fact, water is second only to the automobile among accidental causes of death in childhood."

Adults are victims of drowning also. These drownings occur in swimming pools; fast moving water in rivers; along beaches with strong tides or currents, usually while surfing or boating. Both adults and children are also falling victim to mishaps in hot tubs.

Dr. Schieffelin suggests the following safety rules for recreational activities that are associated with water:

1. Never leave babies and toddlers alone in the bathtub.

2. Never allow children to play alone near an unfenced or unguarded pool.

3. All pools should be adequately fenced to prevent access to toddlers.

4. In households where the risk of drowning to toddlers is especially high and unavoidable (such as a house with a swimming pool), one should consider special instruction to teach the child to float on his back.

5. No one should ever swim alone.

6. Lifeguards should supervise swimming in every public pool.

7. Never drink alcohol and swim. Never drink alcohol and go boating. Alcohol and cold water are an especially dangerous combination. Alcohol dilates the superficial capillaries, giving the victim a false sense of warmth while increasing the rapidity with which cold water lowers the body temperature to a point where coordination is lost.

8. When boating in a small boat, make sure the boat is capable of floating when swamped and that it is equipped with proper flotation devices.

9. It is usually safer to remain with a boat when it swamps than to swim to the shore.

10. Hyperventilation (holding one's breath) is very dangerous before swimming. Hyperventilating lowers the $CO_2$, lowering the respiratory drive to the point where the body may run out of oxygen, resulting in the swimmer suddenly losing consciousness. It is important that children be taught never to hyperventilate before racing or swimming under water.

11. Body surfing is a dangerous sport and should never be practiced in a rough surf.

The following case of Luanne and Paul illustrates how guilt and blame can complicate a grief. The case also demonstrates the necessity for allowing the bereaved to sort out the problem for himself. Luanne accomplished this painful piece of grief work; Paul did not. But he was also allowed to set his own priorities: he denied and delayed his grief despite the alternatives suggested by his wife and the counselor. Nothing worthwhile could have resulted from insisting upon a rejection of his doubts and denials. After all, denial can be an important factor in survival.

Luanne and Paul asked for help when their small child drowned in their swimming pool, and the body was found by one of their other children. After the funeral, Paul withdrew from the family into his work and was home very little. Luanne was left in the home with the other children and with the swimming pool as a constant reminder of what had happened.

There had been a carefully kept household regulation regarding a mechanical device that shut the pool off from the rest of the play area. The parents' anguish centered on who or what was responsible for the mechanical failure. A search for the cause of the failure was thorough and painful for it led them repeatedly to human error within the family. At first, the parents blamed each other; then each secretly blamed a child. The undercurrents of this relentless search affected the children who could not know what was troubling the parents. Both children sensed neither parent was himself. Everything seemed changed, and the atmosphere in the home was heavy and morose.

It took Luanne a long time to realize that this search was making her ill, her husband angry and irritable, and the children bewildered. In addition to losing a lovely child and brother, the entire family had lost each other. It took a long time for Luanne to acknowledge and talk realistically about the excessive uneasiness and suspicion in the family. Finally, she asked herself, "If I am the one who was negligent, what do the others think of me?" Several sessions were spent discussing her feelings about this and allowing her to project the question on each of the other family members. What was its effect upon them? She struggled through the effect it would have upon her marriage if she and her husband allowed a human error to drive a wedge between them. She also struggled with the effect that blame for negligence would have upon the children. She cried at the thought of using the child's death to *punish* herself, her husband, or one of the children. She cried with relief that the search had not yet gone far enough to allow that to happen. *Then* she cried for the loss of the child and for the sadness felt by her husband and the children.

Paul never allowed himself to be brought into these painful later sessions. He remained aloof and depressed. Nor would he seek professional help. Luanne felt that she had gained enough insight into the situation to accept human error as the cause of the death without directing blame upon any family member. With help, she thought she could lead the children into their grief for their brother without burdening them with a lifelong sense of guilt or blame.

Paul's grief is still being delayed. Perhaps he will never grieve until another loss or separation comes upon him, or perhaps he will settle down in the pattern of the workaholic who substitutes keeping busy for accepting the need to work through grief.

## POISONS

Accidental poisonings affect thousands of children every year. Alan Lundberg (1977), a member of the Pediatrics Department at the Kaiser-Permanente Medical Center in Sacramento, California, lists these six ways parents can help prevent the poisoning of a child or help a child so that no permanent damage is caused.

1. Have syrup of ipecac handy in your home. This may be purchased without prescription at a drug store. This medicine will make your child vomit. Most times this is the best treatment of a poisoning, but one must be sure to get medical advice from a pediatrician or poison control center before giving syrup of ipecac. If given in the wrong cases, it can worsen the condition. Having this syrup of ipecac available at home has saved the lives of many children. If you do not have this medicine, buy some now so you will be prepared. If you leave your child with a regular babysitter, purchase a bottle for her, also.

2. Aspirin is still the most common poison children find. Although aspirin is sold in smaller quantities today, this small amount may still be enough to kill a child.

3. Although many medicines and household cleaners now have childproof caps, these caps do not always prevent children from opening the container. You still must use caution in storing poisons and medicines even if you have a special childproof cap.

4. Keep gasoline, cleaning fluids, and household cleaners, as well as medicines, out of the reach of children. Children are climbers and just putting something up high is not always enough. If possible, lock it up. Don't keep household cleaners under the kitchen sink. It is also important to know that the recommended treatments listed on some

of these cleaners are not current and may worsen the effects of the poison. Call your pediatrician for the most current antidote information.

5. Keep all medicines, household cleaners and poisons in carefully labelled containers, never in unlabelled or mislabelled bottles or boxes. A soda bottle is not a good place to store gasoline for the lawn mower.

6. Know the number to call should you suspect your child has been poisoned. Write it down where it will be readily available in case of a poisoning emergency.

This number should be that of your pediatrician or the poison control center for your region. If you do not have these numbers, telephone your local Crisis Center.

### ALCOHOL ABUSE

Grief counselors have become acutely aware of an additional problem that arises in work with the bereaved of sudden deaths. This is the problem of alcohol abuse by the deceased. Alcohol abuse may be looked upon as a slow means of suiciding, an increased hazard for the likelihood of accidental deaths of many kinds (falls, choking on food, drowning, traffic accidents, etc.) or as an aggravation to many kinds of diseases, such as cardiovascular episodes, emphysema, high blood pressure, in fact, chronic diseases of all kinds.

In our experience, the majority of alcohol abusers of both sexes are in their fifties and sixties, although there are some in their forties, a few in their thirties, and a smaller number still in their teens.

In addition to being a contributing factor in many kinds of sudden death, alcohol abuse adds a new dimension to the problems facing the bereaved and the grief counselors. The most common reactions to such a death complicated by alcohol abuse are either a sense of relief that the long, downward spiral of the increased social complications of the alcoholic is now over or a tremendous sense of guilt. This sense of guilt has been fostered by the deceased during his lifetime in order to throw the burden of responsibility for his alcoholism upon his spouse. In either case, the bereaved is often unwilling to admit to feelings of relief (which, under the circumstances, is a normal reaction), or the bereaved is burdened with guilt feelings that obstruct the normal need to grieve.

## REFERENCES

Liebgold, Howard B., "Motorcycles — The Two-Wheeled Monster," *Planning for Health, 20*(2), 1977.

Lundberg, Alan, "Poisonings, How Parents Can Prevent Accidents," *20*(4), 1977.

Schieffelin, John W., "Drowning: Common Sense Can Protect Your Family," *Planning for Health, 20*(3), 1977.

## Chapter 7

# INDUSTRIAL ACCIDENTS

### Introduction

INDUSTRIAL accidents are those accidents that occur in an industrial plant, on a construction site, or some other kind of work situation. These accidents may be the result of human error or the failure of plant equipment or machinery or some unforeseen combination of circumstances that leads to the death of a worker or workers. If more than five persons are killed in the same accident, it is classified as a disaster. Other situations may also be classified as disasters if five or more persons are killed by the same means—fire, earthquake, flood, the collapse of an existing building (as opposed to one under construction), tornado, or hurricane. We are concerned here with those deaths that occur in an industrial or employment situation in which fewer than five persons are killed by the same cause.

Working conditions in the United States have been the concern of governmental agencies for a long time. The State of California added amendments to the State Constitution in 1911 and in 1918 to cover the health and occupational safety of employees. An updated Occupational Safety and Health Act was passed in 1973. The federal government has also been protective in this area and updated its concern in 1970 by passing a new Federal Occupational Safety and Health Act.

This federal act covers virtually every employer in the country. It requires each employer to furnish his employees a place of employment free from recognized hazards that are causing or likely to cause death or serious physical harm. These employers are required to comply with the provisions of this Act. States have their own provisions but are also expected to implement

90

the federal act by complying to federal standards for worker safety and health, job safety and health. States are expected to have compliance safety engineers and industrial hygienists who investigate workplace fatalities, serious industrial injuries, and complaints of workplace hazards. They must also conduct inspections as part of an ongoing program of accident prevention, as well as be responsible for the enforcement of the State and Federal Acts.

There is also a great deal of activity by individual companies and groups of industries to form associations and councils that actively participate in industrial accident prevention classes, inspections, drills, etc. Such classes and workshops are given in the communities surrounding large industrial complexes, in community high schools and colleges. Labor unions have also begun to be involved in classes, inspections, and accident prevention programs.

Despite the state and federal laws and local preparedness, industrial accidents do happen. Numerically, these accidents generally comprise a small portion of the sudden deaths that occur locally. In part, this low incidence is a result of both the federal and state laws which are generally rigidly enforced, and partially perhaps it reflects an overly optimistic picture of what is happening. We are all increasingly aware of the unseen industrial hazards that are mounting throughout the country. These hazards include industrial waste disposal problems, the transportation of toxic wastes, toxic chemicals, and explosives for industrial or military use throughout areas of high population density. There are also the problems of exposure to toxic substances that do not affect those exposed to them until perhaps twenty years later, as in the case of asbestos. The possibility of exposure to radiation or chemical and nuclear wastes has alarmed and alerted the public to the fact that industrial workers and even the surrounding population may already be exposed to substances that may be detrimental to public safety and health years hence. There is also a realization that industrial engineering and technology have surpassed the education and training of the workers who are responsible for the daily operation and maintenance of highly specialized equipment and machinery.

## SPECIAL PROBLEMS THAT AFFECT THE BEREAVED IN INDUSTRIAL ACCIDENT DEATHS

1. How the death is announced by officials is a matter requiring diplomacy, compassion, and courtesy, no matter what the mode of death. It is a difficult task when the deceased's body is disfigured or wholly or partially destroyed. If this information is not given in a dignified or compassionate manner, the bereavement is almost certain to be complicated in the early stages.

2. The condition of the body strongly affects the bereaved. This feeling is immediately communicated to the rest of the family. Family members then realize that something terrible has happened. The immediate problems of what to tell the young children is a great burden. Children sense that this is something much worse than a bad automobile accident, even if they have never seen one. The next-of-kin need encouragement and guidance to tell the children the truth without going into any of the morbid details. More complete information can be given children as they become older and ask more questions.

For the present, a simple statement that "Daddy died in an accident at the plant" will suffice. Questions about what happened? how?, etc., may be answered briefly by, "There was an explosion," or "A piece of machinery hit (ran over him)," or "He fell," without elaborating on what he fell over or into.

Older children can be given more information depending upon their ages. Truthful, but protective, direct answers are best through the preadolescent years.

3. Nevertheless, this cannot always be handled in this way because plant accidents are written about in the newspapers or appear on local TV and radio and are discussed by the children's friends.

4. As in any death, the surviving parent is encouraged to notify the child's school. Such a call enables the teacher to be prepared for the questions her pupils will ask. She will also be able to help her pupils discuss the death and to deal with subsequent questions that will arise. Enlightened teach-

ers can use this occasion as an opportunity to further the children's understanding of death and to be receptive to ways of responding to their classmate's return to school following the funeral.

5. Death by an industrial accident inevitably leads to problems of insurance, pensions, or legal suits. Counselors must recognize their limitations and incompetence in dealing with such complicated financial and legal affairs. Their role as an advocate to the bereaved must be limited to (a) discussing and hearing the bereaved's thoughts on these matters, (b) urging the client to seek legal or financial help, and (c) continuing to stay with the client in order to help focus on grief problems that are likely to get set aside because of the pressing legal and financial emergencies. Counselors remain with clients when they have been referred to medical, psychological, or psychiatric help; the same helpfulness is needed during times when the client is involved with legal assistance.

The following case illustrates how normal grief counseling efforts may have to be modified during bereavement following an industrial accident:

Sylvia had just returned from the hospital following a heart attack. She was under medical supervision, and there was the expectation that she would return for major heart surgery. Shortly after her arrival home, she was told that her husband had been killed in an industrial accident. Her relatives (there were no children) and friends kept from her the horrendous details of the death in order to spare her perhaps another heart attack.

She readily accepted a grief counselor. Most of their preliminary conversations were related to her own condition, medication, and precautionary measures that needed to be taken. It was obvious that she was in a fragile condition. No effort was made to discuss the death unless she brought up the subject. Of course no effort was made to draw from her any emotions that might ordinarily be appropriate for a person recently made aware of the death of a loved one.

Sylvia realized that her own survival depended upon her ability to refrain from any severe crying (only tears), anger, anxiety, or inquiry into what had happened at the industrial plant. The widest scope her sadness could be allowed was participation in the plans for the funeral and her heroic command of herself during the funeral.

Counseling matters stayed on a fairly even keel in this way for several weeks. Then it was clear that a suit needed to be brought in order to obtain the financial benefits from such a death. Sylvia and her family selected an attorney. It was not until a subsequent session with her attorney that she was made aware of the details of the accident. By that time she was in sufficient control of herself to handle this information, but she did require additional medical help at that time.

Weeks passed. During this time Sylvia and the counselor discussed what plans the attorney was making, the pros and cons of each issue as seen by the family, her own reactions to these plans, and her own progress in stabilizing her health. There was frank recognition by both parties in this counseling situation that Sylvia's complete grief expression must wait until her health allowed her some emotional release.

The following conversation between a counselor and a client bereaved by an industrial accident illustrates how a parent and the counselor focused on how the death affected the young children:

*Miriam:*      I'm glad you're here today. Things haven't gone very well lately. Both the children act so strange, and they don't seem to hear me no matter what I say.

*Counselor:*  That doesn't sound like them, does it?

*Miriam:*      No. And since they've never been like this before, I don't know where to take hold. It's as though they're suddenly not paying any attention to anything.

*C:*              Like they're withdrawn into their own thoughts?

*Miriam:*      Well, they don't seem like they're *here*.

*C:*              Have you thought that they may be grieving?

*Miriam:*      Grieving? At their age? No.

*C:*              Children can grieve at almost any age. It just takes on different forms at different ages.

*Miriam:*      Really? I never knew that.

*C:*              Remember how you felt when you first learned that the industrial accident Bob was in would likely be fatal? Remember how you felt all numb and just wanted to be alone to think about it?

*Miriam:*      You mean Tommy and Susan are going through that?

C:          Very likely. You see, they didn't know the serious-
            ness of Bob's injuries for a long time. It just came
            upon them slowly, and soon after that he was no
            longer alive. They have much to think about.

Miriam:     Oh God, I hope they aren't having such a time as I
            had then. Do you suppose they are?

C:          I don't know. How much have you talked to them
            about Bob's death?

Miriam:     Well, not much, I guess. I've been so busy with all
            the details of the funeral and my own feelings. . . .

C:          Yes, it's hard to have so many important things to
            think about and to do something about, all at the
            same time. Perhaps if you remember to talk to Tom-
            my and Susan about a number of these things it will
            make it easier both for you and for them?

Miriam:     What will talking to them about whether to sell this
            house do for them?

C:          Talking to them about it on their level will help you
            separate some of the important details from the un-
            important ones, and it will give them a feeling of
            participating in the decision.

Miriam:     How can they participate in the decision?

C:          The way they were brought into the details about the
            funeral. Remember how we spoke then of keeping
            them informed of what was scheduled to take place
            and where and who would be there and why they
            came? It's the same with the house. Getting the feel-
            ing that they are consulted, brought into the de-
            cision, gives them a feeling of security and of being
            valued.

Miriam:     You mean when we talk about some of the details
            about the house it will help them talk about how
            they feel about Bob's death?

C:          It will likely help them talk about Bob and you and
            some of their feelings. Right now I expect they feel
            pretty insecure. After all, Bob isn't here any more,
            and they haven't figured out yet why he isn't. It's up

to you to provide opportunities for them to ask questions or to express how they are feeling. As you
know, grief is a new emotion for you. It is for them
also. Talking about how much you miss Bob can
break loose some of the emotions that they need to
let out.

*Miriam:*      Sounds like an awful lot at a time like this. I guess
I didn't really think that the kids would grieve.

*C:*      Yes, they grieve but in different ways, and it often
takes longer for them to pass through their grief.
You couldn't believe Bob was dead, and you tried
and tried to regain him. Tommy and Susan may
still be having that feeling.

*Miriam:*      Why do you say that?

*C:*      Well, you knew for a time that Bob's injuries were
serious, and then it dawned on you that they would
be fatal. During that period you had some time to
work through some of the emotions you had then. . . .
Why Bob? Why is this happening to me? What am I
going to do? Why didn't Bob and I make some plans
for insurance? Why couldn't the doctors come up
with something helpful?

*Miriam:*      Oh, and Tommy and Susan are being hit now by
*that?*

*C:*      Very likely, some version of that. And it's hard being a child. They haven't the language yet to express these new emotions. They can only act out
their aggressive feelings. You can talk about your
emotions and the new problems with which Bob's
death confronts you. Tommy and Susan can only
punch somebody or do something inappropriate for
the time or the place or not mind or not pay attention.

*Miriam:*      Oh God, and I've been scolding them!

*C:*      Let them know it is OK with you for them to experience this new emotion of sadness and loss. You and
I know this emotion is natural, inevitable, and high-

ly desirable. You need to provide the opportunity for them to share in your grief—to realize that it is normal to cry, to express anger and wonder. Allow Tommy and Susan to find their own ways to express these things. By expressing them, they will also be better able to lessen their own guilt feelings.

*Miriam:* What guilt feelings could Tommy and Susan have?

*C:* Since children believe in magic, they often feel that something they said or did caused a death. They know when they are naughty they get scolded or punished in some way. When a death occurs, they know at once that something bad for them has happened, and so the death must be a punishment for something they said, did, or thought. It is likely that Tommy and Susan are feeling guilty in some way. You can help relieve this feeling by casually mentioning that nothing they said or did or thought caused Bob's death. His death was not a punishment for any wrongdoing of theirs.

*Miriam:* Do children raise questions about guilt and death?

*C:* They may raise them. If they don't, assume they are there. Create an atmosphere in which they can ask any questions they want; raise doubts; express wonder, anger, or sadness. Help them to bring out in the open their doubts and questions about whether their behavior had anything to do with Bob's death. They may wonder whether Bob abandoned them deliberately or if anything they said or did may have influenced Bob's death.

*Miriam:* How can I teach Tommy and Susan to accept my answers about death?

*C:* None of us should feel the need to have a child accept our answers. After all, we adults *know* we don't have all the answers to questions about life and death. It is better to encourage Tommy and Susan to believe that you do not have any final answers but that you are willing to help search for some explanations.  But in the meantime, all three of you feel very sad that Bob died, and now the three of you must continue to live without him.  Assure them that you are going to do your best and so are they, and you are confident that the three of you will be successful.

*Miriam:*  That's a large order.

*C:*  It's tough all right, but I'm sure you can do it.

*Chapter 8*

# HOMICIDE

IN AN UNPUBLISHED PAPER entitled "The Epidemiology and Prevention of Homicide," Nancy H. Allen (1978) points out that the homicide rate in the United States in 1973 was 8.3 per 100,000. The United States' homicide rate ranks the third highest in the world—behind El Savador (31.2) and Mexico (17.5). She points out that in 1975, 51 percent of the homicides in the United States were committed with handguns.

These figures may come as a surprise to most readers. They *are* dramatic. Writers in the field of homicide are often accused of writing "purple prose," but the facts bear out what is being reported. Richard Lewis Clutterbuck, a retired military general in Great Britain who has written extensively on the subject of terrorism, recently made this statement to a reporter for the *New Yorker* (June 12, 1978):

> Detroit has a population about equal to that of the whole of Northern Ireland—a million and a half. For all the lethal skirmishing between the I.R.A. and its adversaries, there were two hundred and fifty homicides in Northern Ireland in 1973, as opposed to seven hundred and fifty-one that year in Detroit; in 1977, the ratio increased from three to one to almost five to one. Anyone who goes to Belfast these days stands a chance of being killed, but the risk is three times as great in Washington, D.C. One reason I suppose, is that so many Americans consider gun-carrying the right of a citizen. By European standards, the number of guns in the United States is staggering.

It should be pointed out that the dubious title of the homicide capitol of the United States has now passed from Detroit to Houston.

Donald T. Lunde (1975, 1976, 1977) adds to the picture of

the magnitude of this slaughter. He reports that "Americans are killing each other off twice as fast as they did twenty years ago so that . . . over the course of a normal life span, more than one in every two hundred of us may be murdered . . . . More of us were slain during the last four years than were killed in the Vietnam War" (1976). How does Professor Lunde account for this increased rate? His explanation centers on economic slumps.

> Whereas murder rates used to go down and suicides up during economic slumps, the opposite seems true today. This reversal may have come about because Americans no longer blame themselves for their material misfortunes. When traditional values and the Protestant Ethic reigned in America, we took out our frustrations on ourselves; many committed suicide during the Depression, for instance. Now we expect society to provide us with two cars in every garage, two chickens in every pot, and when it doesn't, we strike out at others. The police, political leaders, and others in positions of authority do not seem to recognize that increasing economic expectations combined with a depressed economy have something to do with the growing murder rate. Many believe that tougher criminal penalties, increased rehabilitation programs, and more money to beef up police forces will stem the bloody tide. They assume falsely that there is a "criminal element" in this country that can be identified and then either killed or cured (1975).

Professor Lunde also tells us some interesting facts about who commits these homicides:

1. For the most part, they are husbands, wives, lovers, neighbors, friends, and acquaintances—persons who can no longer endure chronic dissatisfaction and frustration. These people rarely try to escape; they are easily caught and confess.

2. Most of these killers have little to gain from their crimes, financially or otherwise.

3. The publicity surrounding bizarre or mass murders leads the public to believe that a majority of killers are insane. This is not true; less than 4 percent of them are judged to be criminally insane.

4. Since one-fourth of all murderers and their victims are related, more than 40 percent of homicide victims are killed in their homes. Of these murderers, half are hus-

bands killing their wives or vice versa. More women die in their own bedrooms than anywhere else; husbands die in their kitchens where the wife has access to knives.

5. Women who kill their infants or young children are usually severely disturbed. Fathers rarely kill their children, but when they do, they often turn out to be child abusers. Fathers are more likely to kill their teenage sons. These men are marginally adequate husbands and feel inferior and frustrated by life. Guns and alcohol play a significant role in their lives. They are simply explosive individuals who kill impulsively; they are not persons with a history of psychiatric illness.

6. Older children who kill their younger siblings are expressing displaced aggression—the victim serves as a substitute for a parent who is the true object of rage.

7. From time immemorial, homicide has been committed in the context of frustrated sexual passions, jealousy, or adultery.

8. Persons who kill casual acquaintances usually grow up in what is called a "subculture of violence." The killer is often a young adult male who regularly carries a lethal weapon, like his friends do, and is used to settling accounts by direct action.

9. Probably because they lack physical strength, murderers under fifteen and over fifty use guns almost exclusively.

10. More white people than black people plan murders or anticipate fights, arming themselves in advance with guns.

11. Idleness is a contributing factor to homicide. Few homicides occur during business hours, but on weekends or during holidays—making the title "Saturday Night Special" an appropriate name for a handgun.

12. There are geographical variations in the homicide rate. Of all recent murders, 44 percent occurred in southern states, 22 percent in north central states, 19 percent in northeastern states, and 15 percent in western states.

Homicide rates increase as population density increases. Residents of a large city are twice as likely to become victims as those in a rural or suburban area. But homicides are unevenly distributed throughout large cities; they tend to clump together in a few sections of the city.

13. Homicide is a pursuit of youth. Less than one out of ten victims is killed by someone over fifty, and more than half are slain by persons under thirty-five. The average murderer has always been young, but he is getting younger; ten or fifteen years ago he was thirty, now he is closer to twenty. Most victims are also under the age of thirty.

14. Homicide statistics also vary according to the color of your skin. If you are black, you are more likely to become a target. Black men are ten times more vulnerable than white males, and black females five times more in danger than white women. The races keep homicide mostly segregated. In more than nine out of ten homicides, killer and victim are the same race. In the few instances where racial lines are crossed, it is more often whites murdering blacks then the reverse.

15. In a significant number of cases the victim actually contributes to his own death. An unfaithful husband or wife, a drunk who dares his foe to shoot, a provocative or seductive woman may all goad or push their antagonist to homicide.

16. While there are homicides committed by persons who are egocentric, impulsive, rebellious, or sadistic and cannot control their emotions, there are also vicious crimes committed by persons whom friends and relatives describe as mildmannered, religious, and kind to children. The latter persons could be either "overcontrolled" or "undercontrolled"—either they inhibited their aggressive impulses or they were unable to control them. The latter never developed internal taboos against lashing out when provoked and have few inhibitions about satisfying their acquisitive or sexual desires aggressively. These killers tend to be chronic criminal offenders.

The overcontrolled offenders tend to find unsatisfactory, even socially acceptable, outlets for aggression, such as swearing or pounding a table. They let nothing out, so their hostility builds until they reach a breaking point and commit an act of unspeakable violence. Perhaps the archetype of the overcontrolled murderer is the long-suffering parent or the restricted teenager who suddenly murders his entire family. Stricken with grief, he then commits suicide.

Our experience has been that there is an increasing amount of homicide where the victim is not known to the offender. The victim is killed either by a sniper or by a person who commits homicide in the process of committing a felony.

Lunde explains the homicide committed by a total stranger by suggesting that while he may not know the victim, he knows him in a context of his own. His victim is a member of a group (the rich) or type (young girls) who torment him in his delusions. The victims themselves are unaware of their place in his scheme or sexual fantasies.

In the face of mounting homicide rates, how can each of us protect ourselves from becoming an unwitting victim of a homicide? Ms. Allen (1978) lists some useful techniques to avoid such an occurrence:

1. Keep away from firearms when possible.
2. Avoid areas with high crime rates when possible.
3. Stay away from potentially dangerous persons or situations.
4. Do not hitchhike, and do not pick up hitchhikers.
5. Walk in groups of two or more. Do not walk alone at night.
6. Carry a whistle.
7. Don't provoke. Consider the other person may become angry easily, and he may be carrying a weapon.
8. When provoked, don't respond.
9. Don't leave valuables in sight, and carry only as much money as necessary.
10. Keep all doors of home, apartment, and car locked.
11. Know the location of nearest police station.
12. Keep emergency police telephone number posted by or on each phone.

13. Use extreme caution when placing ads in a newspaper or on bulletin boards.

If attacked, follow these instructions:

1. Try to stay calm. The assailant will be less likely to attack you if you appear controlled and confident.
2. Run and scream or blow whistle if possible.
3. Don't resist robbery.
4. Get a description (see following text) of the perpetrator, report and prosecute.
5. Defend yourself only as a last resort.

If others are attacked, follow these instructions:

1. Shout and blow whistle to get help.
2. Gather others to help.
3. Call the police.
4. Cooperate in the prosecution.
5. Get a description of perpetrator and vehicle (see following text) if a car is involved.

She recommends the recall acronym, ARREST HIM, for use in identifying the personal characteristics of the one committing the crime. CYMBOL is a term developed by California Attorney General Younger's Office (1977) that may help one to be a good witness when a car is involved.

A —Age, as close as possible.
R —Race: white, Asian, black, Chicano.
R —Rags, term used in clothing business; how dressed.
E —Eyes: color, large, small; glasses; eyebrows.
S —Sex.
T —Tatoos.

H—Height, hair.
I —Impediments, scars, limp, etc.
M—Movements (ran, drove away, in what direction), mannerisms.

C —Color of car.
Y —Year (as close as you can guess).

M—Make of car.
B —Body style (station wagon, etc.) .
O —Occupants (how many? description if possible) .
L —License.

## GRIEF AND HOMICIDE

After a homicide, grief is frequently arrested or delayed. This is especially true when the homicide is committed with no apparent reason by someone not yet in custody or someone who has performed additional violent acts, such as rape. The bereaved is often unable to experience grief owing to his anger and rage. The police investigation may be time-consuming and compound this situation. With each periodic check with the family about new developments and suspects, the reality of anger is awakened. It is often unbearable for the family to have these old wounds reopened. The family becomes frozen at the level of imagining the violence with which their relative died. They find it difficult to deal with the death *in terms of their own loss and sadness.*

A counselor must possess qualities of compassion, restraint, and diplomacy in order to deal with the family's anger, allow it to continue for a necessary amount of time, and recognize when that time is past. Empathy is very important initially. Nearly everyone experiencing such a loss would feel the same way; it is easy to identify with their hurt. Yet the time comes when this outrage is no longer fitting, and the bereaved must be shown other methods that are more beneficial in working through grief.

Usually, the bereaved is not receptive to such a change. He has been denying his grief by immersing himself in the hope the offender will be brought to justice through the efforts of the police and the courts. The bereaved is frequently unable to work through his grief unaided in cases where the offender is never apprehended. Counselors must be aware of their own limitations and make proper referrals to professionals when they themselves cannot perform the service required.

Bereaved persons sometimes approach homicide in a different fashion; from the very beginning they speak of their desire that the offender be found *in order that he may be helped.* They speak of forgiveness; they want society to help the offender so that he will never again be tempted to perform such a crime. They do not talk of vengence or punishment but of love and forgiveness. They may be in this frame of mind for several months, then anger and outrage possesses them. But now they are embarrassed by their earlier feelings of compassion for the criminal; now they experience a need to hide their real feelings. This compounds the problem of doing justice to their feelings while simultaneously working through their grief.

It may be helpful to remind the client that love can still exist in the midst of angry feelings if there is a conflict between forgiveness and anger or love and justice. It is possible to maintain self-esteem for finding the act so low. Later, we suggest methods by which the bereaved may use this awful experience to help himself as well as others become involved in projects, activities, courses of study, or self-awareness. At this later time, we often bring together groups of people who have been beset by grief stemming from similar modes of death. These meetings provide the bereaved with the opportunity to discuss feelings at the time of the loss and things that helped them most with others who experienced the same sort of loss. This mutual help also aids the bereaved in consolidating advances they have been aiming for in their grief. We had no such opportunity with Elaine.

In the case of Elaine, one can clearly see how the grieving process was delayed by the police investigation and her own family and friends.

> Elaine lived alone with her infant daughter. Her home was broken into, her baby was killed, and she was raped.
>
> During the investigation, Elaine felt she was so "hassled" by the police about the rape that her life became unbearable. The police felt that she must certainly have known the rapist or perhaps encouraged him. She felt that the police investigation raised too many doubts about her role in this double jeopardy to her emotions. She responded by believing that her family, friends, and neighbors had lost confidence in her. She felt socially astracized and alone.
>
> Because the queries and examinations took up a good deal of time, Elaine was never free of the onus of being the victim of a rape. There seemed to be no time to become engaged in her great loss as a mother. In the meantime, well-meaning friends and relatives took

over the management of the house, the funeral, and burial. In this way Elaine was removed physically and mentally from the normal expectancy of being the center of a household in mourning for an infant that died violently. Elaine's grief was delayed and delayed. When the investigations were over, so was the funeral, and Elaine returned to a tidy, empty house.

She packed her bag and left. No one knew where she went. No one close to her helped her, comforted her, shared her loss with her. We do not know where she went. She is "out there, somewhere," her delayed grief ticking away within her, undoubtedly angry and hurt at a social system that allowed this to happen and at friends and relatives who never reached her as a grieving mother.

## REFERENCES

Allen, Nancy H., "The Epidemiology and Prevention of Homicide," an unpublished paper given at the Annual Meeting of the American Association of Suicidology at New Orleans, 1978.

Lunde, Donald T., "Our Murder Boom," *Psychology Today*, July, 1975, pp. 35–42.

———, *Murder and Madness.* San Francisco: S F Bk Co, 1976.

———, Interview with Nancy Faber of *People* regarding "Son of Sam," Spring, 1977.

## Chapter 9

# SUICIDE — AN OVERVIEW

### Introduction

D URING THE LAST DECADE, between 220,000 and 500,000 people in the United States have committed suicide. If we had a greater understanding of the effective ways to intervene in suicidal crises, some of those lives might have been saved. Suicide is not a new phenomenon. No one knows, but probably suicides began very early in the history of man and will continue to be with us. The Bible specifically mentions six suicides (those of Abimelech, Saul, Saul's armour bearer, Achitophel, Zimerie, and Samson) all in the Old Testament.

In Chapters 1 and 2 I have already stated that grief caused by the death of a significant person is one of the most powerful and painful complexes of emotion with which we all have to cope. Such a grief can encompass despair, rage, guilt, relief, and depression. At the same time, survivors must continue to live, work, and love successfully. A sudden death is much more difficult to cope with than one where the death is expected, as in a long illness. When the sudden death is intentional, as it is in suicide, the survivors are faced with the most difficult process of all.

This chapter will deal with some of the myths and facts of suicide, the epidemiology of suicide, the psychodynamics of suicide, special tactics of intervention, how to assess the potentiality and lethality of a suicide threat, and the costs of suicide.

### MYTHS AND FACTS

Suicide has always been considered a taboo subject. Such a mode of death seems to engender a tremendous residue of guilt, blame, shame, and a desire to deny the very existence of the suicide. Consequently there have grown up over the centuries many misconceptions about suicide that every generation needs to unlearn. These misconceptions, misbeliefs, or myths interfere at every turn in dealing with persons who are themselves suicidal and their significant others following a suicide.

Each generation needs to learn the myths and facts about suicide. Listed are eight myths and opposite them are listed the facts that are supported by research and study:

| *Myths* | *Facts* |
|---|---|
| 1. People who talk about suicide don't commit suicide. | 1. Of any ten people who kill themselves, eight have given definite warnings of their suicidal intentions. Suicide threats and attempts *must* be taken seriously. |
| 2. Suicide happens without warning. | 2. Studies reveal that the suicidal person gives many clues and warnings regarding his suicidal intentions. Alertness to these cries for help may prevent suicidal behavior. |
| 3. Suicidal people are fully intent on dying. | 3. Most suicidal people are undecided about living or dying, and they gamble with death, leaving it to others to save them. Almost no one commits suicide without letting others know how he is feeling. Often this "cry for help" is given in "code." These distress signals can be used to save lives. |
| 4. Once a person is suicidal, he is suicidal forever. | 4. Happily, individuals who wish to kill themselves are "suicidal" only for a lim- |

ited period of time. If
they are saved from self-
destruction, they can go on
to lead useful lives.

5. Suicide strikes more often among the rich—or, conversely, it occurs more frequently among the poor.

5. Suicide is neither the rich man's disease nor the poor man's curse. Suicide is represented proportionately among all levels of society.

6. Improvement following a suicidal crisis means that the suicidal risk is over.

6. Most suicides occur within three months following the beginning of "improvement," when the individual has the energy to put his morbid thoughts and feelings into effect. Relatives and physicians should be especially vigilant during this period.

7. Suicide is inherited or "runs" in the family.

7. Suicide does *not* run in families. It is an individual matter and can be prevented.

8. All suicidal individuals are mentally ill, and suicide is always the act of a psychotic person.

8. Studies of hundreds of genuine suicide notes indicate that although the suicidal person is extremely unhappy, he is not necessarily mentally ill. His overpowering unhappiness may result from a temporary emotional upset, a long and painful illness, or a complete loss of hope. It is circular reasoning to say that "suicide is an insane act," and therefore all suicidal people are psychotic.

Dr. Carden's contribution, which follows, presents an overview of the subject of suicide that the general reader may not have encountered.

### SUICIDE
NORMAN L. CARDEN, M.D.

The major aspects of the problem of suicide may be briefly summarized. These four aspects are the distribution and epidemiology of suicide, the assessment of lethality, the psychodynamics, and intervention techniques with specific suggestions.

### Epidemiology of Suicide

Statistics most recently available from the World Health Organization (WHO) the Department of Health, Education, and Welfare (HEW) suggest that there is a rather wide variation in reported suicides throughout the world. These statistics are to be viewed with skepticism since in some countries the sophistication of data-gathering techniques is minimal, and various religious or cultural taboos lead to an avoidance of reporting suicide as the cause of death. The countries reporting to WHO with the highest suicide rates (10 to 20 per 100,000 population) are Hungary, West Germany, Austria, Czechoslovakia, Japan, Denmark, Finland, Sweden, and Switzerland. Countries that are at the low end of the scale (less than 10, greater than 6 per 100,000 population) include Italy, the Netherlands, and Spain. The lowest end of the reported scale (with rates less than 6 per 100,000 population) are Ireland, Chile, and New Zealand. The United States ranks approximately tenth in suicide rates, with a reported incidence between 10 and 12 per 100,000 population. In the United States, these statistics are felt to be approximately one-half of the actual suicide rate because it is speculated that 50 percent of suicides are recorded by the family and doctors as due to other causes. In the United States, the state with the highest suicide rate is Nevada; the state with the lowest suicide rate is Mississippi, and the city with the highest suicide rate is Las Vegas, Nevada. The highest suicide rate in the entire world is in West Berlin.

Suicide rates in the world and the United States are changing. Overall, there was a decrease in the suicide rate between the increase in suicide among young black males, so that the rate is approximately the same as that of young white males. In older black males, suicide continues to be less prevalent than in the white male population. Of the ethnic groups within the United States, the American Indian population has the highest rate.

Socioeconomic status and its relationship to the suicide potential of an individual is difficult to assess. Until approximately 1977, it was commonly reported that suicide rates in the United States were greater in the lower economic strata than in the higher; whereas in Europe, they were greater in the higher economic strata than in the lower. Recent statistics fail to support this, and now it appears there is no consistent relationship in the United States between economic status and the incidence of suicide.

Until 1977, it was reported that suicide occurred more frequently in urban centers than in rural and bedroom communities. The most recent evidence suggests that there is no relationship between high suicide rates and city dwelling. A review of these statistics suggested that many suicides in rural settings were reported by the coroner's office in the nearest urban center, thus skewing the data.

Occupations appear to have some significance in that those occupations giving access to more convenient or popular modes of suicide are associated with a higher incidence, such as policemen and military personnel with access to firearms, and medical, dental, and pharmaceutical personnel with access to medications.

The relationship of religious affiliation to suicide is inconsistent. Until recently, it was reported that Protestants had a higher incidence than Roman Catholics. More recent evidence fails to support this, and instead it appears that the firmness or steadfastness of one's affiliation with any organized religion is associated with a lower incidence, and only nominal or no religious affiliation of any type is associated with a higher incidence.

Marital status is a significant factor in the epidemiology of suicide. Ranging from the highest to the lowest incidence of suicide is as follows: (1) divorced, (2) widowed, (3) never married, and (4) married. These categories apply equally to males and females.

The season of the year appears to play some role. The common idea that suicides are more frequently around the time of the full moon has not been statistically substantiated. However, there does appear to be a somewhat higher incidence around the times of significant holidays, anniversaries, and the spring season of the year.

Almost all epidemiological studies of suicide state that physical illness of a severe nature is associated with a higher suicide rate. In spite of this, there is lack of significant statistics indicating that people with diagnosed terminal illnesses, such as cancer, have a higher suicide rate.

### Assessment of Lethality

Lethality is an attempt to assess the intensity of the suicide risk. The age, race, marital status, etc., as noted in the paragraphs on epidemiology, are to be considered in the assessment of lethality. In addition, the following aspects of the individual are significant. These are listed not necessarily in order of degree of importance but rather should be assessed as a group.

1. Family history. The loss of a father, mother, or surrogate parent by suicide is associated with a higher risk. In general, the loss of a parent by death from any cause prior to age thirteen is associated with a higher suicide risk.

2. Having a specific plan and means (gun, pills, etc.).

3. Access to the specific means. If the individual's specific plan is to use a gun, the lethality factor is greater if the individual has access to a gun.

4. Absence of plans and/or hopelessness regarding the future in general.

5. A lack of any meaningful interpersonal relationships that might reinforce the person's desire to live.

6. A history of prior suicide attempts. A long term follow-up study indicated that at five years after an initial attempt, 5 percent had made a second attempt. Longer than five years after the first attempt, 10 percent actually died by committing suicide.

7. Concomitant use of alcohol or central nervous system drugs (sleeping pills, tranquilizers, etc.) at the time of the lethality assessment. The vast majority of suicide attempts are associated

with the ingestion of alcohol.

8. The presence of symptoms of depression. These include subjective feelings of depression or significant sadness, change in sleep patterns, change in eating patterns, change in weight, generalized loss of interest in the environment, decreased sexual interest, generalized lethargy, apathy, or agitation, and social withdrawal.

9. A recent loss. The loss can be a person, money, health, status, etc.

10. Unemployment or employment of less than six months at the present job or having more than two jobs in less than two years.

11. Individuals who have lived at their present residence for less than six months.

12. Individuals who live alone.

### Psychodynamics of Suicide

One of the earliest explanations for suicide was offered in 1851 by Durkheim (1951) who utilized a sociological approach. He classified suicides into three general categories. First, the altruistic suicide was the type of individual who was so integrated into a cultural group, whether it be a nuclear or extended family or some other collective body, that he felt a loss of his own identity. Second was the egoistic suicide who was essentially the opposite of the altruistic individual; he had remained basically a loner, never becoming integrated into any type of group. And third was the anomic suicide type of individual, one who had a change in group integration—for example, an individual who was divorced or experienced a loss due to death, job, or money.

The individual psychological or psychodynamic explanations of suicide are usually categorized as follows:

1. Retaliatory abandonment. This type of suicidal individual feels that he has been rejected or abandoned by a "significant other" in his life. These people use their own death, their suicide, as the ultimate means of getting even by rejecting the "significant other" who previously abandoned them. Often there is the attitude "they will finally realize how badly they treated me

and will have the burden of my death upon their shoulders."

2. Reunion. In this category, the individual sees suicide as a form of reunion with a dead loved one. This is one of the significant reasons for suicide in retirement homes, where individuals feel alone as a result of loss through death of a majority of friends, their spouse, or those with whom they felt a continued link with life. Through suicide they hope they will be reunited with loved ones in the hereafter.

3. Rebirth. This form is psychologically linked to childlike or primitive forms of thought processes that essentially state, "For something new to occur, something old has to die." This theme of death and rebirth is also found in mythology. Thus, the individual who feels disillusioned with life will sometimes attempt suicide as a means of achieving a fresh start in the hereafter.

4. Retroflexed murder. This is most prevalent in individuals who have experienced the loss of a significant other toward whom they had strong ambivalent feelings with a considerable negative aspect, i.e. hate, hostility, anger. Unconsciously, the negative feelings are internalized. Thus, by committing suicide, the individual finds a way of killing the symbolically internalized aspect or image of the person or the situation who has made him angry.

5. Omnipotent control over death. This essentially is an exaggeration of the knowledge that we are all going to die sooner or later. Some individuals, especially when they feel impotent or powerless in their life situation, attempt to regain control over their life by controlling the time, mode, and place of their death. It is an ultimate statement that "I am in control of my destiny."

6. Expiation. This is an attempt to win back the love that an individual feels he has lost by virtue of some (real or imagined) act of omission or commission. Such an individual sees his death as a means of buying back love that he has lost. He sees his love object as accepting his death as payment for any wrongdoing and that the loved one will once again be his.

7. Self-punishment. This often takes the form of expiation as just noted and is a punishment for some situation for which he feels extreme guilt or as a punishment for having failed in achieving specific life goals that were either internally or externally set for him (most commonly internally established). Both this form

and the expiation form of suicide are often connected with dramatic recovery if an individual does not die as the result of the attempt. Such an individual may attempt suicide only once, seeing the close brush with death as sufficient punishment or expiation.

8. Suicide of an already dead (emotionally) person. This is the individual who views suicide as the accomplishment of a phenomenon that has, in an emotional sense, already taken place. He essentially feels emotionally dead, feels no sense of pleasure in anything, and is going through life numb and zombielike. These individuals are often either psychotic or extremely depressed. Such individuals have a relatively poor prognosis even if their suicide is prevented at the time of the acute attempt.

### Intervention

A basic premise of intervention is that suicide is a time limited crisis and is not inevitable. Most people who attempt suicide have made prior pleas for help. Studies show that most have contacted family, doctor, friends, or clergy within the thirty to ninety days prior to the attempt, communicating their suicidal thoughts directly or indirectly. People who attempt suicide are ambivalent no matter how vehemently they may state suicidal intent. There is an aspect of their psyche that pleads to go on living. When the individual's crisis is resolved, suicidal ideation is replaced by a desire for life.

Thus, specific tactics in the intervention of the suicidal crisis basically consist of two components: a) buying time—getting the individual through the specific crisis, and b) activating and reinforcing the nonsuicidal component of the individual's ambivalence. The following are some useful intervention techniques that are based upon the general psychodynamics of suicide as described previously.

1. If in doubt, specifically confront the individual regarding his suicidal intent. Asking if someone is suicidal will not initiate or institute such ideas.

2. Aid the individual in recognizing and externalizing feelings of hostility. Usually he will deny awareness of any such feelings, stating that "no one cares" or "the world would be better off without me," or bemoaning a significant loss. Behind such state-

ments is a relatively less conscious feeling of anger associated with a general attitude of "why me?" or anger with a specific individual, situation, fate, or God. Any of these feelings can be mobilized and verbalized. Explore with him who he feels would be most hurt by his death as a further means of mobilizing this hostility; that is, point out that the ultimate way of hurting someone is to kill them or yourself.

3. Almost universally, no matter which of the psychodynamic explanations one feels is applicable for a specific attempt, the suicidal individual has a tendency to "glorify" his death and to see it as a means of achieving "peace." An effective way of undermining his continued desire to die is to question his concept of the "realities" of his own death. This can be done by exploring with him what his concept of death and dying is and what happens after death. This may or may not have religious implications regarding the hereafter. If there are nonreligious implications, focusing on the practical details of his death often leads to a rapid reevaluation of his fantasy of "peace" or "glamour," or "escape" via suicide. It is effective to question him pointedly and in great detail about the circumstances of his fantasized funeral, asking such questions as, what kind of coffin, how he would like to be dressed, who would attend the funeral, what the clergyman or other individual officiating would say, what friends and relatives would say, etc. It is often helpful to focus especially on the general idea that, although people may be polite and say kind things about the dead individual, many people have the idea that "anyone who commits suicide must be crazy." Although this is psychiatrically not accurate, most people find it disconcerting to be thought of in such a fashion and react by externalization of hostility or in a dramatic expression of tears, emotion, and a reassessment of their desire to die.

4. Attempt to help them in a search for alternatives to cope with their own dilemma.

5. Attempt to establish a link with life. The most effective link is through meaningful interpersonal relationships. During the time of the acute crisis, it may be important to establish a meaningful interpersonal relationship between yourself and the individual going through the crisis. This may be reinforced by

establishing a schedule in which you will have him continue to call and make further contacts until it appears the crisis is over. It is very important that you avoid stating that one reason for him not to commit suicide is to please you. This is specifically mentioned because it is a frequent ploy of someone going through a suicidal crisis to state that "No one cares, why shouldn't I die?" and ask the imperative question, "Who would really care about me?" Often crisis intervention workers respond by stating "I care" or something similar. This is a potential for manipulative acting out by the suicidal individual who might at some later point (for rational or irrational reasons) wish to express hostility toward you and make a further suicidal attempt either to hurt you or to test the validity of the statement that you are a significant reason for him not to. (Of course, it is understood on a nonverbal level that your empathy and stated interest in his situation is a means of expressing your caring.)

6. Make follow-up contact, even after the immediate crisis is over.

7. Refer to an appropriate treatment resource at the earliest appropriate moment.

The implicit message in suicide intervention is that "life is worth living," and this is accomplished by establishing a meaningful interpersonal relationship with a significantly important other living human being, who, during the time of the acute crisis, may be you.

## ASSESSMENT OF SUICIDE POTENTIALITY

The Los Angeles Suicide Prevention Center has for many years used a rating schedule of its own for determining the potentiality and lethality of a possible suicide. Our grief counselors use this schedule to determine the suicide potential for our clients who are suicidal.

Name_____ Age____ Sex_____ Date_____

Rater_____ Evaluation_____ 1 2  3 4 5 6  7 8 (9)

                                                      L       M     H

### SUICIDE PREVENTION CENTER
### ASSESSMENT OF SUICIDAL POTENTIALITY

This schedule rates suicide potentiality. By "suicidal potentiality" is meant generally the possibility that the person might destroy himself. In general, the rating is for the present or the immediate future.

Listed below are categories with descriptive items which have been found to be useful in evaluating suicidal potentiality. The list is not meant to be inclusive, but rather suggestive. Some items imply high suicidal potentiality, while others imply low suicidal potentiality. Some items may be either high or low, depending on other factors in the individual case.

The number in parentheses after each item *suggested* the most common range of values or weights to be assigned that item. Nine is highest, or most seriously suicidal, while one is lowest, or least seriously suicidal. The rating assigned will depend on the individual case. The rater will note that some categories range only from one to seven.

For each category the rater should select the item(s) which apply and place the weight he would assign it in the parentheses at the right of the item. (More than one item may apply.) The rater should then indicate his evaluation of his subject in the *category* by placing a number from one to nine (or one to seven) in the column headed, Rating for Category. In those categories where the descriptive item is not present for the subject being rated, write the item in and assign a weight in the parentheses following.

The overall suicidal potential rating may be found by entering the weights assigned for each category in the box, front page, totaling, and dividing by the number of categories rated. This number, rounded to the nearest whole number, should also be circled at the top of the front page.

---

SUICIDAL POTENTIAL:

| | |
|---|---|
| A&S | _____ |
| Sy | _____ |
| St | _____ |
| AvC | _____ |
| SIP | _____      TOTAL _____ |
| Res | _____ |
| PSB | _____      No. of categories rated _____ |
| MedSta | _____ |
| Comm | _____      Average _____ |
| RoSO | _____ |

### STRUCTURE 1

1. AGE AND SEX (1-9)                    Rating for Category
   *Note:*                                    ( )

   The sex and age ratings for Category 1 have been changed
   from the figures given in the Los Angeles Assessment.
   These changes are adjustments in the range of values or
   weights to be assigned to the sex and age item which more
   nearly reflect our local conditions as reported yearly in
   our county suicide statistics. Each locality may also wish
   to make such changes, depending upon whether accurate
   and up-to-date local suicide information is available.

| Male  |       | Female |       |
|-------|-------|--------|-------|
| 7–13  | (1–3) | 7–13   | (1–3) |
| 14–19 | (7–9) | 14–19  | (6–8) |
| 20–29 | (7–9) | 20–29  | (7–9) |
| 30–39 | (7–9) | 30–39  | (7–9) |
| 40–49 | (6–8) | 40–49  | (6–8) |
| 50–59 | (6–8) | 50–59  | (6–8) |
| 60–90 | (7–9) | 60–69  | (4–6) |
|       |       | 70–90  | (1–3) |

2. SYMPTOMS (1–9)                       Rating for Category
                                               ( )

Severe depression: sleep disorder,
   weight loss, withdrawal, despondent,
   loss of interest, apathy. (7–9)          ( )
Feelings of hopelessness, helpless-
   ness, exhaustion. (7–9)                  ( )
Delusions, hallucinations, loss of
   contact, disorientation. (6–8)           ( )
Compulsive gambler. (6–8)                   ( )
Disorganization, confusion, chaos.
   (5–7)                                    ( )
Alcoholism, drug addiction,
   homosexuality. (4–7)                     ( )
Agitation, tension, anxiety. (4–6)          ( )
Guilt, shame, embarrassment. (4–6)          ( )
Feelings of rage, anger, hostility,
   revenge. (4–6)                           ( )

Poor impulse control, poor judg-
ment. (4–6)                         ( )
Frustrated dependency. (4–6)        ( )
Other (describe):                   ( )

3. STRESS (1–9)                     Rating for Category
                                          ( )

Loss of loved person by death, divorce,
or separation. (5–9)                ( )
Loss of job, money, prestige, status.
(4–8)                               ( )       ( )
Sickness, serious illness, surgery,
accident, loss of limb. (3–7)       ( )
Threat of prosecution, criminal in-
involvement, exposure. (4–6)        ( )
Change(s) in life, environment,
setting. (4–6)                      ( )
Success, promotion, increased
responsibilities. (2–5)             ( )
No significant stress. (1–3)        ( )
Other (describe):                   ( )

4. ACUTE VERSUS CHRONIC (1–9)    Rating for Category
                                          ( )

Sharp, noticeable, and sudden onset of
specific symptoms. (1–9)            ( )
Recurrent outbreak of similar
symptoms. (4–9)                     ( )
Recent increase in long-standing
traits. (4–7)                       ( )
No specific recent change. (1–4)    ( )
Other (describe):                   ( )

5. SUICIDAL PLAN (1–9)              Rating for Category
                                          ( )

Lethality of proposed method—gun,
jump, hanging, drowning, knife,
poison, pills, aspirin. (1–9)       ( )
Availability of means in proposed
method. (1–9)                       ( )

Specific detail and clarity in organiza-
   zation of plan.   (1–9)                    ( )
Specificity in time planned.   (1–9)        ( )
Bizarre plans.   (4–6)                       ( )
Rating of previous suicide attempt(s) .
   (1–9)                                     ( )
No plans.   (1–3)                            ( )
Other (describe) :                           ( )

6. RESOURCES  (1–9)                    Rating for Category
                                              ( )

No sources of support  (family, friends,
   agencies, employment) .   (7–9)         ( )
Family and friends available, unwill-
   ing to help.   (4–7)                     ( )
Financial problem.   (4–7)                   ( )
Available professional help, agency or
   therapist.   (2–4)                       ( )
Family and/or friends willing to
   help.   (1–3)                            ( )
Stable life history.   (1–3)                 ( )
Physician or clergy available.   (1–3)       ( )
Employed.   (1–3)                            ( )
Finances no problem.   (1–3)                 ( )
Other (describe) :                           ( )

7. SUICIDAL BEHAVIOR  (1–7)        Rating  for  Category
                                              ( )

One or more prior attempts of high
   lethality.   (6–7)                       ( )
One or more prior attempts of low
   lethality.   (4–5)                       ( )
History of repeated threats and
   depression.   (3–5)                      ( )
No prior suicidal or depressed history.
   (1–3)                                    ( )
Other (describe) :                           ( )

8. MEDICAL STATUS (1–7)            Rating for Category
                                            ( )

Chronic debilitating illness. (5–7)     ( )
Pattern of failure in previous therapy.
  (4–6)                                 ( )
Many repeated unsuccessful experiences
  with doctors. (4–6)                   ( )
Psychosomatic illness, e.g. asthma,
  ulcer, etc. (2–4)                     ( )
Chronic minor illness complaints,
  hypochondria. (1–3)                   ( )
No medical problems. (1–2)              ( )
Other (describe) :                      ( )

9. COMMUNICATION ASPECTS (1–7)   Rating for Category
                                            ( )

Communication broken with rejection
  of efforts to re-establish by both
  patient and others. (5–7)            ( )
Communications have internalized goal,
  e.g. declaration of guilt, feelings of
  worthless, blame, shame. (4–7)       ( )
Communications have interpersonalized
  goal, e.g. to cause guilt in others to
  force behavior, etc. (2–4)           ( )
Communications directed toward
  world and people in general
  (3–5)                                ( )
Communications directed toward one
  or more specific persons. (1–3)      ( )
Other (describe) :                     ( )

10. REACTION OF SIGNIFICANT
    OTHER (1–7)                         Rating for Category
                                            ( )

Defensive, paranoid, rejected, punish-
  ing attitude. (5–7)                  ( )

Denial of own or patient's need for
help.  (5–7)                                      (   )
No feelings of concern about the
patient does not understand the
patient.  (4–6)                                   (   )
Indecisiveness, feelings of
helplessness.  (3–5)                              (   )
Alternation between feelings of anger
and rejection and feelings of responsibility and desire to help.
(2–4)                                             (   )
Sympathy and concern plus admission
of need for help.  (1–3)                          (   )
Other (describe) :                                (   )

## THE COSTS OF SUICIDE

The following information appeared in the Hot Line (1976) and is based on Nancy Allen's monograph (1973) .

The estimated cost of each suicide ranges from $50,000 to $300,000.  The burdens to the family and community are considerable.  These costs begin with the ambulance fee, coroner's time and facilities.  Then there are the needs of welfare assistance, social security benefits, and for community mental health services. To this can be added the loss of tax revenues—taxes to the State and Federal governments—that the deceased would have paid in during the potentially remaining earning years.  There are also the long-range costs involved when disturbed families require increased police, probation, court, and justice system services.

In one county in California, it was estimated that the county spent approximately $75,000 a year for emergency psychiatric hospitalization for suicide attempters.  This psychiatric hospitalization does not include the medical costs for gastric lavage, suturing, emergency life-saving procedures, and all the staff time and facilities necessary to provide them.  The $75,000 figure applies only to the amount spent on "Holding Unit" wards to hospitalize people for whom the major reason for admission was suicide attempt.  Hospitalization for physical recovery and its attendant costs were not investigated.

Unfortunately, statistics on how many of these hospitalized suicidal persons were repeaters is not available. Probably a good number of these clients were "chronics"—people who have developed the habit of dealing with emotional crisis by making serious suicide attempts or suicide gestures. The attempts are less serious, but equally frightening, painful, and costly.

The high cost of suicide in our society runs fourth, behind heart disease, cancer, and accidents. In California for 1968 (the last year calculated), the cost was 300.2 million dollars in lifetime earnings lost through suicide.

It is time to spend more on creative, innovative suicide-crisis programs so that less money, time, and pain need be spent on after-the-fact ministering to suicide victims and survivors. Primary prevention in the schools, social clubs, fraternal organizations, and churches is an alternative to this "revolving door" policy now in practice. Another secondary preventive measure is assistance to suicide-crisis hotlines. Both alternatives need additional innovative programs that marshall the clients' and the communities' human resources into innovative programs for helping the suicidal person.

### SUICIDE PREVENTION

We are indebted to Professor Seiden (1977) for his thoughtful article on "Suicide Prevention: A Public Health/Public Policy Approach." In this article, Seiden approaches the incidence of suicide not only by method but also by relative availablity and lethality of the method. He ranks four methods of suicide in this way:

| Method | Availability | Lethality |
|--------|--------------|-----------|
| Firearms | Moderate | High |
| Ingestion | Moderate | Low |
| Coke gas | Low | High |
| Golden Gate Bridge | High | High |

He then points out what public policy control measures could do to reduce the availability of these suicide methods and how the lethality could be reduced by the following less lethal substitutions.

*Suicide Methods: Public Policy Control Measures*

| Method | Availability | (Lesser) Lethality |
|---|---|---|
| Firearms | Gun control and registration | TASER, pellet guns, etc. |
| Ingestion | Tightened rules on prescriptions (especially barbiturates) | Pharmacologically "safe" drugs |
| Coke gas | Change to natural gas | Detoxify coke gas |
| G.G. Bridge | Hardware barrier | Widened second deck |

Seiden points to the fact that firearm studies indicate that the "easy availability of a highly lethal means of violence like a gun raises the risk of suicide as well as the risk of accidental and homicidal gun deaths." In this connection, he cites the recommendation of the National Advisory Committee on Criminal Justice Standards and Goals (1973) that "the manufacture, sale and private possession of handguns should be prohibited for all persons other than law enforcement and military personnel.

He suggests that there is need for some "regulation of manufacture, prescription and dispensing of [certain drugs] . . . to limit their availability as a method of suicide. At the manufacturing level some greater regulation appears necessary to stop over-production. For example, in 1969 the pharmaceutical industry produced ten billion doses of barbiturates or enough to have provided each man, woman and child in this land with fifty barbs. At least half of the supply gets into the illicit market."

Coke gas is rarely used as a suicide method in the United States because of its limited availability, but it is widely used in Europe and was once a preferred method of suicide in Great Britain. Seiden (1977) states

In approximately the mid 1960's there was a substitution of non-poisonous natural gas from the North Sea for use as a domestic fuel. This adventitious change has contributed to a reduction of Britain's annual suicide rate by about one-third against a background of rising rates world-wide. Since 1963 the British rates have fallen steadily and there has not been any switch to other available methods to make up the difference. Reducing the *lethality* of coke gas has also provided comparable results. The City of Birmingham, England while not yet on natural gas, altered the carbon monoxide content of their gas-making feedstock from 20 per cent to 2.5 per cent. Suicides droped 45 per cent during the study period (1963-69) and have remained at the reduced level.

The Golden Gate Bridge in San Francisco is infamous from coast to coast as the "number one suicide spot in the world." Plans to build a second deck in order to reduce the *lethality* of this bridge were proposed and finally scrapped. There have also been plans to widen the lower deck and to seal off this lower level with a barrier that would extend from top to bottom. Presently, there is another proposed measure that would create a hardware barrier to control the *availability* of the bridge as a suicidal method. Seiden, who has written extensively on the subject of suicide, concludes his plans for public policy control of lethality and availability in this way:

> . . . we know very well that suicidal people are typically very ambivalent in the midst of a life and death crisis and that the risk period is transient, often directly related to acute situations. If the person can weather that crisis, the suicidal danger passes, often never to return. Considering the transitory nature of suicidal crises, the presence of a highly lethal and easily available means such as the bridge must be regarded as equivalent to a loaded gun around the house ready to be used in an impulsive outburst. Such impulsive suicides are very characteristic of younger people which makes it all the more significant to note that the average age of suicides at the bridge has dropped from the mid-fifties during the years after the bridge was first opened to the middle twenties at the present time.

By following Professor Seiden's model for proposed public health/public policy control of both lethality and availability of common methods of suicides, there could be provided an important deterrent to some kinds of suicides. In addition, such controls might act as deterrents in the incidence of some accidental deaths (by overdose and handguns) and many homicides (handguns).

A good many suicides could also be prevented by more and better community education in the area of identifying certain premonitory clues, such as are outlined in this chapter (see pp. 120-124 and pp. 148-151).

## REFERENCES

Allen, Nancy H., *Suicide in California, 1960–1970.* Sacramento:  California State Department of Public Health, 1973.

Durkheim, Emile, *Suicide, A Study in Sociology.*  Translated by John A. Spaulding and George Simpson, edited with an introduction by George Simpson.  New York:  Free Pr, 1951.

*Hotline,* "Cost of Suicide."  Walnut Creek, California:  Contra Costa Crisis and Suicide Intervention Service, 1976.

Seiden, Richard, "Suicide Prevention:  A Public Health/Public Policy Approach," *Omega, 8:3,* 1977.

## Chapter 10

# SUICIDE – THE YOUNG AND
# THE ELDERLY

### TEENAGE SUICIDE

ONE OF THE most disturbing statistics to come out of the decade of the 70s is the alarming increase in the rate of suicides in the 15–19 age group. The incidence of suicide has nearly tripled over the past twenty years (Lee and Ross, 1977). This sharp shift in the age group that most frequently suicides is in contrast to previous years when the person most likely to suicide was the white male between the ages of 45 and 50. This shift in the age and frequency of suicide for young people gives rightful cause for all of us to be alarmed and frightened by the fact that the young, who are viewed by society as having everything to live for and look forward to, are taking their own lives in increasing numbers.

Why are these youths who are entering the most vigorous and prime time of their lives, often with a potentially good future, suddenly filled with the desire to end their lives? Depression among the young is much more prevalent than adults realize. But why should youths—in the most carefree portion of life—be depressed? If one looks closely, one observes that the lives of teenagers are not all that carefree. They are confronted by a galaxy of problems, some not of their making, that are disturbing.

### Some Important Tasks for Youth

One of the foremost tasks that confronts a teenager is to develop his own self-identity. This is a difficult and necessary undertaking in a society that has largely wiped out other forms of

129

social identity, such as birthright, wealth, ethnic group, etc. The young are left in a desperate struggle to develop their own identity. In a society where many families have a single parent, a youth may not have a rolemodel of the same sex. Moreover, sex roles are changing considerably, and there are many bewildering decisions to make with not much guidance from the adults in their lives.

The young must also take the responsibility for learning how to disengage from their parents. This is an important step that has to be taken by everyone, but presently a real dilemma exists for teenagers in this regard. The time for being dependent upon the family is continually being extended through added schooling and unemployment. There are also misguided alternatives that seem to promise the teenager new freedoms but entrap him in further dependency—drugs, alcohol, promiscuity.

Youth has always needed to look toward the selection and completion of appropriate vocational aspirations. How to acquire the necessary training and skills in order to qualify as a self-sufficient, employed adult has always been a major problem for youth. Even if the training and skills are somehow obtained, and frequently they are not, youths are most severely handicapped by the staggering rate of teenage unemployment. This teenage unemployment hits minority young blacks much harder than white youths.

### Parental Expectations

The tasks that have always confronted young people in the process of growing up are complicated by the fact that today the family frequently lays an additional burden upon children by its own unbridled emphasis upon success for the family and for the children. Parents who are high achievers frequently compound the difficulties of growing up by insisting that the young excel as much as they did or surpass the accomplishments of the parents. Parents who are not high achievers often insist on their children excelling in a way they were never able to do. In short, the children need to compensate for the parent's own failures, inadequacies, and insecurities. Neither the high nor the low achiever family is likely to accept failure in their children. This is a harsh expectation since we all must learn through the errors we make growing up.

Parental approval based on such unreal expectations has too high a price tag. If the youth succumbs to the enticements of the parents, he gives up his own identity, preference for work, training, skills and does what the parents want done. Failure to live up to the parents' expectations is a frequent cause of considerable humiliation for the child. Seiden (1977) says, "These parental expectations are far more intense than the usual wishes for success that most parents have for their children. They represent a total lack of acceptance of their children as they are."

## What To Watch For

Under the circumstances just described, a child may experience early on tremendous feelings of unhappiness, frustration, or failure that are unacceptable to the parents. These feelings are either denied by the parents or, even worse, ignored or met by hostility. Constant reminders of "After all we have done for you" push a child into a constantly eroding self-image and a position of isolation in the family. Under such circumstances, who wouldn't become depressed?

Some young people, rather than becoming depressed, seek a new image, a new release of energy, etc., through drugs or alcohol and sexual promiscuity. In any event and for whatever reason, not being appreciated or understood by the family seems to be the most common factor in the general unhappiness and perturbation that take place in a suicidal youth's life.

The general inability to get along with others can also lead a presuicidal youth into confrontations with teachers and the school, his own friends, the law, and other authority types. A good many suicidal youths have had physical fights with their families. There also seems to be a considerable amount of physical and assaultive behavior among family members.

The other side of this rebellious or violent behavior shows the teenager withdrawn, a loner, without friends or supportive family members. Whichever route, he ends up being enormously unhappy. He lacks self-confidence, hope for the future and, in the end, feels miserable and helpless. Dr. Herbert Hendin, director of psychosocial studies at the Center for Policy Research in New York City, recently remarked (1978), "Worry about the kids 15, 16 and 17 years old who are alone, sitting in their rooms listening to rock music, not talking to anybody and not getting into trouble. The most seriously suicidal kids have stopped complaining. They only complain through their suicide attempts."

Dr. Hendin describes these young people as "deadened or numbed" to life. They may be outwardly cheerful and cooperative, but they have already adopted death as a defense against life. What they have in common, he says, are much isolation and loneliness in their lives; contacts with people don't touch them deeply; using work as a barrier against life, although it is often a pleasureless preoccupation.

Young people should *always* be taken seriously when, under these circumstances, they attempt to make some philosophical statement about what life is all about and comments and ruminations about life's purposelessness, boredom, and "being tired of it all." One should immediately begin to talk and listen attentively to what that young person says. One needs to be attentive to any signs of intense withdrawal, remarks about the pervasiveness of unhappiness, disturbances in appetite or sleep, loss of interest in sports, marked decline in school performance, giving away meaningful objects, and any mention of suicide, even in a joking or lighthearted way.

### Talking It Over

Nothing is ever lost by trying to talk. Since troubled youths feel that other people do not understand how they feel, it is sometimes much more important to allow them to talk and try to be reassuring to them rather than preach. It can also be a put-down to suggest that the youth "snap out of it." He cannot snap out of it so the best one can do is to be accessible and reasonable. It is reassuring for him to hear you say, "I know you're feeling down and in time it will get better." Then give him time to talk, have his say, as you listen attentively. At this time, you can ask a series of concerned, yet supportive questions, such as, "Is something bothering you? You don't seem to be yourself lately. You appear to be kind of down. Are you feeling kind of depressed? Do you sometimes wake up in the morning and wish you didn't have to wake up, wish you were dead?" A "Yes" here leads you to, "Have you been thinking about killing yourself? Has suicide been on your mind?"

These questions should be spaced out in a low-key, kindly conversation about the youth's feelings and difficulties. His replies can lead you to become convinced that he is contemplating suicide. *Now you continue to talk to him* in the same thoughtful, nonjudgmental way about seeking help. Help is available at the nearest Crisis and Suicide Intervention Center in your community and from your clergy, doctor, psychologist, or mental health counselor. Adolescence can be a time of depression, but no matter how hopeless or self-defeated a young person may feel, strong family support can help deter most who are on a disaster course.

## SUICIDE AND THE VERY YOUNG

Suicide by children of kindergarten and grade school ages—from 5 to 14—is an emerging problem in the field of mental health. Some experts believe that even infants can intentionally kill themselves.

The National Center for Health Statistics reported 170 confirmed child suicides in 1975, the most recent year for which data are available. "That figure is demonstrably inaccurate," commented Dr. Ari Kiev, developer of the Crisis Intervention Clinic at Cornell Medical College (1978). "There has always been a stigma attached to suicide, particularly child suicide. As a result it is concealed and it is not accurately reported."

There are also suicides that go undetected—deaths that appear to be accidental. Dr. Joaquin Puig-Antich, chief of the Child Depression Clinic at Columbia-Presbyterian's Psychiatric Institute in New York, said (1978), "Children commit suicide for many of the same reasons as adolescents and adults, mainly while in deep depression, which may take many forms and come from many causes. Some may kill themselves in the hope of rejoining a parent who has died. In achievement-oriented families, children have tried to kill themselves rather than come home with poor grades."

One of the most debated elements of child suicide is whether children recognize that death is final. "Children do not develop mature ideas about death until middle childhood," says Dr. David Shaffer, formerly of the Institute of Psychiatry in London, where he conducted a "psychological postmortem" of thirty child suicides (1978). "Half the children in the 6 to 11 age group in one study believed death to be reversible. In the 11 to 13 group, 13 per cent still believed this."

There are also questions asked among the experts about whether children and adults with emotional problems understand death. Dr. Daniel Casriel, founder of New York's Casriel Institute, stated his position this way (1978), "It isn't so much that the suicide wants to die, but that he doesn't want to live anymore. A child who is severely depressed feels as though he has an emotional spear in his belly. It isn't that he feels he would be happier dead, just that there would be less pain."

There are those who believe that childhood depression is the most common cause of behavior problems in youngsters. Sometimes depression is brought on by tremendous stress or trauma, such as the loss of a parent, a close friend, or even a pet. Perhaps the most common cause of childhood depression is a lack of love from parents who may be too disturbed by pressing problems of their own to give the child the time and love he needs. Parents may love the child but may be totally unaware that they have changed in their attitude toward the child. Parents should not assume that childhood depression is unimportant or that it will soon pass. A child who is frequently or chronically sad needs professional attention. Parents too usually need help because they are apt to assume that their child's state of emptiness and sadness is their fault. This is not necessarily so.

These brief observations about suicide and the very young point up the importance of acknowledging the presence of depression in the young, identifying it, and getting the child and his parents directed to professional help.

### Cases

The following case illustrates some of the complicated aspects of suicide among the young: family and peer pressures, romantic or mysterious events that become magnified, the elusive qualities of suicide contagion, and the lack of recognition by everyone that this group of young people share powerful thoughts and fantasies about suicide.

## The Pied Piper of Rio Seco

Phil phoned shortly after his brother Ben, 18, suicided. Phil, who said he was more like a father than a brother, spent many hours discussing the case and digging for information that might have shed some light on Ben's suicide.

At the time of his suicide, Ben was a college student and one of a tightly knit group of eleven young people who were friends during their entire high school experience. This group met most weekend nights to listen to records, both rock and classical, discuss books they were reading, and "to shoot the breeze." There apparently was no use of drugs at these gatherings, but plenty of beer and an occasional joint of marijuana. They were all good students—bright, curious, gregarious. The only thing that was out of the ordinary for such a group was that for the last three years Ben would often suggest, at the end of an evening of music and talk, that they go for a ride to a place that was "really far out." He led the caravan to a cemetery. Other cemeteries were added to the list until this group had visited all the cemeteries in their locality, plus a few farther away. On these occasions, they would pile into their cars and drive to the cemetery where they would walk to a location that Ben had previously selected and sit there for hours—sometimes talking, sometimes sitting quietly.

One Saturday night while they were having a noisy, argumentative session at a friend's house, an older man wandered in from the street and joined them. Each person felt that this man was invited by somebody in the group—rather like the uninvited guest at a New Year's Eve party—so his presence was never questioned by anyone. He entered into their conversation, and they were charmed by his "style," his knowledge of the books they were interested in, and the account of his various travels to distant and exciting places. He returned several times to their sessions, and during one he told of an experience he had following an operation. He said he had died during the operation but that he had "come back." He did not like it here and he wished he had remained "there" where it was beautiful and wonderful. Everyone was fascinated by his account of this experience. Death, dying, afterlife, cemeteries, and "how I'd like to die" conversations and sessions became more and more absorbing and frequent. Just as suddenly as he appeared, their mysterious visitor disappeared. They looked for him about town, but since they did not know his name or where he lived, they never found him. But his "aura" was present, and they spoke often of him. They found his thoughts about "the other side" to be especially provocative, and the group was absorbed for most of a year in an ongoing discussion of these new ideas.

Changes occurred in the group. As some of the participants graduated and moved on to college, travel, or jobs, the group diminished in number but still retained its cohesive quality and became a kind of magnet for the ones who returned home for a visit. During the next three years, three of the group suicided—one at college, one at work, and Ben—just about a year apart. Only Ben left a note indicating his intention to suicide.

There remained five young men, two young women students, and another young woman who had moved away. Phil held sessions with all of those remaining in the community, keeping in touch with us for suggestions, ideas, and questions to raise with them. They were all aware of our participation with Phil. Without his role as an investigator, few of the following facts and occurrences would ever have been revealed.

Three young women were romantically attached to Ben: one had moved away, another who came from a strong, supportive family had recently broken off with him, and the third was still dating Ben. The latter two young women were seen by us. There seemed to be a straightforward effort to break with Ben by the one friend. She recognized that Ben needed help and said she had persuaded him to ask his mother to help him seek a psychologist. When his mother refused to do this, saying that all he needed was to concentrate more on going to church, she had broken off their relationship.

The other girlfriend said as a child she had been punished by her mother by having her head shaved on several occasions. She indicated that Ben had physically abused her on occasion, but because she loved him, she allowed it and waited out his affairs with the other two girlfriends. Her self-image was poor. She vacillated between thinking God was helping her and being terribly anxious about the next full moon. She was studying criminology because she wanted to become a cop and added, with unusual emphasis that as a cop she would kill people in the line of duty. She declined help from us or a referral elsewhere. (Later Ben's parents spoke of her as a "devil" who was moody, on drugs, suicidal, and pushing Ben toward death by way of books, reading, talk sessions, and the cemetery visits.) Both of the girlfriends spoke of the mortuary as being Ben's "loveland." These girlfriends agreed that for a while Ben was "into" prescription drugs. He obtained the drugs from a doctor who had treated him following an operation and a dentist who had performed dental surgery. He complained about pain to both these professionals and was given considerable quantities of codeine.

There were five young men friends. One, according to Phil, had his "head on straight"; another was quiet, reluctant to talk, and had always been dependent on Ben and went to him whenever anything went wrong. Two were unknown to Phil until he met them at meetings where they spoke up and participated with the others. Another had known of Ben's use of prescription drugs and had tried to straighten him out. This friend said he had had suicidal thoughts himself, liked to talk a lot about heaven, and did not realize that Ben was going in the direction of suicide. None of these young men responded to Phil's suggestion that they seek help from a minister, counselor, or us.

Ben's own family was affected by suicide. Ben's father was 16 when his older brother suicided. Ben's father said he had hoped and prayed for years that none of his sons would take the route of suicide. An older brother of Ben's said he had often sat where Ben last sat, holding a gun himself, and pondering taking his life. Another brother said that he had often had suicidal thoughts and toyed with a gun but that he had always "snapped out of it." This brother never kept any of his numerous appointments with us.

Ben's father was a self-made man, conservative, proud of his financial success and his ability to provide generously for his family. He used financial gifts to control his sons' lives. Ben's mother said her mother never loved her. She was religious almost to the point of being a fanatic. She tried to project her religion on her sons. While Phil offered considerable resistance to her ideas, Ben often went with her to church. He also painted pictures of crosses and Jesus. Both parents accepted Ben's death stoically and were already speaking of having three remaining sons and six grandchildren "to help and guide." They accepted grief counseling to the extent they were able. The father felt that he needed to get back to work as soon as possible. The mother felt that she needed to concern herself more intensely with her religion. Neither opened up their grief to the point of crying but concerned themselves with "how to help Ben's friends."

Phil concentrated on asking for help for his family, his older brother's family, and his younger brother. The two family groups were interested in help for their children and the effect of Ben's death upon them. They were also interested in how to discuss the death with the children. Good progress was made with these two families.

Near the anniversary date, arrangements were made for seeing again the members of the family whom we had seen and the young women. The latter were no longer in the area. Neither of the parents wanted to be seen. The father was ill and the mother, according to Phil, was assuming the fathers' role as provider, giftgiver, and controller of the clan. The two younger families were grateful for the help given them and felt they had made good progress during the year.

Phil reported that he was fine too. He had gotten in the habit of visiting Ben's grave and, strangely for him, he thought, was spending more and more time there. He also admitted that his wife did not know the extent of time he spent there. He offered the information that at those times he just sat there feeling the quiet, the sweetness of the breeze and the closeness of the stars. Sometimes, he said, he thought Ben was lucky to be on "the other side," and he often thought about what it must be like and felt himself drawn toward wanting to be "there" with Ben. Otherwise, he said his life was uneventful. Even though his work was going well and his family also, he was feeling guilty about spending so much time away from them at Ben's grave. He said he was going to try to spend more time with his family.

Three years later, Phil phoned to ask for some help for a friend's son. After discussing these problems, the talk drifted to Phil and his activities. He said everything was fine. Then he added,` laughingly, that he was really addicted to visiting cemeteries. He still goes to the one where Ben was buried. He also spends considerable time thinking about "all those young people and that stranger they liked so much." Phil thinks he does not see Death as the stranger, but he cannot forget the stranger, even though he personally never saw or heard him. He is certain it is the stranger who draws him toward Ben's grave and keeps prompting him about the beauties of "the other side."

One can see from this case that there were many factors that complicated an understanding of Ben's suicide. There were family conflicts and misunderstandings, unshared experiences, unwillingness to seek help, and a lack of recognition by the young people and the family that something was occurring in this group that fostered thoughts of suicide. No one thought it strange that three young people had suicided.

Phil gathered a good deal of information, but it carried little meaning since none of the surviving young people would face what was happening to them or what had happened in their group meetings. As a result, Phil was confused himself about what happened. He and the two families with small children learned a good deal about their feelings and how to share them with each other. The parents never appeared to be grieving, although they must have been hurting.

The following case is interesting because it shows how a family that originally felt it did not want to expose itself to an outsider did manage to come through the first session. By expressing what they felt—exasperation, anger, frustration, and intolerance of other's views—this family found a kind of accommodation that allowed them to share their hurt. Subsequent visits with individual members and with the family opened up ways they could share their grief. In the process of sharing this grief, they learned to support each other.

### Excerpts From A Home Visit

The seventeen-year-old son in the family suicided. Present at the visit were the surviving members of the family—the parents and four siblings. At the time of death, the deceased was a runaway and a truant.

| | |
|---|---|
| *Father:* | How did you happen to send us a letter? |
| *Counselor:* | Our agency reads the files of the suicides and other sudden deaths in the coroner's office. Your name appeared in the file as the next-of-kin. We send such a letter to family members or to close friends and neighbors of all traumatic deaths that occur in the county. |
| *Father:* | Well, if you're from the coroner's office, I've got news for you. I think that office stinks. What they did is no way to run an investigation. Do you know what they did? |
| *C:* | No. |
| *Father:* | Well, they never took fingerprints of our boy or took them from the gun. If you are part of that bunch, I doubt if we have much to talk about. |
| *C:* | While we read the files in the coroner's office, we are in no way connected with that office or a part of any investigation. We are volunteers who work for the Crisis Center, and that Center is concerned with a crisis such as sudden death or suicide. |

*Father:* Would you believe that they never looked into the two guys who were last seen with our boy? It was for them that he came back here for the gun. Wouldn't you think they'd follow up a hot lead like that?

*C:* You mean you think your son was killed by those fellows?

*Father:* He could have been. And that's what I keep telling them. But I reckon he killed himself all right, but if he didn't, they'd never find out.

*C:* Well, the reason I am here is not to talk about the investigation. I expect that the deputy has advised you about your rights and how to proceed to bring your point of view to the attention of the coroner. I thought perhaps I could help you in another way. All of you have had a sudden and grievous loss. You have lost a son and a brother and you are probably hurting a lot.

*Mother:* This is not a family to show much emotion. Everybody goes his own way and is expected to do the right thing without complaining or feeling sorry for himself.

*Father:* One thing I've tried to teach this bunch is to stand on their own two feet. That's pretty much what we do. We don't give help, and we don't ask for it.

*C:* Nevertheless, I expect at a time like this you feel a closeness perhaps you never felt before—perhaps a desire to seek help or to give it?

*Father:* Well, I can tell you how I felt when I got your letter. I threw it in the fire. "Damn," I said, "that's one piece of b.s. I don't need." I thought that was the end of it. But then the Mrs. comes along and says you talked to her on the phone. I don't know what kind of route it took, but everybody here has been involved in the hassle. Nobody wanted you, but here you are because we asked for you. How's that for a big joke on us?

*C:* Since I never knew your son, tell me something about him so I'll have an idea what kind of person he was.

|           | Will each of you tell me something about him? |
|-----------|--------|
| *Mother:* | He was a quiet boy. He didn't do well in school recently. His grades went down very badly this year. But then he was under a great deal of pressure. |
| *C:* | What kind of pressure? |
| *Mother:* | He was on the _____ team and one of their best. I think they put a lot of pressure on him to win, to practice, to do special training, and I don't know what all. _____, you were once on the team, what do you think? |
| *Sibling 1:* | We all know what the pressure is. _____ isn't a team sport. It's man against man and it's all up to you. If you win, you're the greatest, but if you lose, there isn't any team to help you talk it out, share the blame, or cuss out the opposition for playing dirty. If you lose, it's *you* that loses and nobody else. That's pretty hard to take. (The father was also in this sport when he was young. His sons resemble him in build, stance, and bearing.) |
| *C:* | Do you think _____ took too hard some of the matches he lost? |
| *Father:* | Who knows? There was a lot happening around here. It could have been almost anything. His mother was too easy on him. |
| *Mother:* | Well, I can't always be nagging and scolding. I've been sick a good deal, and there are times when I just have to have peace and quiet. The arguing and bitterness around here was too much for me sometimes. |
| *C:* | What do you remember most about your brother? |
| *Sibling 2:* | It's hard to say. We didn't see much of each other. Since my accident, I've been confined to the house a lot and he was always on the go. He didn't spend much time at home. |
| *Sibling 1:* | Yeah, he hated it around here. |
| *Father:* | What do you mean by that? I know he disliked doing anything anyone suggested, but I never thought he hated anything. What did he hate? |

*Sibling 1:*    Why, he hated the house—it was a kind of prison, and he hated you because you were always riding him about something.

*Father:*       I know there was a lot going on, but I didn't think he hated it here. Why should he do that?

*Sibling 1:*    Well, you know he wanted to quit school. He wasn't doing anything there but all that sports stuff, and that was getting him down. He had some money, and he wanted to leave. He planned to go as soon as he turned 18.

*Father:*       Fat chance he'd have anywhere. Mrs., he was the limit. Here was this big, fine athlete, with a body of a man, and under all that meat was a little kid who didn't know anything about this world. He was really innocent. He didn't know what it took to get through school, to get a job and hold it, to make money, or to hang on to it.

*Sibling 1:*    Well, he still had several hundred dollars he'd made.

*Father:*       He had no idea what he wanted to do, no ideas what there is even to do. He had to be told everything. . . .

*Sibling 1:*    Well, you told him everything. To get up, to go to school, to come home, to study, to do this, to do that. He used to lie in bed and wait until he heard you reach a certain tone of voice before he'd get up. He said there was no use getting up until you got to the right point. He didn't want to disappoint you.
                (The phone rings.)

*Father:*       I told you that we are not accepting any calls tonight. We're going to sit here and talk about this. But no one is going to hang on the phone.

(During the course of the evening the telephone rang several times for different members of the family and each time the father's response was the same until a call came for him. Then he got up and excused himself "to take a business call." A strange look passed from one family member to another. While he was speaking on the telephone, one son got up from his position on the floor and sat in his father's chair. When the phone call was completed, I could see the father in another room, and he was aware that his chair was occupied. He called into the room, "I'm finished with the call now." The son did not move. I could see the father circling through the other rooms. Again he called and said he'd be in in a couple of minutes. No move from the chair. Still circling, this time he called, "If you aren't out of my chair by the time I get there, I'll break both your legs." It was only when the father stood immediately in front of his chair that the son relinquished it.)

| | |
|---|---|
| *Father:* | You see, these kids have no respect for their father, and their mother's being sick all the time hasn't helped much. |
| *C:* | Have you been ill long? |
| *Mother:* | Yes, I have had a nervous breakdown. I had just begun to think the end was in sight when this happened. It is very difficult for me to keep from crying. |
| *C:* | Perhaps crying might help. Letting the emotions out at a time like this can be helpful. Have you had a good cry? |
| *Mother:* | Yes, but only at times when I was alone. |
| *C:* | Perhaps the children might like to cry with you. (To the children) Have you cried? |
| | (Shaking of all heads except the one who found the body.) |
| *Father:* | Well, I cried. And if I wasn't full of tranquilizers, I'd probably not be able to sit here this calm. . . . |
| *Sibling 1:* | You've cried? |
| *Father:* | Many times. I guess I've got a lot on my mind. I suppose you'd say I feel guilty. I did ride the kid pretty hard. But how is one to know how they're supposed to take it? I thought I was teaching him to be strong and self-reliant. I had to be, and I handled it all starting at about his age. I never knew how to reach him, I guess. Oh, God, what a mess this all is. |

(Both younger sons begin to cry, one sitting upright in his chair with the tears coursing down his cheeks, the other one flung full length with his head under the coffee table where he would be unseen.  Only his convulsed shoulders revealed his sobs.)

| | |
|---|---|
| *Mother:* | You haven't felt well yourself, you know.  You haven't been well either, and I know you have been tired and irritable. |
| *C:* | Each one in the family is experiencing a new emotion—grief.  It is a bewildering experience.  Moreover, I expect each of you has also some feelings of personal guilt or blame? |
| *Sibling 2:* | I know I do.  He always wanted to talk to me, and I didn't like to hear about all sports talk.  What good would it do to hear all that?  I couldn't help him.  I can't *do* anything. |
| *C:* | And now you feel that it might have helped him just to talk, even if you only listened? |
| *Sibling 2:* | I guess so . . . (beginning to cry) . |
| *Sibling 1:* | Well, look at this.  Everybody crying but me.  No one wanted to do this but Mom, and look at everybody crying.  You know, we all did a lot of bargaining before you came? |
| *C:* | I don't know what you mean.  Tell me. |
| *Sibling 1:* | Well, no one wanted you to come.  _____ is dead, and there's nothing we can do about it now.  What good would a stranger be coming here?  But each of us saw an advantage for ourselves if you came.  For instance, I agreed because I'm against air pollution. . . . |
| *C:* | How does that come in? |
| *Sibling 1:* | Smoking.  I agreed to sit through all this if Mom would agree to quit smoking.  She thought it would help everybody so she agreed.  Sis agreed if she could just sit there and not say anything.  _____ agreed if Dad would stay off his back.  _____ is the only one who may need you; after all, he found him.  That's a messy deal. |
| *C:* | Do you regret the bargain you made? |
| *Father:* | I think we've all got our bargain and then some.  We're actually crying.  Together.  And smiling too.  What's going on here? |

C:            Perhaps it feels good to share your grief with someone in the family?

*Sibling 1:*    Well, it hasn't hit me. But I'd rather hurt the way I
do now than hurt the way he did before he killed
himself.

C:            I hope it does hit you and soon.

*Mother:*    What are we to do now?

C:            Maybe the ice is broken now, and the family can begin not only to share its grief but to help each other
bear that grief. Try listening to each other, helping
each other.

*Mother:*    Will you come again?

C:            Of course, if you wish. Right now I expect you don't
know what you want. But each one can think it over
for a few days. If you wish to talk to me singly, we
can do that. Or we can meet again as a group—whatever you decide you want. Here is our telephone
number; you can reach me there any time. But I'll
call you in a few days.

(The father escorted me to the car where he proceeded to tell me
the nature of his wife's illness. Because of her illness, he had lost
a job he valued greatly. Now, doing something not to his liking,
he found his irritability mounting whenever he thought of his
recent disappointment. While we were talking beside the car, the
youngest son appeared.)

*Father:*    What do you want? You think we're going to say
something you'll miss?

C:            _____, I expect you miss your brother very much.
You were called upon to perform a very grown-up
task and not an easy one at that. I expect your father
is proud of the manly way you conducted yourself
during the investigation and especially during the
identification of the body. I know I admire you very
much. (He begins to cry and I reach out and take
his hand and hold it while I talk with his father.)

C:            Your wife mentioned you're not feeling well. How
is your health?

*Father:*    Well, I'm tired all the time and losing weight and feeling lousy.  So I went to see what is the matter.  They don't know yet so they're running all kinds of tests and so I don't know either.

*C:*         Why are they running the tests?

*Father:*    They found this lump and they just want to satisfy themselves that it's nothing, and when they know that I'll probably feel a lot better.

*C:*         But right now you are pretty worried, I expect.  Full of anxiety and uncertainty?

*Father:*    Yeah.  I'll be glad when it blows over.  Thanks for coming.  You really opened up a hornet's nest tonight.  Learned things I didn't know were going on right in my own house.

(When last seen the father was walking back toward the house with his arm flung across the shoulder of his youngest son.)

The most significant point that this interview makes is one that most grief counselors need to take seriously:  When one is meeting with a family group, *one should not make efforts to keep the family from showing anger, disagreement, frustration, or anxiety.*  Generally, the helping person feels that if he allows the family members to "blow up," he has somehow contributed to an unruly scene and that *he* will be in hot water beyond his depth.  Unsavory as these sessions can often be, it is important to allow these scenes to develop—for family members to hear (perhaps for the first time) the complaints and frustrations each holds.  Allowing the family "to get it all out in the open" clears the way for an honest discussion of what the family difficulties are—how each member has legitimate (or not) reasons of his own, how some differences can lead to new understandings and develop new insights into how family members are hurting (like oneself).  These *shared* "scenes" can lead to attempts to share one's grief, express one's anger and, in the process, give support and nurture to other family members.

## SUICIDE AND THE ELDERLY

The elderly—10 percent of the total population in the United States—account for approximately 25% of reported suicides, about 5,000 to 8,000 yearly. The highest suicide rate is found among white males in their 80s; for white females it is between the ages of 45 and 60. One is immediately aware of the fact that this high rate of suicide among the elderly is due to the suicides of white males and females. The discrepancy between the rates for elderly white males and females and elderly black males and females has a societal relationship. Elderly white males as a group suffer a severe loss of status. As a group they have held the greatest power and prestige and exerted the most influence on society. Elderly black males and females have a much lower suicide rate because they have long been accustomed to lesser status (racism and sexism) and, ironically, do not suffer such a drastic change in old age.

Indicators of potentially suicidal older individuals include such things as previous suicide attempts; statements about self-destruction or suicidal tendencies; depression; withdrawal and isolation; purposelessness (no pleasure or meaning to life) ; decreased self-regard; and actual physical changes, such as in sleep patterns, loss of appetite, and loss of weight. These indicators can reflect a number of social causes and cultural factors that are commonly associated with the elderly.

In the first place, these elderly persons are generally retired. As a result of their retirement, they have experienced a drastic reduction in income. They are living on fixed incomes that cannot be readily adjusted to a rapid rate of inflation. In an effort to make some kind of adjustment, they have had to change their housing, often several times. If mobility in search of adequate housing at prices they can afford is not sufficient to enable them to make ends meet, the next step is a reduction in their outlay for food. A decline in their general health can be the result of this effort, for already they have lost a good deal of their motivation for eating. If they are alone or just a couple, they may give up "cooking" and resort to "snacking" in order to reduce fuel costs. If fuel economies become urgent, they may also be cold, less clean, and their general health deteriorates. Neither are they able—either physically or socially—to find extra employment for the extra dollars they need. Ageism and employment discrimination against the elderly keep them from small jobs they could perform and benefit from.

They have also been subjected to numerous losses. Socially they are becoming isolated because they are experiencing losses of a spouse, friends, and colleagues. Such diminished contacts take a great toll, for there now seems to be no one they "know," and they are forced into spending more and more time either alone or just "watching" the scene about them or on television. Moreover, there are other losses that are physical in nature. Their hearing and eyesight are diminished; rheumatism, arthritis, or cardiovascular diseases impede their mobility. Indeed, the quality of life is rapidly disintegrating through lack of income, medical care, housing, self-help groups, even lack of household help. Such numerous losses and deprivations lead to feelings of uselessness and alienation which bring on a genuine depressed state.

### Depression and the Elderly

Depression is a common experience for the elderly, but it is not always identified because of the social isolation and alienation that shield the elderly from close scrutiny. Friends, neighbors, physicians, and social workers or senior citizen center hostesses need to be aware of the symptoms of depression. If these persons would check these symptoms by casual questions and conversation, they could do a great deal to help alleviate the depression through better nutrition, increased exercise and social contacts, medical attention, and an increase in some kind of sociability.

The symptoms of depression in the elderly to watch for are:

1. Sleep disorder, loss of appetite, weight loss, withdrawal, loss of communication, despondency, loss of interest, apathy, feelings of hopelessness and helplessness, and exhaustion.

2. The individual may feel or look sad, cry a good deal; he may have poor facial expression, a monotonous voice, long pauses between sentences, slow speech, faint voice or low tone of voice; may possibly exhibit crying fits or be almost altogether stuporous.

3. There may be strong guilt feelings or strong anxieties that reveal a strong sense of shame at being unable to cover up a feeling of humiliation. A conversation may reveal a phobic re-

action, disturbed concentration, or a state of panic; strong mental stress; absolute insecurity as revealed by suspiciousness, tendency for paranoid thoughts; disorganized, agitated speech.

4. There may be a strong theme of frustration as a center of his interest, and he may be able to discuss with difficulty any other subject.

5. There can be a permanent aggressiveness accompanied by rage, anger, hostility, and revenge, with little or almost no provocation. This may be accompanied by poor impulse control, poor judgment.

6. Frustrated dependency upon certain behavior may develop —such as becoming a compulsive gambler, alcoholic, drug addict.

### Stress and the Elderly

The elderly are not without stress. Some common stressful situations include the loss of a significant person by death, divorce, separation; sickness or serious illness, surgery, accident, loss of a limb; the threat of prosecution, crime involvement, exposure; and changes in life, environment, or present location. When such stress and/or depression are acute, it is imperative that counselors seek to determine whether suicidal thoughts and fantasies also exist. Casual conversation and questions can reveal such thoughts. Listen for clue words or gestures, such as "not wanting to be a burden to anyone," "can't face the prospect of any more pain," wishing "to join a deceased spouse or friend," making funeral plans, payments, giving away prized and sentimental possessions.

If there is a suicidal plan, the counselor must assess the resources available to the suicidal person. Does he have family, friends, or agencies that can help him? Does he have such support? Is that support available but unwilling? Willing but unavailable? Some arrangement must be made so that the client is either not alone or has someone who looks in on him at regular intervals.

Counselors need to be aware that life can be harder for widowers than for widows (Kohn, 1978). Men are more likely than women to suffer loneliness, low morale, and an inability to carry on a normal life after the death of a spouse. While widows outnumber widowers four to one, they tend to be younger. This difference in age can mean that widows may get more social support from their female friends whose husbands have already died.

A study of the elderly by Carol Barrett and presented to the 1978 American Psychological Association shows that men and women consistently show different responses in six major areas of life after the death of a spouse. Widowers are more likely than widows to experience low morale, to feel lonely and dissatisfied with life, to predict poor future health, to need help with household responsibilities; to have difficulty obtaining necessary medical appointments, to eat poorly, and to experience negative attitudes toward their own continued learning.

Moreover, widowers are less likely than widows to want or seek a confidant or to want to talk about their widowhood or death. Ms. Barrett said her study showed that "elderly men whose wives are still alive do not suffer similar problems. . . . These unique differences between the reactions of the sexes does not mean that widows should not be a center of our concern. Rather, it should raise our concern about elderly widowers. Their relative situation is likely to be an obstacle in social services and other treatment attempts."

In planning for helpful techniques in uncovering the potentially suicidal elderly, community resources need to be assessed, evaluated, and encouraged to

1. develop friendly visitors programs, using visitors trained in suicide techniques
2. use a crisis telephone communication system
3. disseminate information about suicide prevention
4. utilize Senior Centers as case-finding sources.

An effort to educate the public in ways to prevent or intervene in elderly suicides will require the full cooperation of community resources, such as the medical/public health personnel, private and public housing, public and private crisis and suicide intervention, and the clergy. A well-organized and action oriented approach to the needs of the elderly would be a proper response to a frequently asked question in certain sectors of our society: Should suicide always be prevented in old age? There are those who believe that elderly suicide is a realistic reaction to a meaningless life—a resolution of existential guilt. The elderly need not have a meaningless old age because they are subject to depression or economic and social displacement. Suicide for such reasons is beneath the tolerance of a society such as ours, just as euthanasia can never become an issue if proper steps are taken to insure that the elderly can be granted a relatively pain free final illness.

## REFERENCES

### Suicide Among the Young

Casriel, Daniel, Associated Press Release, February 5, 1978.

Hendon, Herbert, Associated Press Release, February 5, 1978.

Kiev, Ari, Associated Press Release, February 5, 1978.

Puig-Antich, Joaquin, Associated Press Release, February 5, 1978.

Ross, Charlotte and A. Russell Lee, *Suicide in Youth and What You Can Do About It.* West Point, Pennsylvania: Am Assn Suicidology, 1977.

Seiden, Richard H., "Suicide Prevention: A Public Health/Public Policy Approach," *Omega, 8:3,* 1977.

Shaffer, David, Associated Press Release, February 5, 1978.

### Suicide Among the Elderly

Cumming, E. and W. E. Henry, *Growing Old: The Process of Disengagement.* New York: Basic, 1961.

Kohn, June Burgess and Willard K. Kohn, *The Widower.* Boston: Beacon Pr, 1978.

Lynch, James J., *The Broken Heart.* New York: Basic, 1977.

Senick, Daniel, *Counseling Older Persons.* New York: Human Sci Pr, 1971.

*Section III*

# COUNSELING THE BEREAVED

## Introduction

IN THE FIRST section of this book, I have attempted to give the reader an understanding of the grief process for adults and children by *describing* the process—the pain, anguish, anger, and sadness that accompany the bereaved for a long time. I have also indicated what can happen if the bereaved does not resolve this grief: "If these adjustments toward adaptation and completion are not made, the outcome is likely to be long-term despair or depression, an impairment of the capacity to love again, or various irrational attitudes toward death and destruction."

Now you are wondering what this has to do with the counseling process. What is the process, how does one progress in the process—even, why bother? *Why* do grief counseling at all?

If one has understood even a part of the grieving process, he is aware that this kind of grief happens to us all *if* we have made ourselves vulnerable to it by loving deeply—a spouse, a lover, a child, a parent—someone who is emotionally important to our well-being. Grief is inevitable under these circumstances, as inevitable as death itself. Grief counseling is, first of all, an attempt to help the bereaved recognize that the pain and anguish he is experiencing is a wholesome, normal reaction to his loss. But just being able to recognize what is happening is not enough. The grief process is faced by both the bereaved and the counselor to encourage the fullest expression of that pain, anguish, anger, etc., in order to become free enough, eventually, to face life *without* that loved one. The bereaved must be able to pick up the strands of his life and move forward toward a new life *without* that person but with the full knowledge that life is now richer for having had that experience. One can say that one of the reasons for doing grief counseling is *to help others face life and grow*.

It would be dishonest of me not to include here that counselors report that this aspect of grief work makes counseling a rewarding experience for them. It enriches their lives and causes them to reexamine their own lives for additional ways of new growth.

Because the grief process takes place when the bereaved is perhaps at his lowest emotional ebb, the bereaved is not only confronted with his present grief but is also deeply troubled by some of his previous losses and separations or some of the pre-existing conditions that are listed on page 68 of the Introduction to Sudden Death. These old losses and separations or preexisting conditions enter into the picture, if the counselor is wise. There is a time within the grief process and in the grief counseling for these old wounds to be discussed and dealt with. And it is precisely here that the most rewarding things happen to the bereaved, for it is here that *the mental health aspects of what is done become most apparent*. By confronting the problems that arise from the grief itself and also those problems that are a holdover from previous years, the bereaved and the counselor can work over, discuss and, in the end, hopefully resolve a combination of factors that can mean a better, more wholesome mental health outlook for the bereaved.

In the second section of this book, I have tried to familiarize the reader with the kinds of sudden death that occur and have noted special areas that become difficult for the bereaved as a result of that particular mode of death. And I have indicated a deep concern that some of these deaths are troublesome to both the bereaved and to the counselor because *they could have been prevented*. In the last analysis, that is really what grief counseling is all about and why grief counseling is done—prevention. It is prevention of future problems by taking care *now* of the trouble areas of a grief; prevention of future problems by teaching the bereaved *now* how to handle a crisis situation, how to set priorities, how to ask for help, how to know where to go for help; prevention of future problems by helping the bereaved face the old problems *now* in order to become disengaged from them once and for all or to get them into a perspective that will make them less obtrusive.

That is what grief counseling is all about—prevention of mental health problems. This orientation not only permeates the counseling sessions but is given high priority in all the preparations for counseling: the screening of prospective counselors, their training, and their care of themselves. It is as important to promote sound mental health for our counselors as it is to promote it for our clients. Consequently, our approach to grief counseling is tilted in that direction, and it has produced an unusual approach to instruction in grief work. As the reader has already observed, most chapters contain case material that illustrates what is being presented. The same approach is made during the training period. When a prospective counselor asks, What if . . .? How does one . . .? What happens when a client . . .? These questions are immediately dealt with in the light of cases that illustrate the problem raised. The same approach is used with you readers. Consequently, there is material on how to counsel the bereaved interspersed among many of the chapters of this book. To keep cases from becoming too numerous here, the reader is directed to additional sources in the bibliography and suggested reading.

*Chapter 11*

# HOW TO COUNSEL THE BEREAVED

## BASIC NEEDS OF THE BEREAVED

D URING THE time of intense grieving, the bereaved has many
basic needs that require attention by those who want to give
him the support and assistance that will be most helpful. Such
needs are

1. A need for companionship and privacy—neither a house
filled with people nor an empty one but a balance between the
two. He needs people to talk to occasionally and then for them
to return to their homes and leave him alone for awhile. Some
people cannot express their grief, cry, or give vent to their anger
in the presence of others. It is difficult to express these emotions
before persons who have previously looked to the bereaved for
strength and encouragement.

2. An opportunity for the expression of grief without embarrassment or reticence. Tears, anger, protest, hostility, (whatever emotions he is feeling) should be expressed without fear of
embarrassment.

3. The bereaved needs to be among people who recognize that
intense grieving brings about in many the same physical changes
that occur during or after a serious illness, e.g. loss of sleep,
appetite, strength, and motivation. An understanding of these
physical changes can help friends and relatives be more tolerant
of the bereaved's inconsistencies of behavior.

4. Social support and assistance need to be given in a climate
of trust, where regularity of appointments and arrangements regarding domestic or business situations are honored. For example, the bereaved needs to know that people will be dependable,

for the bereaved has to make a great effort to pull himself together in order to face new situations. Failure to honor such commitments regularly and punctually can cause the bereaved to regress and, perhaps, break down.

5. A firm focus should be placed on the crisis of his loss without the feeling that this is an illness or a personality disorder that is disturbing him.

6. Special assistance should be given to make and meet satisfactory personal, business, or legal relationships. In our work, we find that we are assisting in the resocialization of the bereaved in many ways that do not seem to be related to grief counseling (Fulton, 1970). These additional ways of helping include talking about the health and nutrition of the bereaved and his family, his probate problems, Social Security, insurance, pensions, disposing of the deceased's effects, the pros and cons of moving or making a change in life-style, jobs, etc. By giving attention to these important topics, the mourner gets resocialized, gets back in the main stream of living life. It is important that friends, relatives, counselors, or clergy help and support him while he gets there. Later in this period, we suggest that the bereaved join clubs, attend classes, join in charitable work, even get a pet—for *to have no one to care for is one of the deprivations of the bereaved.*

## HOW ONE HELPS THE BEREAVED

Bereavement seldom requires therapeutic intervention. What is required is the recognition that grief is a normal response to the loss of a beloved person; it is of fundamental importance to work through the grieving process, and this process should be completed without harmful interference or repression.

The bereaved must be allowed to talk, to tell details of the last weeks and days again and again. Listening is important—to the old losses and separations, to the psychological crosscurrents in the family. Hear the reaction of the bereaved to his loss; help him express his anger, protest, resentment, and grief. Give him complete access to tears. Those who are bereaved need to talk, complain, mope, and to realize that they are being *actively* listened to. Such important sharing is facilitated by a good listener—the grief counselor.

If the appropriate anger is not expressed, it needs to be gently provoked. Anger is often a natural component of any death. Since death is an abandonment of a kind, the anger at being abandoned needs to be focused upon and allowed expression. The gradual reworking of old memories, good and bad, is essential. For it is only by remembrance and release that the desired autonomy of the bereaved can be achieved. Unfortunately, our society usually does not recognize this need. It gives the message of "Be brave, don't cry" to all ages and both sexes. Often the bereaved has to be taught to give himself permission to express the loss and separation that are agonizing him.

There are requirements when a marriage comes to an end because of the death of a spouse. Pincus (1974) outlines them, and a good counselor should attend to them. The following requirements also delineate the steps that need to be taken in order to "internalize" the deceased spouse.

1. Allow the surviving partner to relive experiences of earlier attachments and losses in order to be free for new, realistic relationships.

2. Help the bereaved partner to understand and modify the ongoing interaction between himself and the internalized deceased.

3. Help him face the difficult task of accepting the reality of the loss and yet hold on to the memory of the lost partner. This is an important step toward helping the bereaved.

4. Only by achieving this autonomy can the bereaved regrow the ability for new attachment and become free enough for new life.

## Active Listening

By active listening I mean that you are very much on the alert to indicate to the client that you hear and understand what he has said. Your understanding may be expressed by briefly restating what has just been said by the client. In that way, the client knows that you heard what he said and you understand it. If, however, you do not understand what he has said or cannot seem to get it sorted out, then you say that it is not clear to you and that you would like either a repetition of that part or a bit more clarification.

It is important to do this exchange of listening, hearing, and/ or asking for clarification in brief segments.  If you allow too much information to accumulate without understanding what went on, the sequence, or the actual persons involved, then you run the risk of discouraging the client by asking him to repeat *too much,* and he will be likely to give up and say nothing more.  If you do it in small segments and restate what you have heard as briefly as you can, your client will hear that you got each step and will be encouraged to go on.  You can do this kind of summarizing for perhaps every five or ten sentences of the narration you are hearing.

When you are in doubt about whether you got his story straight, state what you understand and ask if that is correct.  In that way, you begin an exchange of information, a give-and-take that will facilitate the flow of the narration, etc.  In this way, you can also summarize a whole flood of explanations about feelings by expressing the feelings that you understand the client is experiencing.  For example, you can summarize by saying, "I understand that what made you feel really bad was the way that made you feel put down.  Is that right?"

You will know you are on the right track when your client confirms your summary by saying, "That's right" or "No, what happened was . . ." and immediately goes deeper into the subject or begins another issue related to the one you summarized.  Often just a nod from the client indicates that your summary is correct; at another time, he may just give a big sigh of relief and then proceed with his narration.  Conversely, you will know you are not on the right track if the client repeats exactly what he said before.  Now you must listen to see where *you* are confused and not seeing the difference between what he said and what you heard.  Then you can summarize again and inquire, "But that's not right, somehow?"

You are also not doing it properly if the client looks confused or anxious about your summary.  Stop and ask again what there is about your statement that is not correct or does not reflect his own feeling.  If you do not do this, the client is likely to change the subject entirely because he realizes he is not getting his ideas across to you. When this occurs say, "I'm not getting it right and I want to. Please repeat the part about. . . ." Do not allow the client to speculate about what *you* have said and get drawn into a discussion of generalities. Bring him back to the personal point you were working on before. ("You were saying . . ., and I was trying to feel what it felt like to you. Tell me again.") Do not feel that you should receive credit for getting it right. That is what you are supposed to do! Your intention is to hear what he is saying, get the sequence right, and hear how he felt about it. If it takes several tries to get it right, that is okay also.

The counselor should also keep in contact with his own feelings as much as possible and reflect them, within limits, to the client. If the situation is sad and you feel sad, it is fine to show tears or to weep with the client. If what the client says is scary and you feel scary too, acknowledge this, for it will allow the client to go further into his feelings about the scariness. You may also need to say to *yourself*, "That's scary" or "That's what is getting me (confused, disappointed, scared, bewildered). Perhaps if we talk about *that* it will help the client also." Allow time for such exchanges as these to occur. It will be helpful to both of you to get it out in the open rather than allow a whole mass of confusion or tightness or anxiety to build up.

Do not be afraid for silences to occur. The client needs this space for gathering his thoughts together or for pacing himself or for relieving the strain of too much talking. You will feel better too if you use these silences for centering yourself, taking three deep breaths, and readying yourself for what lies ahead.

### SPECIFIC STEPS IN GRIEF COUNSELING

REMEMBER: If you wonder whether a client is suicidal—ask him! This is a fundamental question to keep in mind for every age level—for the young, the teenager, the young adult, the middle-aged, and the elderly. Ask about his suicidal thoughts and fantasies. When in doubt about your assessment of these thoughts, fill out the Los Angeles Suicide Potential Assessment (See Chapter 9 on Suicide). The client is not brought into this assessment personally. You make the rating on the basis of what you have seen and heard from the client. If the assessment is medium to high for suicide potential, you know you have much important work to do with the client. But this work *does not* include discussing the assessment rating as such with the client. *This assessment rating is for your use only.*

Listed are some specific steps that a good grief counselor is expected to follow and to keep abreast of.

1. Hear the account of what happened, how family members reacted, what was said. Allow the bereaved to retell this in different ways and to express his shock, protest, and anger—along with the tears—in any way he chooses.

2. Listen for accounts of previous losses and separations, how the client coped with them, whether the client indicates a satisfactory closure or whether there is still unfinished business with these losses.

3. Mentally obtain data regarding family members, ages, relationships, who has been told of the death, how this was done, what was said. Listen for clue words, and watch for behavior that reveals signs of denial, guilt, anger, depression. *No notes are taken during client-counselor sessions.*

4. Pay special attention to children who are living in the home. Be aware of those who do not live at home. Inquire what has been told them, by whom, what was said, and the reaction to this information.

5. Look for indications of willingness of adults to share and communicate their shock and grief with others, especially minor children. Explain to the adults *why* you are interested in these facts regarding the children.

6. Look, watch, and listen for special strengths the client displays in order to build upon them later. In addition, inquire about and listen for special persons and systems—friends, family, neighbors, church—he already has available. These are the social and financial support systems of primary importance.

7. Allow the client to enumerate the stressful problems that will need to be dealt with as a result of this death. *Help him make the list.*

8. Help the client decide for himself the priorities he assigns to these problems. Indicate your confidence in his ability to select

the most pressing problem that needs attention *now*.

9. Express your willingness to help the client work through this problem until he feels more comfortable and better satisfied with it. *Deal with one problem at a time.*

10. Use your counseling skill to give the client self-assurance and confidence in his ability to deal with this problem. Do not rush in with community or individual referrals for help until you are sure yourself that you know what his most pressing problems are, which ones he feels need attention immediately, and which ones he may need help with later on. Provide the opportunity and the ambience for him to do as much as possible of the groundwork himself. (A good counselor does not do all the work or all the talking.) Save your referrals for later and for those problems for which neither he nor you has control or the competence that is required.

11. Other short-term or acute problems may arise as a result of any one of the problems he has specified as urgent. These emergencies arise and are to be expected. People in crisis need to discuss their extra, special, or unexpected problems. It is for this reason that the client is given twenty-four-hour access to the counselor. A telephone call to you can bring into focus for the client the dimensions of his new problem, what needs to be done, what can be done. He also needs your reassurance that he can handle this new problem. One of the advantages of our kind of counseling is that the counselor *is available* for these anticipated emergencies. The number of these calls will normally diminish as time progresses.

12. As these emergencies diminish, plan to guide your client into the next phase of his priority listing.

13. Throughout these emergencies, you will have had adequate time to become knowledgeable about his personal reactions to this death. What is his *personal* difficulty? It is guilt, shame, anger, depression, lack of self-confidence, dependency? Encourage him to talk about these difficulties. Let him *hear himself*. Let him also know that you are actively listening to him, that you have confidence in his ability to handle these new bewildering emotions. Again, let him choose which of these emotional reac-

tions he thinks most important to deal with first. You and he marshall your resources and begin to work on them—*one at a time.*

14. Make it clear to your client that you will respect the confidentiality of the sessions you have with him. Make it clear also that you will always consult with him when you believe that some of the confidential information needs to be shared with someone else *for his own benefit.* (This is sometimes necessary in situations that involve strong suicidal or homicidal feelings.)

15. In every situation, emphasize to the client that the death he has experienced does lead to anxieties and fears about what to do and what will happen to him and his family; doubts as to whether he can cope with the myriad problems now confronting him. Whenever possible, assure him of your confidence that he *can* cope with these matters. Convey to him your belief in his strength and ability to manage his problems. Share with him the possibility that exists that he may become stronger, more confident and able to function at a better level than he did previous to the death. Remind him that time is on his side. Assure him that you will remain with him long enough for him to feel more comfortable in handling these daily decisions.

A statement has been adopted for the purpose of having a uniform policy for the guidance of the counselors involved in our program. The following policies are those that relate to the client-counselor relationship:

1. Counselors are expected to be friendly but not to socialize with the client.

2. Crisis situations arising during grief that involve drugs, alcohol, lethal weapons, marital or personality problems must be referred at once to the proper agency or therapist, and the counselor must not become personally involved.

3. Grief counselors must work to eliminate client dependency on the counselor. The job of the counselor is to aid the client's progress in working through his grief, at which time the relationship is closed. If the counselor has been unsuccessful in attaining this goal, he must refer the client to other appropriate sources of help.

4. Clients are not transported by counselors for any reason. There is no insurance coverage for this activity.

Counselors are supervised in the work they do with the client. The forms that they use to report the progress of their work are to be found in the Appendix. During the twice monthly two-hour sessions the counselors spend in ongoing training, there is ample opportunity for them to discuss their work, to ask for suggestions and criticism, and to receive help in working through their own anxieties. Grief work is heavy work, and counselors are vulnerable to many anxieties themselves. Chapter 19 will summarize some of the ways counselors are encouraged to understand themselves and to prevent stressful emotions from interfering with either their work or their lives.

### REFERENCES

Fulton, Robert, "Death, Grief and Social Recuperation," *Omega, 1*:23–28, 1970.

Pincus, Lily, *Death and the Family, the Importance of Mourning.* New York: Pantheon, 1974.

## Chapter 12

# THE ANNIVERSARY INTERVIEW

M UCH HAS been written of the emotional heritage of the survivor of a suicide. In addition to the doubts and questions the
survivor is heir to, he also suffers emotional shock and trauma,
displacement of long-accepted family routines, and financial hard-
ship. There is also a sense of having come too close to a situation
for which our society lacks understanding and feels apprehensive
about.

The anniversary date of a suicide may likely be the last anticipated emotional outpost the survivor has to pass. An interview
at this time can also be an important part of the grief counseling
program. The anniversary date is not only a significant time in
the lives of bereaved clients, but from this vantage point both
the survivor and the counselor can assess how the pattern of life
has shifted or changed—what has been resolved or continued to
plague the survivor. The anniversary date is also seen as a suitable time to terminate the association with the client.

For the first year of our program, out of 88 next-of-kin (spouse,
children, siblings, or other relatives) residents in our county
eligible for a letter from us, 17 or 19.3 percent, could not be
reached because of moving away, disconnecting the telephone,
leaving town indefinitely, etc. At the time, we thought this a
lamentably high percentage but an understandable one, since 72
percent of the suicides that year occurred in the home, and the
body was discovered by a spouse or family member.

A list of questions was drawn up as an aid to the counselors
during the anniversary interview. Generally, we allow the client
to talk about what he feels is important or what he felt met some

166

need of his. During such a friendly, spontaneous conversation, there is seldom any difficulty in rewording the questions in this list to fit the circumstances or need of the conversation. A list of the questions follows.

1. How have the children in the family reacted during the year?
2. Do the children and adults speak naturally and comfortably about the deceased?
3. Does the client feel there is any problem with any particular child?
4. Is the client in good health? The children?
5. Is the client satisfied with his own grief progress during the year?
6. What is the client doing now? New job, relocated, new friends, remarried, etc.?
7. What does the client think was the hardest thing he had to do during the year?
8. What does the client think was the most help to him during this time?
9. Are there other persons—children, friends, or neighbors— who could have benefitted from our service but were unknown to us?
10. What suggestions has the client concerning how we could have been more helpful?
11. What did we do that "bugged" the client?

The foregoing questions were developed on the basis of our counseling experience and not on the basis of any specific hypothesis to be tested. We attempted to organize the responses to see if they could be related in a meaningful way to existing material in the field. We concluded that the data should be considered initially in relation to the work of Holmes and Masuda (1972) involving what they term "The Life Event Rating" (see Appendix C for this rating and Chapter 3 for a discussion). This rating scale seemed a reasonable way to compare the family condition of the survivors at the time of our initial contact with the condition at the time of the anniversary interview.

## THE LIFE EVENT RATING SCALE

The life events of the first year following the suicide were listed and assigned points after a rereading of the anniversary interview. Neither of these ratings—at the time of the suicide or a year later—purports to be in any way complete since no formal life history was ever taken. They are indicative only of the information that seemed important during the grief counseling interview.

Looking at these comparative figures, we see that at the time of our initial contact, the life events rating for our clients fall between the scores of 740 and 94, the median being 198 which would indicate that there would be some impact of stress with physical symptoms. The rating for these clients at the time of the anniversary interview fell between the scores of 394 and zero, with the median being 20, indicating a "mild" problem. Of the anniversary interviews conducted, nine did not reveal anything at all about the current life events.

For both interviews, there were certain life events that were repetitive for most clients. The first interview, of course, was marked by the suicidal event itself, which carried the highest value and the numerous events that accompany the death-grief situation. These accompanying events include the change in health of a family member, change in financial condition, revision of personal habits, change in living condition, change in sleeping and in eating habits. For the anniversary interview, there were also life events that were repetitive and that we shall look at in more detail: illness, change of residence, persistent grief difficulties, change in job situation or marital status, contagion, suicide, and the effect upon the children.

Of the anniversary interviewees, 25 percent experienced illness during the year following the suicide. These illnesses ranged from arthritis, high blood pressure, and emphysema to fainting spells, heart attacks, malnutrition, and becoming overweight. Also widely mentioned were depression, guilt, nerves, and dependence on pills. There were 15 percent who were ill enough to be hospitalized some time during the year for appendectomy, broken bones, depression, gall bladder, victim of homicide attempt, malnutrition, mastectomy, and prescription drug withdrawal. This incidence of illness following the traumatic experience of a suicide in the family confirms what Holmes and Masuda concluded in their study: ". . . that clusters of life events do help cause illness. Life change events can be considered necessary to the occurrence of disease but not sufficient, all by themselves, to cause disease. . . . If it takes too much effort to cope with the environment, we have less to spare for preventing disease" (Holmes, 1972).

It comes as no surprise that there is considerable illness even one year after suicide. Persons involved in grief work know how depressed and inadequate for everyday coping the bereaved is during the first three months of grief. For most bereaved, these months are a time of intense grief, of social disorientation, physical illness and feelings of personal inadequacy. Indeed, the bereaved is in a precarious situation where he needs more social support than at any time since his childhood. "Survivors do not always get over a serious loss and return to 'normal,' without first suffering a great deal. Sometimes bereavement leads to serious somatic and psychological symptoms during the next year or two" (Parkes, 1972).

Anniversary interviewees displayed discontent with their place of residence; 1.5 percent of them moved to another location in the county, most for financial reasons and change of life-style. About 1 percent had a change of jobs or were fired from a job. A change in marital status also occurred. Two persons were divorced (these were next-of-kin of adolescent or young adult suicides), two remarried, and two stated they were presently looking for another spouse. While these percentages are small, they indicate ways the interviewees found to withdraw from familiar family routines into new ones not related to the suicide.

There were 50 percent who stated their grief symptoms were allayed, while 25 percent were still experiencing a grief problem. The remaining 25 percent were noncommittal about the progress of their grief. Clients who still had a grief problem displayed patterns that were largely concerned with weeping, unwillingness to recall the deceased, or inability to talk with a stranger about the death. These persons made statements or recounted experiences that pointed toward a tendency to hold onto resentment, an inability to forgive, a poor self-image, or an inability to seek or to develop meaningful long-term relationships. (Of these persons, four were still in therapy two years after the suicide.)

There were eleven persons who had declined to be seen at the time of the initial interview. At the time of the anniversary interview, six of the eleven regretted their earlier decision and responded fully to our inquiry. There were two others who did not regret their decision, one because he still felt there had been no suicide and the other because she felt that she would probably call us later when she felt more ready to talk.

The most common difficulty experienced during this year was loneliness, followed by depression, guilt, and having "to pick up and go on." The family, friends, and relatives were mentioned most frequently as the greatest source of help during this time; two ministers were mentioned by name, and three spoke warmly of their therapists. The grief counseling program received warm praise from the majority of those responding to this question. Some even expressed the hope that sometime they could participate in the program as counselors.

There were three individuals who spoke of their psychic experiences during this year—two by seeing and speaking with the deceased through a medium or in dreams and one by a keenly developed precognition that at times was either bothersome or outright upsetting.

At the time of initial contact, 9, or 11.84 percent, of our clients were touched by contagion; 11, or 14.52 percent, were themselves suicidal. (Suicide contagion is the ready acceptance of suicide as a means of solving perplexing life problems by some members of a family, clan, living group, or neighborhood.) By the time of the anniversary interview, 18 percent were now touched by contagion and described behavior in the family—threats, talk of suicide, attempts—that points toward probable future involvement in heavily stressful situations.

A client suicided three months after the anniversary interview. The numerous clients who reported that their grief and despair led them into heavy drinking were no longer talking about this at anniversary time. Drinking was apparently a crutch they used temporarily for six to eight weeks. A few who were heavy drinkers before the event continued to drink heavily. No referrals to Alcoholics Anonymous or rehabilitation were necessary at the time of the anniversary interview.

It was difficult for the counselors to impress upon the surviving parent the possible serious effect of the suicidal act upon the children. Difficult as the suicide is for the surviving spouse, it provides an almost unknown burden for the surviving children. Bettie Arthur describes the process when she states

> A parent suicide affects the spouse and the children who survive, with each in his own way, suffering both an intensely personal guilt and having to repeatedly experience doubts about the other surviving members of the family and their part in the suicide. Too often this in turn is followed by the further guilt attendant on such thoughts. Thus an intricately constructed web of doubt, suspicion and guilt is woven of the fragments of direct personal experience with the victim and the fragments of witnessed experiences between the other members of the immediate family. The survivors are each condemned not only to a sense of loss but to additional conflict based on an incomplete and biased account of what actually led to the suicidal act. A parent suicide is indeed a family affair, but one with exceptionally vicious consequences for those who survive it. (Cain, 1972)

There were 126 children survivors involved in the families we interviewed, 21 of whom we assisted by talking to their parents about ways of discussing death with children. The number involved grew to 145 children by the time of the anniversary interview. The increased number is due to those who declined to see us at the time of the suicide but later changed their minds and by the number of children who were temporarily out of the home at the time of the suicide and thus not reported initially.

The parents reported that twenty-four of these children were still having problems—eleven were described as having behavioral difficulties, such as frequent anger flare-ups, quarrels, and excessive fighting with peers and siblings; four were withdrawn; two were still having nightmares; and there were single examples of suicide threats, runaways, ulcers, special school difficulties, learning difficulties, and excessive secretiveness and bitterness. In other words, these children were experiencing what Shneidman expressed when he wrote (1969), "The person who commits suicide puts his psychological skeleton in the survivor's emotional closet—he sentences the survivor to a complex of negative feelings and, most importantly, to obsessing about the reasons for the suicide death."

## Conclusions

The anniversary interview shows that

1. According to the Holmes-Masuda rating scale, the life events rating at the anniversary date was considerably below the level of the rating at the time of the suicide. In other words, stressful situations in their lives had begun to diminish by the end of the year following the suicide.

2. There were death-grief situations, however, that were stressful to the clients, such as changes in financial conditions, living conditions, and sleeping and eating habits.

3. The suicide and its accompanying life events led to illness, change of residence, persistent grief difficulties, changes in jobs and marital status, suicide, and contagion.

4. All of these situations affected the children in the home. There was evidence of behavioral difficulties, withdrawal, nightmares, school difficulties, running away, and excessive secretiveness and bitterness.

5. By reaching both parents and children, the hope arises that this timely assistance will help diminish the despair and anxieties that follow a death by suicide.

### REFERENCES

Cain, Albert C. (Ed.), *Survivors of Suicide.* Springfield: Thomas, 1972.
Holmes, Thomas H. and Mineru Masuda, "Psychosomatic Syndrome," *Psychology Today,* April, 1972.
Parkes, Colin Murray, *Bereavement, Studies of Grief in Adult Life.* New York: Intl Univs Pr, 1972.
Shneidman, Edwin S. (Ed.), *On the Nature of Suicide.* San Francisco: Jossey-Bass, 1969.

## Chapter 13

# THE CORONER'S ROLE IN
# GRIEF COUNSELING

Lt. Al Moore

THE CORONER is one of the first persons to meet survivors and discuss the death of someone who has died suddenly or unusually. (This includes virtually all the deaths that occur outside of medical facilities or when the deceased has not been attended by a physician for twenty days prior to the death.) The coroner is most often the person making the notification of death and bearing the brunt of the initial outpouring of sudden shock and grief.

A professional who notifies the next-of-kin regarding a death anticipates that there will be considerable shock. The investigative officers are not prepared, however, to offer any real comfort or hope for the days, weeks, and years to come. The coroner usually tries to secure some immediate help by getting other family members, clergymen, physicians, psychologists, or friends to be with the survivors, but most coroners would admit they offer very little comfort in the grief process simply because the resources are not available in most areas. Coroners often receive calls from grieving relatives who have no place to turn to express their grief.

Professional counseling, when available, is expensive, and in many areas it is not even available. Untrained, well-meaning individuals may do more harm than good when they make innocent statements (such as, "You still have your other children" or "You won't have to worry about him any more") that are quite devastating. Where does this leave the coroner, who is funded by tax dollars and limited to the scope of his duties by law?

The duty of the coroner is to determine cause, manner, and means of death in certain circumstances which are reportable by law. We conclude from this that the legislators who enact the laws governing the coroner are not concerned with the grief process of the survivors and do not mandate any activity in that area by the coroner. The grief process must be handled either without any help, with paid professional help, with volunteer help, or a combination of these.

Although there is no lawful duty or requirement for the coroner to work with or assist grief counseling volunteers, it can be mutually beneficial and a much more effective service if the grief counselors and the coroner have a good working relationship. This has been proven in Contra Costa County, California, where such a program has existed for seven years.

The coroner has provided working space and access to files in cases of sudden deaths. Volunteers have provided the time and resources to do the grief counseling. This has been of little inconvenience to the coroner, who provides office space for the volunteers coming to the coroner's office once a week. The review of the records is accomplished in two or three hours with no disruption of the coroner's routine. Coroner's records in California are public records, so allowing access to files does not present a confidentiality problem. Survivors have rarely questioned the coroner about giving out information on a case to grief counselors.

The advantage to the coroner in this type of program is the feedback from grief counselors on the impressions survivors have of coroner's deputies and other staff members with whom they have had contact. The grief counselor might relay the disagreement on the part of a survivor to the coroner who has made a determination of a mode of death with which the survivor disagrees. This is particularly true in suicide and accident classifications when a survivor refuses to believe his loved one has committed suicide.

Without the cooperation of the coroner, a grief counseling

service has little chance to work well since accessibility to the records is an absolute necessity. It is imperative, however, that the coroner and his staff remain independent from the mechanics of grief counseling or providing the grief counseling. A definite conflict of interest is possible if the coroner wears two hats—investigator and counselor. There is a confidential relationship between a counselor and client that does not exist between the investigator and witness, although the client and witness may be the same person. There is also a danger when the coroner selects which survivors in which cases need the counseling. This should be left to the professionals and paraprofessionals.

The autopsy procedure, discussed from the pathologist's perspective in another chapter (see Chapter 14) is an essential part of the investigation and subject to many misconceptions by most people. Doctors, family, grief counselors, peace officers, and others who are involved in death investigations are often misinformed or assume on their own things about autopsies that are not true. The decision whether or not to autopsy should be made by a forensic pathologist based on his evaluation of the investigation, medical records available, and type of case.

California law permits the coroner to perform an autopsy over the objections of the next-of-kin; in fact, he may perform an autopsy without permission from anyone. A private physician, on the contrary, must have written permission from the next-of-kin before an autopsy can be done. To do his job properly, a coroner must have the authority to do autopsies over the objection of families. Without this authority, it would be quite easy to cover up a homicide or suicide. A coroner could hardly be expected to sign a death certificate stating a cause of death without first eliminating all other possible causes. The single car accident where a car leaves the roadway and hits a tree is an example. Apparently, traumatic injuries have caused the death, but without an autopsy, a pathologist could not state with any certainty that the person had not suffered a heart attack or other natural phenomenon that would have caused the death. This makes a big difference in classifying the mode or manner of death.

The difference between accidental and natural death for in-

**CERTIFICATE OF DEATH**
STATE OF CALIFORNIA

STATE FILE NUMBER — LOCAL REGISTRATION DISTRICT AND CERTIFICATE NUMBER

**DECEDENT PERSONAL DATA**
1A. NAME OF DECEDENT—FIRST | 1B. MIDDLE | 1C. LAST | 2A. DATE OF DEATH (MONTH, DAY, YEAR) | 2B. HOUR
3. SEX | 4. RACE | 5. ETHNICITY | 6. DATE OF BIRTH | 7. AGE YEARS | IF UNDER 1 YEAR MONTHS | DAYS | IF UNDER 24 HOURS HOURS | MINUTES
8. BIRTHPLACE OF DECEDENT (STATE OR FOREIGN COUNTRY) | 9. NAME AND BIRTHPLACE OF FATHER | 10. BIRTH NAME AND BIRTHPLACE OF MOTHER
11. CITIZEN OF WHAT COUNTRY | 12. SOCIAL SECURITY NUMBER | 13. MARITAL STATUS | 14. NAME OF SURVIVING SPOUSE (IF WIFE, ENTER BIRTH NAME)
15. PRIMARY OCCUPATION | 16. NUMBER OF YEARS THIS OCCUPATION | 17. EMPLOYER (IF SELF-EMPLOYED, SO STATE) | 18. KIND OF INDUSTRY OR BUSINESS

**USUAL RESIDENCE**
19A. USUAL RESIDENCE—STREET ADDRESS (STREET AND NUMBER OR LOCATION) | 19B. | 19C. CITY OR TOWN
19D COUNTY | 19E. STATE | 20. NAME AND ADDRESS OF INFORMANT—RELATIONSHIP

**PLACE OF DEATH**
21A. PLACE OF DEATH | 21B. COUNTY
21C. STREET ADDRESS (STREET AND NUMBER OR LOCATION) | 21D. CITY OR TOWN

**CAUSE OF DEATH**
22. DEATH WAS CAUSED BY: (ENTER ONLY ONE CAUSE PER LINE FOR A, B, AND C)
IMMEDIATE CAUSE (A)
CONDITIONS, IF ANY, WHICH GAVE RISE TO THE IMMEDIATE CAUSE, STATING THE UNDERLYING CAUSE LAST
DUE TO, OR AS A CONSEQUENCE OF (B)
DUE TO, OR AS A CONSEQUENCE OF (C)
APPROXIMATE INTERVAL BETWEEN ONSET AND DEATH
24. WAS DEATH REPORTED TO CORONER?
25. WAS BIOPSY PERFORMED?
26. WAS AUTOPSY PERFORMED?
23. OTHER CONDITIONS CONTRIBUTING BUT NOT RELATED TO THE IMMEDIATE CAUSE OF DEATH | 27. WAS OPERATION PERFORMED FOR ANY CONDITION IN ITEMS 22 OR 23? TYPE OF OPERATION | DATE

**PHYSICIAN'S CERTIFICATION**
28A. I CERTIFY THAT DEATH OCCURRED AT THE HOUR, DATE AND PLACE STATED FROM THE CAUSES STATED. I ATTENDED DECEDENT SINCE (ENTER MO, DA, YR.) | I LAST SAW DECEDENT ALIVE (ENTER MO, DA, YR.) | 28B. PHYSICIAN—SIGNATURE AND DEGREE OR TITLE | 28C. DATE SIGNED | 28D. PHYSICIAN'S LICENSE NUMBER
28E. TYPE PHYSICIAN'S NAME AND ADDRESS

**INJURY INFORMATION**
29. SPECIFY ACCIDENT, SUICIDE, ETC. | 30. PLACE OF INJURY | 31. INJURY AT WORK | 32A. DATE OF INJURY—MONTH, DAY, YEAR | 32B. HOUR
33. LOCATION (STREET AND NUMBER OR LOCATION AND CITY OR TOWN) | 34. DESCRIBE HOW INJURY OCCURRED (EVENTS WHICH RESULTED IN INJURY)

**CORONER'S USE ONLY**
35A. I CERTIFY THAT DEATH OCCURRED AT THE HOUR, DATE AND PLACE STATED FROM THE CAUSES STATED. AS REQUIRED BY LAW I HAVE HELD AN (INQUEST-INVESTIGATION) | 35B. CORONER—SIGNATURE AND DEGREE OR TITLE | 35C. DATE SIGNED

36. DISPOSITION | 37. DATE—MONTH, DAY, YEAR | 38. NAME AND ADDRESS OF CEMETERY OR CREMATORY | 39. EMBALMER'S LICENSE NUMBER AND SIGNATURE
40. NAME OF FUNERAL DIRECTOR (OR PERSON ACTING AS SUCH) | 41. LOCAL REGISTRAR—SIGNATURE | 42. DATE ACCEPTED BY LOCAL REGISTRAR

**STATE REGISTRAR** A. | B. | C. | D. | E. | F.

VS-11 (10-78)

Figure 1: Copy of a Certificate of Death.

surance purposes can be quite significant. The question, "Why did you have to autopsy when the cause of death is so obvious?" is often asked. A gunshot suicide, for example, might not seem like the kind of death that would require an autopsy, but the very reason for the suicide might be found at autopsy. A cancer, tumor, or other disorder that caused pain and anxiety might give a person reason to commit suicide.

Some circumstances of death can be quite bizarre, and what appears to be quite apparent often turns out to be something quite different. (An apparent suicide, where a note was left and there was an indication that drugs and alcohol were the means of suicide, may be proved to be a natural death after a complete autopsy and toxicologic study.) These are examples of why it is important to autopsy all trauma or suspected trauma related cases.

While there might be an objection to an autopsy immediately after death, the long-term effect of not doing the autopsy might be much more difficult to live with. Without an autopsy, there is room for doubt about the cause of death that can never be resolved later. As an example, consider the case of a two-month-old infant who is found dead in its crib after being put down for a nap. There is no medical history of any problems that would give a clue as to why it died. The pediatrician cannot sign a death certificate with any specific cause of death but is willing to sign stating cause as sudden infant death syndrome. The parents object to an autopsy and are experiencing severe guilt and grief. The immediate feeling of the parents is "The baby is dead and nothing can bring it back. Let's get the funeral over with."

Should this baby be autopsied? The answer is an unqualified YES for at least three good reasons. The first is to determine if there was a congenital defect that would not only explain the death but would also help relieve the guilt feelings of the parents (even if there is no reason for guilt feelings). Besides the immediate relief, there is a long-range effect if the couple decides to have another child. Most parents of SIDS babies and those suspected of SIDS have admitted later that the autopsy was beneficial by proving the diagnosed cause of death. One other possibility to consider is infanticide, which could be accomplished without any obvious signs of trauma, such as smothering. The person responsible for the death would obviously not want an autopsy performed. This is a very rare situation but one that should not be overlooked.

The most obvious reason for autopsy is to confirm the suspicion that the cause of death was not specific and it was, in fact, sudden infant death syndrome. After a visual and microscopic examination and toxicologic or biologic tests prove negative, it can be stated with some certainty that no obvious cause of death was found. Most pediatricians agree with the need for an autopsy and would be reluctant to sign a death certificate even where permitted by law.

Being part of the policy-making process of the Grief Counseling Service is beneficial to both the coroner and the counseling agency. By this, I refer to membership on the Board of Trustees and perhaps the Executive Committee. This allows input from the coroner and a personal relationship and an exchange of ideas between other board members and the coroner. Suggestions about proposed policy can be dealt with much faster and easier when the coroner or his representative participates. It is also quite helpful to the coroner to know the inside workings of the agency and the rationale behind the goals and direction in which it is moving.

A pitfall to be avoided by the coroner, as well as by the grief counselors, is the reversal of roles. The coroner while dealing with grieving survivors cannot assume the role of grief counselor. The coroner's function is investigation of reported deaths. The function of grief counselors is to help survivors deal with their grief. If the grief counselors assume the role of investigator, they will most probably alienate the coroner and the clients they are trying to help.

Exchanging impressions about cases can be useful to either the coroner or the grief counselor but must always be done on a confidential basis. Any information appearing in a coroner's report that came from a grief counselor source could be an embarrassment to both. Strict confidentiality must be maintained when discussing cases.

The relationship between the coroner and grief counselors must be smooth if the progress is going to work well or work at all. Setting the ground rules at the inception of the program and maintaining good lines of communication will insure a good start, and there should be no hurdle too high to stop further growth.

My personal feeling is that there has been virtually no grief counseling of survivors in most areas and that it is a much needed service.

*Chapter 14*

# THE AUTOPSY

WILLIAM M. BOGART, M.D.

A MEMBER of your family has died. You, as a very close friend or the nearest relation of this person, have suddenly been informed that the case will be handled by the Office of the Coroner. The death of this family member or loved one may have been expected, or it may have been quite unexpected. In either case, you are left in a state of not only grief but of confusion and concern. A young man or young woman will arrive at your residence and, if your composure seems to them to be rather well under control, you may be asked several questions at this time. The person to whom you will be talking is an investigative officer from the coroner's office of the county. This person, although a law enforcement officer, is not at your residence or the place of death because of any infraction of the law by you or anyone else concerned. He or she is there merely to obtain pertinent information relative to the death of the family member or friend. This investigator has been sent to your residence because the death of the person mentioned has been reported to the office of the coroner for any one of several reasons.

The majority of the cases reported are those in which individuals have expired as the result of so-called natural causes. In other cases, the death has been referred to the coroner's office by the physician's office, a hospital, or some other authority, usually because the physician has not attended the person for a considerable period of time. Any number of other reasons would result in such an investigation, including cases such as homicide

179

and suicide and injuries from accidents such as falls or motor vehicle accidents.

During the discussion with the investigator, the term "autopsy" may suddenly enter the conversation. This particular word or the mention of such often arouses repulsive thoughts and feelings in the minds of many people. One of the main reasons for this feeling or attitude is the lack of knowledge of the actual procedure and what the pathologist will attempt to accomplish by performing the postmortem examination. The procedure, a medicolegal autopsy, is an examination that is performed under the law, on order by the medical examiner or coroner, for one or more of the following purposes: (1) determining the cause and the manner of the death; (2) separating death due to disease from death due to external causes, for the protection of the innocent; (3) providing interpretation and correlation of facts and circumstances related to death; (4) providing a factual and objective report for law enforcement, prosecution, and defense agencies, if needed.

The autopsy performed in the hospital is an examination that is done with the consent of the deceased person's relatives for the purpose of (1) determining the cause of death, (2) providing correlation of clinical diagnosis and clinical symptoms, (3) determining the effectiveness of treatment, (4) studying the natural course of disease processes, and (5) for educational purposes.

The medicolegal autopsy attempts to gain information such as has been listed under the objectives of the hospital autopsy but, in addition, to perform an extremely thorough examination, both externally and internally, of all features of the case, whatever they may be. A very detailed documentation of this examination is made, and this can prove later to be of great importance, especially if the case may be brought into the courts or if pertinent information relative to insurance payments arises. The written report of the pathologist performing this medicolegal examination is a professional report without bias.

The terms "pathology" and "pathologist" have been used. The word pathology in its literal meaning is basically the study of disease. However, as one might well see, this is a rather wide and extensive definition. All of medicine in its many specialities and subspecialities is dedicated to an attempt to learn ways to prevent, as well as to cure, disease processes. The pathologist is a medical doctor who has received special formal training in a field that is basically "laboratory medicine." One of the categories of pathology is clinical pathology. Surgical pathology is another field, and this is a situation where a specimen, removed from the human body either in the physician's office or in a hospital, is examined very carefully by an expert in this field in order to determine the presence or absence of any disease process and if such is present, the nature of the disease. Another category, and this relates to our main subject, is postmortem pathology and the performance of an autopsy. In our particular county, the autopsies are performed by well-trained and experienced certified pathologists in this particular field of forensic medicine. The forensic pathologist is the one who has had special training and experience in the examination of decedents from a medicolegal standpoint. The examination of the decedent is carried out under the jurisdiction of the coroner or medical examiner and performed by a forensic pathologist. This in no way means that the death has any medicolegal implications. The purpose of the examination is to establish the true cause of death and to indicate the manner in which this death occurred. The forensic pathologist does not neglect to observe those particular features that have been listed as the purpose of the hospital autopsy. The medicolegal autopsy, however, involves much more, as will be seen.

The medicolegal autopsy is an examination of a decedent, carried out in a precise, uniform, thorough, and scientific manner. The forensic pathologist attempts to perform his examination in the most professional manner possible and attempts also to proceed in a manner very similar to that of a surgeon who has entered the interior of the body for the purpose of correcting some malfunction. Because of the necessity to accumulate a large amount of information, however, the pathologist must perform an unusually extensive examination. This does not involve what is often believed to be mutilation of the body. It is obviously necessary in the autopsy to remove and examine carefully and thoroughly organs and tissues in order to secure the required information and to establish the proper cause of death and the manner in which it occurred. When such examination is done in a proper manner, there is no reason why the exhibition or "showing" of the decedent may not be done at a mortuary or funeral home, providing the proper procedures are carried out by the mortician and embalmer. Over a period of many years I have heard it stated that the autopsy makes the embalming procedure more difficult. In discussing the situation with many morticians and embalmers, I find that a large number of them and some of the best of them actually prefer that an autopsy be done, for this actually somewhat simplifies their preparation work at the mortuary.

The actual autopsy procedure is one in which the name of the decedent must be identified to the pathologist. A careful documentation of the date, time, and place of autopsy must also be made. Any pertinent information prior to the autopsy examination, as well as the medical history, is certainly desirable. Photographs play a very important part in many situations. These are used to document certain types of alterations in body structure, especially injuries. X-ray examinations are made almost routinely in cases where one must attempt to locate foreign objects, such as bullets, and also to detect any anatomic deformities and features, such as fractures.

The first portion of the protocol (the autopsy report), following the general heading of the various pertinent pieces of information necessary, is actually an external examination of the body, and this is carried out in great detail; the features are documented either by written record or by direct dictation into a recording machine, such as is done at the Central Morgue in Contra Costa County. Normal as well as abnormal features are observed and related.

Following the detailed external examination, the interior of the body is entered. This is done by an incision similar to that which may be made by a surgeon, although it is obviously somewhat more extensive in order to present a greater exposure of the interior structures of the body itself, such as the heart, lungs, liver, and various organs within the abdomen. These organs are described according to their positions, whether normal or abnormal. They are described relative to size and shape. The majority of the organs are actually weighed during the examination, and a record is made. A description of each of the individual organs is made in detail, including not only normal features but any abnormalities that may be encountered. The same procedure applies to the examination of the structures of the neck where there may be some suspicion of the presence of a foreign body within the air passages, such as a portion of meat that may have been aspirated. The examination also includes, in many cases, a detailed observation of the brain in all areas, making a very careful note of not only the normal features but any abnormalities.

During the autopsy procedure, very small portions of the various organs are collected and placed in a fixative solution for possible study after preparation of microscopic slides, or the portions may merely be held in such a fixative solution in case such studies are considered necessary at a later time.

Other types of specimens are collected during the examination, these include a sample of the heart blood, urine which may be found in the urinary bladder and, in certain cases, the contents of the stomach may be removed to be analyzed for any medications that may have been taken in excess amount. Other materials removed may include portions of the liver, and frequently the contents of the gall bladder are removed and placed in a container.

Following the extensive examinations that have been described, the individual organs and tissues are placed in a clean plastic container and are then replaced within the body cavity. The incisions that have been made are then sutured in order to close the opened cavities. The exterior of the body is then cleansed thoroughly and dried carefully with toweling. A sheet is placed over the remains and, in our particular facility, the remains are then placed in a refrigeration unit. The purpose of this is to maintain the integrity of the tissues and prevent any decomposition.

The pathologist, as soon as his examination has been completed, issues a brief report of his findings and his opinion as to the cause of death in the case, if such a decision can be made at this time without further studies. This report is given directly to the investigator or the individual in charge of the office.

If a funeral director of choice has been selected prior to this time, an immediate call is made to this director informing him that he may come to the morgue and remove the body of the decedent to his establishment for whatever preparation he may be required to do.

A copy of the complete autopsy report is available to the family member or members at their request at a nominal charge; a copy of such report is issued to the attending physician at his request, and if the death has occurred in a hospital, the hospital receives a copy of the report.

An attempt is made by the pathologist to give, near the end of his report, an opinion as to the cause of death that can be understood by the average layperson. The pathologist also gives a conclusion in medical terminology, this particular information being that which will appear on the Certificate of Death (see Fig. 1 in Chapter 13 for a copy of this certificate).

Frequently, an individual may not understand the reason for the decedent having been removed to the office of the coroner, neither can they understand the reason for the autopsy examination. The forensic pathologist performing the examination is certainly willing at any time to discuss the findings with family members in an attempt to clarify any confusion or misunderstanding that may occur. One may question why an autopsy is necessary. It is necessary in many instances for the simple reason that without a very thorough examination and documentation, a cause of death may not be possible to establish. This leaves one then in doubt as to the true cause. In some, but relatively few cases, it is possible for the pathologist to state what he considers as a most probable and apparent cause without autopsy examination.

In summary, the forensic postmortem examination or autopsy is a detailed and thorough examination that is done in a very precise, thorough, and scientific manner, yielding information of great value relative to the cause and manner of death of an individual. This information, if no autopsy has been performed, would certainly not be available if one has some reason for proving the cause of death several weeks or months after the death has occurred.

## Chapter 15

# FUNERALS

WHEN A DEATH OCCURS, the relatives of the deceased often find that they are caught up in a number of important financial arrangements for which they are completely unprepared. At that time, relatives are experiencing considerable shock and its accompanying numbness. Nevertheless, arrangements have to be made for the care and disposition of the body, which is very difficult for the bereaved. This chapter will provide information of what is required by law, what is expected, what is optional, and how to proceed in making these arrangements.

Ideally, of course, families should plan ahead for such events, but often inertia, lack of information, or a reluctance to deal with death has prevented the family from the preparations that can be made in advance and that greatly simplify procedures at the time of a death. The inability to discuss death while living blocks the bereaved from knowing what the deceased preferred and also forces the bereaved into a painful experience at a time when it is difficult to concentrate on anything except one's loss.

What are some of the plans that can be made in advance?

1. The will. Making a will is a simple procedure that can be done *if* one takes the trouble to *do it*. Wills can be made by individuals or by an attorney, and the latter are inexpensive in comparison to the loss of money that an intestate (without a will) death often incurs.

> Marjorie's husband died suddenly of a heart attack. She and George had often discussed the disposition of their property, money, and investments. Since theirs was a second marriage for both of them, there were grown children by each previous marriage. Also, each held property in his own name. They had no joint bank accounts.

186

When George became ill, they realized they had no will. They got in touch with their attorney at once and discussed by telephone the disposition of the property, income, pensions, all of which George wanted to be directed to Marjorie. The attorney agreed to draw up the document and bring it out to the house for signatures. George died before the attorney arrived, leaving Marjorie with only her property and what money she had in her purse.

As a result, Marjorie, who was almost completely disabled herself, had to share George's estate with his grown children. To keep the house they had lived in, she had to sell the property in her name and buy out the stepchildren's interest in her own home. After the sale of George's property, there was little left for Marjorie. She was years away from being eligible for Social Security, and she was not disabled enough to be eligible for disability payments. George's intentions to provide well for Marjorie failed completely because of his and Marjorie's negligence in not making a will earlier.

2. Discuss ahead of time what each of you prefers—interment or cremation; a funeral or a memorial service and where it will be held; the kind of service you want, what will be said, sung, or played, and who will be asked to participate in the service. Discuss the cost and determine the limits you want to set on them. Select a funeral home, and tell the director what you want and hold firm on your decision.

Tell a close relative of the arrangements you have made. Advise your clergyman, your attorney, and your physician of your arrangements, and carry this information along with your identification in your wallet.

3. Help each other understand household tasks that are routinely performed by one of you, and provide guidance and supervised practice in these tasks ahead of time. In this category are such things as reconciling a bank statement; keeping checkbook stubs correctly; making out income tax statements; where and from whom you generally purchase household items; where to go for household repairs and improvement, car upkeep, and repairs.

4. Make a list of your property, bank accounts, pensions, insurance policies, and investments. (In most states, if these financial holdings are held jointly by the husband and wife, the financial transition after death is considerably eased.) Know where

this list is kept and where the will is filed.

If you have not made these decisions about the funeral and its expenses ahead of their need, then these affairs must be attended to by you shortly after the death occurs. Do take a trusted friend or relative with you to the funeral home. Such a person can be a great comfort to you; he can also be of invaluable assistance to you in helping select what you want and also in restraining you from going overboard on the expenses.

Deciding how much to pay for the funeral of a deceased spouse is often one of the largest expenditures a person has to decide *under trying and painful circumstances.* The average total expense for a funeral and all funeral related services in this country is about $1,300. Funeral directors are reluctant to quote prices or specific merchandise by telephone and may even limit the discussion of price when you visit them. California has had a law since 1972 that provides that funeral directors must give a complete price disclosure both before entering into an agreement and at the time of billing. A funeral director is required to give you a written list of his prices on an itemized basis *before* an agreement is reached for funeral services. He is also required to announce conspicuously the prices of displayed caskets, with each casket priced individually. He must also display and have available for sale caskets that are included in advertised prices for funeral services. The same legislation prohibits crematories from requiring that human remains be placed in a casket prior to cremation.

Check to see if your state has such legislation. If you encounter any abuses that are prohibited by law, you may file a consumer's complaint by writing to the Executive Secretary, State Board of Funeral Directors and Embalmers or, if you live in California, write to the same board, 1031 O Street, Room A-190, Sacramento, California, 95814.

A certificate of death and a permit for disposition of human remains are required for disposition of the body. The attending physician or the coroner must fill out the medical certification on the death certificate, which must then be filed with the local registry of births and deaths. In California, death certificates cost two dollars, and no funeral director may charge more.

The registry issues the disposition permit to the funeral director or to you, if you are acting as funeral director yourself. On the permit, you must specify either the place the remains are to be buried or entombed or the crematory and final destination of the ashes. You will need the disposition permit to transport, bury, cremate, or otherwise dispose of the body. In 1974, the California legislature eliminated the restrictions on the disposition of ashes that required the ashes be scattered at least three miles off shore and that enurnment or other authorized disposition must occur within thirty days of cremation. Disposition of human ashes outside a cemetery is now permissible as long as the disposition is in keeping with public sensibilities. When disposing of ashes on private property, the disposition permit does not require you to stipulate whether the ashes are buried, scattered, or kept in a box in the closet. It is advisable to obtain written permission of the property owner beforehand.

The legal right and duty to control the final disposition of a body goes to the deceased's spouse, children, parents, and other relatives, in that order. If both the deceased and his survivors are indigent, the county will take over the burial and the expense. In this case, the relatives have to assign social security and other benefits, if any, to the county. If, on the other hand, a relative of yours dies and you are not poor, you not only have the right to arrange and pay for his burial, you have a legal obligation to do so. If you do not, you can be found guilty of a misdemeanor and sued for treble the expenses incurred.

Noncremated bodies may be buried only in "burial parks," plots of land that are already established as commercial, religious, or public cemeteries or are declared by established tradition as family plots. The State Cemetery Board leaves it up to individual cemeteries to determine whether they will require caskets or grave liners. If the gravediggers belong to a union, the cemetery usually requires some type of container. Most cemeteries require a concrete grave liner, which prevents the grave from collapsing, but it does add to the cost. Most burial park graves are priced at $100 for a site without a marker.

There is no law that requires a casket, a funeral director, or a hearse to transport a body. It is legal to transport a body in a station wagon or a truck.   In California, a body need never be embalmed, as long as the body is transported in an airtight container, which costs $250 or more.   The other alternative could be cheaper—shop around.

The body must be cremated, buried in the ground, or entombed, unless it is donated to science.   Neither a casket nor embalming is required for cremation; it is illegal for a crematory to insist on a casket, but some kind of container may be required. A disposition permit must accompany the body.   Ashes may be scattered at sea, provided they are removed from the container before scattering.   This may be done by anyone from a private boat or airplane.   There are also commercial services that do this. The ashes may be buried or scattered in most places in California, in your own back yard or on other private property.   The restrictions here are that there must be no violation of trespass and nuisance laws and that the land is outside the corporate limits of the city.   It is cheaper by far to dispose of a body by cremation, particularly if one is not making any use of a funeral director. At a crematory, the cost runs from $75 to $100.

There are certain restrictions concerning cremation in the case of Catholics.   For more than a decade, the Catholic Church has allowed cremations under certain conditions.   The following statement of these restrictions is taken from *The Catholic Voice,* a publication of the Diocese of Oakland, June 12, 1978:

> According to Christian Burial Guidelines published by the National Catholic Cemetery Conference, cremation may be requested for hygenic, economic or other reasons of a public or private nature. In the case of transfer of remains to a distant place, for example, or possible avoidance of considerable expense, national tradition or custom, or severe psychological or pathological fear of burial in the ground or tomb, the Church will allow cremations . . . .
>
> Burial Guidelines emphasize that the remains of the deceased after cremation must always be treated with respect and placed in consecrated ground.
>
> According to Church instruction, a Catholic may not receive funeral rites of the Church if his request for cremation is motivated by a "denial of Christian dogmas, or because of a sectarian spirit, or through hatred of the Catholic religion or the Church."
>
> The directive is a response to the secret, masonic, antichurch societies of the late Middle Ages that advocated the practice of cremation as

an affront to Church and God.  Cremation for those societies symbol-
ized blasphemy to God—"a challenge to resurrect these ashes, to re-
build the body from dust."

According to tradition, a person who was cremated belonged to
an anti-religious society.

Finally, the guidelines instruct the priest, whose responsibility it is
to perform the funeral, to determine that the reasons for choosing cremation are within those recognized by the Church and not a denial
of Christianity.

Following are some typical funeral costs in the San Francisco
Bay Area; check them with those in your area.  These itemiza-
tions will give you some idea of the *questions you should ask and
things you should look for* when you begin to explore the kind of
funeral and services you wish, hopefully *before* they are required.
These figures are taken from Janice Roberts, "Guide to Funerals," *San Francisco Magazine,* June, 1974, and the price, of course,
is now higher.

| | |
|---|---:|
| Casket | $900.00 |
| (6.5% tax) | 8.50 |
| Professional Services | 650.00* |
| | $1558.50 |

Extras Provided by  the Funeral Home

| | |
|---|---:|
| Clergyman | $ 25.00 |
| Limousines  (4-hour  period) | 50.00 |
| Pallbearers  (each) | 11.50 |
| Obituaries (per line, minimum 7 lines) | 1.48 |
| Copies of death certificates  (each) | 2.00 |
| Flowers | 7.50 and up |

In addition to this look at our local conditions, write to the
Maryland Center for Public Broadcasting, Owings Mills, Mary-
land 21117 for their *Consumer Survival Kit, the Last Rights: A
Look at Funerals,* price one dollar.

---

*The cost for professional services ranged from $600 to $785, depending on the
funeral home.  This includes the following: initial interview, $52; removal of
body, $130; embalming and cosmetic services, $277.50; use of slumber room (3 days),
$78; counseling, $65; use of chapel, $52; care of flowers, $32.50; memorial book,
$13. (These are average, not standard, prices.)

The San Francisco Bay Area is fortunate to have two organizations that have been designed to help the consumer keep down the cost of funerals and at the same time provide basic services with dignity. The Bay Area Funeral Society and the Neptune Society offer a basic service that provides for removal of the body from the place of death, a simple casket, transportation of the body to the cemetery or crematorium, and necessary legal papers. Not included are cremation, embalming, burial costs, or use of the mortuary chapel. For a funeral where cremation is involved, the funeral cost ranges from $195 to $304. The prices vary between the funeral homes, and these societies quote the prices from each in their brochure. If such a society is of interest to you and you live beyond the San Francisco area, make some telephone calls to determine whether such a society exists in your area. Most of these societies are required to belong to the Continental Association of Funeral and Memorial Societies, to which you can also write for information. The address is 1828 L Street, Washington, D.C. 20036.

The funeral and memorial society movement began in 1939 as a reaction to funeral practices of that period but remained little known and relatively dormant until 1963. Then a group of societies met in Chicago to form a national group, the Continental Association of Funeral and Memorial Societies. At about the same time, three important books were being sold that created great interest in the societies by focusing on the practices of the funeral industry and the need for better planning. They included a valuable pamphlet, "A Manual of Death Education and Simple Burial" by Ernest Morgan (1973), a founder of CAFMS; "The High Cost of Dying" by Ruth Mulvey Harmer (1963), who later became president of CAFMS; and "The American Way of Death" by Jessica Mitford (1963), who helped found the Bay Area Funeral Society in California. Also in print at the time was a classic study of the subject, "The Great American Funeral: A Study in Guilt and Sublimity" by Dr. LeRoy Bowman (1964), the first president of CAFMS.

The foregoing literature fired interest in the societies through the 60s and into the 70s when it appeared that nearly every magazine or newspaper had an article on planning for death. The result has been a spurt in the growth of funeral and memorial societies. Interest has also been increasing in the desire of people to help others after death through donation of eyes and other organs, as well as donating the entire body to medical science.

Many people believe that the funeral is a rite designed to give comfort and reassurance to the family and friends of the deceased; others believe that the deceased's wishes should be followed explicitly in planning the funeral; many others do not give the matter any thought until the occasion arises. No matter what category you fall into, you are surely among the majority who feel bewildered and confused as to how to go about planning a funeral or a memorial service. The following form has been designed by J. William Worden and William Proctor (1976). Read this carefully and discuss it with your family. If you know now what it is you want, write down your wishes and also discuss them with your family. Let them know where you will keep the outline so there will be no unnecessary searching when it is needed. Perhaps both you and your spouse can each fill out one of these, indicating your preferences as a guide to your children or relatives. From time to time look over your choices and make additional changes. We do not have just one idea about these things; the more we think about them the more ideas we have, and the more changes we may want to make, and the more up-to-date will be our guidelines for our family and friends.

## FREE TO CELEBRATE

At this point take a few moments and consider what might be an appropriate service to celebrate your life after you die. This is not an easy task, but doing it can put you in touch with some important thoughts and feelings.

I would like my service to take place:

_____ in my church or synagogue.  _____ outdoors.

_____ at home.  _____ at graveside only.

_____ at a funeral chapel.  _____ other _____.

Wherever you decide to have the service, the service should re-

flect you—your uniqueness. Since it will be a time of remembering and recollections, what would you most like people to remember about you? Think about this and make some notes.
What I want people to remember about me:

What has the most meaning in my life? _____

My interest in: _____

My accomplishments: _____

Now consider some procedural issues. Somebody will have to convene the service. Who would you like to do this?

I would like the following person to officiate at my service:

_____ my clergyman.                    _____ a friend.
_____ my funeral director.             _____ a family member.
_____ a psychologist.                  _____ other.

Because of the intensity of emotion that may grip close family members after your death it may be hard for them to publicly participate in your service. Your friends may be in a better position to contribute in your final celebration.

Here are the names of friends I would like to have participate in my service:

1. _____          5. _____
2. _____          6. _____
3. _____          7. _____
4. _____          8. _____

Think of a specific function for each person. Ways they might participate are:


Now think for a moment about the service itself. What would you like it to include:


Some specific things I'd like to have included in my service are:
Music:
Poetry:

Scripture:

Other Readings:

Other features (such as interpretive dance, art forms, etc.)

Religious or philosophical convictions I want expressed in the service:

Things I definitely do not want at my service:

In considering readings and creative presentations for your service, you are choosing material which reflects those things which are important to you. The manner of expressing those beliefs and convictions is limited only by your imagination and sense of taste. Your convictions may include your beliefs as to the meaning of your life and death, where you came from and where you are going. Some people focus on beliefs which sustain them and enable them to function when life gets rough. If you believe that life has a plan and a purpose, share this with those who will be joining in the celebration of your life. Perhaps you might want to write a draft of your own final message.

My final message I would like to be read:

## *OBITUARY*

_____ died today at the age of _____,
a native of _____, he/she died _____
               (birthplace)                   (how you might die)
He/she is survived by _____
                        (the members of your family who survive you)
He/she is best remembered for _____
                       (how people will remember you)
Details of the funeral and the burial are as follows:

The following is an example of how one county in California provides the poor with a dignified burial:

### PROVIDING THE POOR WITH DIGNIFIED BURIAL*

For a mere $335, a man can have a funeral service and be buried in a simple casket in the same cemetery as a man who may have paid ten times that sum.

But that service is reserved for a select group—Contra Costa's poor, who can't afford even the simplest funeral and burial services.

While it might strike some of the county's poor as ironic that they are members of a select group, nevertheless they are, even if they must die to be eligible.

Up until last year, the poor were buried at a lower cost in a small cemetery outside of Pacheco. A dispute with the owner about funeral and burial fees prompted the county to change its policy. Now even the poorest can be assured his final resting place will be a green, landscaped cemetery that will be kept up long after his death.

The $335 authorized by the county includes $200 for mortuary and funeral costs and $135 to purchase the grave site. Upon an indigent's death, the county receives certification of his indigence, and his body is removed to the funeral home of his choice. In cases where no choice is made, the body is taken to the nearest funeral home. At the funeral home, the body is prepared, embalmed, clothed, and placed in a simple casket. The casket is made of wood, is cloth covered and, although simple in appearance, is not demeaning, funeral directors claim. "Gone are the days of the undertaker who went out and nailed some rough boards together, stained them and called it a coffin," said a Richmond funeral director.

The body may be kept at the mortuary for several days if relatives request it. A religious funeral ceremony is provided, with the minister or priest of the family or friend's choice presiding. If the deceased has no friends or relatives, a rare occurrence in this county, a minister still conducts a funeral ceremony.

*By J. Van Lindingham, Lesher News Bureau, *Contra Costa Times*, 1977.

According to funeral directors in Richmond and Pittsburg, where most of the county's indigents are to be found, any outsider walking in on funeral ceremonies probably wouldn't know the deceased was a pauper. The only clue would be the casket and the absence of flowers. No headstone is provided in the county fee, although a temporary marker with the deceased's name and dates of birth and death is provided. These temporary markers are never removed and many still stand.

Anyone who shows he or his family can afford to pay anything for his funeral, even if on a time plan, is not eligible for the county free burial, the funeral directors said. County officials said indigence can be certified only by a social worker, the coroner's office, the hospital, or the district attorney. Because most of the indigents were receiving welfare during their lifetime, it is not difficult to certify them.

The Richmond funeral director complained that it was difficult to find a cemetery that would provide an adult grave for $135, although a child's grave is no problem. He said most of the adult burials were in Antioch's Oakview Cemetery, a nonendowment care cemetery. By endowment care, he meant one where the burial costs also included permanent grave site maintenance. The Pittsburg director said he thought Contra Costa County took better care of its indigent dead than many other counties.

The day of Potter's Field, a burial ground for paupers, criminals, unknown or friendless persons, is gone. And in death, at least, the poor have attained some measure of equality.

### Conclusion

Bereaved families and friends most frequently mention to counselors that a funeral or a memorial service was an occasion for them to begin their grieving process or to begin its closure. When they mention that either the funeral or memorial service interfered with this process, they are making a strong statement against conventional ways of conducting these services. Those friends and relatives who have experienced a Celebration of Life service speak clearly about its value to them beyond the scope of the traditional service. The writer hopes that the suggestions provided in this chapter regarding the Celebration of Life will be helpful to those friends and relatives.  This celebration is another way of providing a meaningful and beautiful service *for the deceased* and achieving also valuable closure experience *for the bereaved*.  The only limitation in its use is your own creative participation.

## REFERENCES

Bowman, LeRoy, *The American Funeral: A Way of Death*.  New York: Paperback Library, 1964.

Harmer, Ruth M., *The High Cost of Dying*.  New York:  MacMillan, 1963.

Mitford, Jessica, *The American Way of Death*.  New York:  Fawcett, 1963.

Morgan, Ernest, *A Manual of Death Education and Simple Burial*.  Burnsville, North Carolina:  Celo Pr, 1973.

Von Lindingham, J., "Providing the Poor with Dignified Burial."  Walnut Creek, California:  *Contra Costa Times,* 1977.

Worden, J. William and William Proctor, *Personal Death Awareness*.  Englewood Cliffs, New Jersey:  P-H, 1976.

## Section IV

# ORGANIZATION AND TRAINING

### Introduction

THE PURPOSE OF THIS SECTION is to help other individuals or agencies, public or private, begin such a service as has been provided by Contra Costa County Crisis and Suicide Intervention Center. It is appropriate to offer this help since this was the first center in the United States to provide grief counseling services to the bereaved of traumatic deaths (coroner's cases) in an entire county. An account is given of some of the problem areas that arise in attempting to start a similar service.

In order to be as informative as possible, this section contains information on how this particular grief counseling program started; how to screen prospective counselors; the specifics of the training classes, session by session; and how to teach counselors to care for themselves.

*Chapter 16*

# HOW THE GRIEF COUNSELING
# PROGRAM BEGAN

## Purpose

IN ADDITION to the traditional hot line service offered by every suicide intervention center, our volunteers have worked in the Coroner's Office since 1971 on a regular basis several hours one day each week. The volunteers have full access to the files of the completed and equivocal suicides and other sudden deaths in the county. This liaison began for the purpose of identifying completed suicides of persons who had used our services. We learned that of the persons who have suicided only a few ever telephoned us, either because they did not know of our service or did not wish to discuss their suicidal thoughts. We also learned that the majority of suicides occur in the home, and the body is found by the spouse or a family member.

The Grief Counseling Service for Contra Costa County* began in November, 1972. The purpose of the project was to provide, free of charge, counseling services to any resident of the county who was a survivor of suicide, regardless of where the suicide occurred. The services of the grief counselors were aimed at (1) giving help and comfort to the survivors of suicide during their period of mourning and (2) giving social support and assistance during the period of despair and into the period of hope and rebuilding. We also hoped that this service would lead to better community mental health by exposing suicide contagion which

---

*Contra Costa Costa County is one of the seven San Francisco Bay Area counties. The present population of this county is 618,200. The county covers a land area of 732.6 square miles.

crops up in our county from year to year.   (Suicide contagion is the ready acceptance of suicide as a means of solving perplexing life problems by some members of a family, clan, living group, or neighborhood.)

## Expanded Program

By 1976, this facet of grief work with the survivors of suicide had earned considerable respect in our community.  With the full cooperation of the Coroner's Office, we expanded our program to *all* sudden deaths that are coroner's cases—homicides, traffic accidents of all kinds, accidental deaths, drownings, industrial accidents, and cardiovascular failures.   Access to the coroner's files for these modes of death are identical with those for suicide cases.

Sudden infant deaths were eliminated because there is a county organization that cooperates with the Coroner's Office in attending to the families where a crib death occurs.   We also temporarily eliminated the cardiovascular failures.   These cases were so numerous we felt we could not maintain our level of quality counseling and care for all of them.   When our counseling group expanded in 1978, the under-fifty age group of cardiovascular failures was added.   The remainder of the ages will be added when our counseling staff is increased.

In 1977, with the full cooperation of the Coroner's Office, the service was expanded again by being designated as the grief counselors to assist the coroner at a time of disaster in our county. A good portion of 1977 was devoted to exploring the literature on disasters and adapting ourselves and our counseling staff to the role we will be asked to fill in case of any disaster in the county.

## THE ROLE OF THE CORONER'S OFFICE

The establishment of a working relationship with the Coroner's Office is *the* important ingredient for the viability of this project; without this relationship,  the project could neither be as far-reaching in its mental health aspects nor as acceptable to the community.  The Sheriff-Coroner's Office was receptive from the beginning.  It took several months of conversations, reports, and waiting for approval from both their department and our agency.  These discussions opened up many issues important to both parties. Each party had much to learn. Our agency had to become informed of the legalities with which the Coroner's Office has to deal and in what sequence in order to fulfill its obligations to the community. The Coroner's Office learned from us the need for the mental health potential of helping bereaved persons who otherwise would be left alone to fend for themselves after a traumatic death. Many conflicts and benefits emerged; all aspects had to be worked into the office schedule of the coroner's unit without interfering with any of its procedures.

Mutual trust and confidence were developed during the first year. The result of the negotiations was that a firm relationship was established and has continued since 1971. Credit must be given to the sheriff-coroner's department for grasping early on the meaning of what we were proposing and for helping make it come to pass at a time when few other coroner's offices in the country were open to this kind of outreach. Our county Coroner's Office recognized this need and stepped in to provide the data we needed.

By mutual consent both parties agreed to work together to provide

1. *Access to the files of the completed suicides and,* later on, to the files of the victims of *all sudden deaths in the county that are coroner's cases.* Our counselors spend several hours one day a week in the Coroner's Office reading files for which death certificates have been signed and recording the information that our agency needs in order to reach the next-of-kin. In cases of suicide, this means that we can reach family members as soon as the death certificate is signed unless there is reason for a long investigation or a series of laboratory tests. There are times when we are able to see these persons on the same day as the suicide or shortly thereafter. This is vital in suicide cases.

2. *Access to the unit commander of the coroner's office for help and assistance* in understanding unusual points of concern to both parties regarding special aspects of a case. This is an important part of the relationship that has existed from the beginning and has made the entire arrangement a matter of mutual concern and interest.

As a result of information sharing, both parties to this agreement have developed a mutual regard for the importance of concepts of confidentiality and the necessity for developing an ongoing respect for each other's need for accuracy, diplomacy, openness, and honesty in dealing with our mutual clients.

Information that is of mutual interest is shared. Counselors may speak to the unit commander about issues they feel need some clarification, e.g. the autopsy, particulars of a case that are perplexing or difficult to understand. Conversely, the unit commander speaks freely to counselors about special cases of persons for whom he feels there is special need for our service. Both parties exchange new material relevant to our mutual needs, such as journal articles, film, etc. In short, it is a friendly and pleasant relationship.

From the beginning of our arrangement with the Coroner's Office, the unit commander has been a member of our Board of Trustees. This is done in order to use his views and reflections on our partnership as a part of our agency's policy-making process.

It is our hope that Coroner's Offices in other parts of the country will try this system of cooperation with crisis/suicide intervention centers. Our experience should encourage them to explore this possibility and to share the vision that our Coroner's Office has displayed.

From reading the files in the Coroner's Office, we also prepare annual statistics of completed suicides of our county as well as those of other types of sudden death. Such statistics include a fairly lengthy report of their implications and the results of our grief counseling with the bereaved.

The suicide rate for Contra Costa County for the past seven years is as follows:

1972—14.5 per 100,000 population
1973—15.0 per 100,000 population
1974—17.7 per 100,000 population
1975—17.3 per 100,000 population
1976—15.7 per 100,000 population
1977—14.5 per 100,000 population
1978—12.9 per 100,000 population

## Board Approval

The grief counseling aspect of our work was an outgrowth of the first two years of work with the Coroner's Office. In the process of compiling statistics on county suicides and the demographic profile of the county suicides, our volunteers noted each year that the majority of the suicides occurred in the home, and the body was found by a spouse or a family member. We realized the heavy burden of shock that fell upon the survivors of suicide at the time of discovering the body and reporting the death. We recommended to our board that our agency might perform a much needed service by helping these significant others talk about their shock, grief, and anger.

The board approved the project, subject to a review of the committee's training by the board's training committee. This approval was given in October, 1972. Members of the committee were trustees whose professional training in the fields of psychology and/or education qualified them to set up the training program for volunteers in the Crisis Center-Suicide Intervention classes. They were guided in their work by specific standards for training that had been adopted by the Bay Area Association of Suicide Prevention Centers.

## HOW GRIEF COUNSELING OPERATES

After a sudden death is reported, a brief friendly letter is sent to the next-of-kin residing in our county (see the Appendix for copies of the forms and records used). This letter is followed by a telephone call from a counselor who has been apprised by the coordinator of the relevant information concerning the death. Often there are several next-of-kin to be called. During this call, the counselor discusses the death with these persons, inquires if there is a need for our service and, if requested, makes an appointment for a home visit. The bereaved may discuss on the telephone any questions he wants to talk about. If the phone call is all that is required or wanted at this time, the counselor states our availability if the person wants help at a later time.

During the home visit, the counselor appraises the situation, the client, the psychological atmosphere of the home, and crosscurrents within the family. The counselor does a great deal of listening, getting the client to talk about the death, the deceased, and his own feelings. In other words, counselors encourage the client to begin the gradual recollection of old thoughts and feelings, a prelude to acceptance of death as a fact. If natural feelings of anger or hostility are not expressed within an appropriate time, the counselor gently provokes the client to express these feelings.

The counselor must be alert, receptive, and responsive in practical ways. Being helpful in practical ways includes discussion of many topics: welfare checks, Social Security, insurance and probate; employment, need for moving, change of life style, the social worker's role, health and nutritional needs of the family, explanation of the role of the coroner in the investigation and the autopsy, disposal of the deceased's effects, etc. This resocialization of the client is concerned with problems that often get overlooked but that are an important step in drawing the client back into the stream of life. Situations that require additional help or consultations with professionals in the community may be identified at this time.

Visits are intended to be a one-to-one friendly discussion and to continue as long as the client needs help, without encouraging dependency. The client has telephone access to the counselor at all times, either through our Hot Line or by having the counselor's own number. The length of the relationship is open ended. The intention is to help the client over the three or four worst months of mourning, with decreasing contacts until the anniversary date (in the case of suicides only).

We are often asked why a one-to-one counseling situation is preferred instead of a team of at least two persons. Our years of experience in the coroner's office have made us aware of the special conditions that occur at such a time of traumatic sudden death. It is possible, at this time, for a home to be almost inundated by teams of workers: the firemen may have come for resuscitation purposes; the police are there, so are one or two investigators from the Coroner's Office; an ambulance has arrived. The house becomes crowded while pictures are taken; drawings made of the site and position of the deceased; fingerprints taken; and a search and inquiry made for a possible note, the weapon used, or for a supply of drugs found in the home. Information is sought concerning the name, age, occupation, etc. of the deceased; names, addresses, etc., of witnesses.

During all of this necessary work, the client is expected to hold himself together during a great deal of questioning. He is in an emotionally vulnerable condition due to his shock, and all of this activity and personnel can be very threatening. If this experience is followed by a team of grief counselors requesting a visit, the next-of-kin is likely to reject their offers for counseling. One friendly call on the telephone and the same friendly person coming as a visitor to the home does not present an additional emotional burden.

A full account of the visit is made to the entire group of grief counselors at their regular, twice-a-month meetings. During these two-hour sessions, counselors may ask for suggestions, criticism, and help for their own anxieties. Records are kept of each telephone call made, of referrals, and of all home visits and counseling calls. A summary record file is kept. (See the Appendix for these record forms.)

We do not carry liability insurance of any kind. We have not encountered any legal problems. This is due to the following reasons: First, our counselors are instructed never to fill in any legal document and second, our cooperative arrangement with the Coroner's Office more or less precludes our getting ourselves into any kind of legal conflict. Since we have been doing this counseling work, we have never had a complaint either to us or to the Coroner's Office about anything we have ever said or done with a client. But both the Coroner's Office and our office have received calls and letters praising our work and its effectiveness.

The respect we have from the Coroner's Office and the community comes from the thoroughness of our counselors' training and the integrity with which we handle the confidentiality of the facts and information we obtain from that office. We always ask the client's permission before we enter into a discussion of his case with any third party, except for material that is used for teaching purposes. Even for teaching purposes, the client's identity is always protected. Our files are kept locked and separate from the files for the Hot Line, and only grief counselors have access to them.

*Chapter 17*

# SCREENING THE PROSPECTIVE
# COUNSELOR

T HE SCREENING interview schedule is arranged in advance by the
secretary who allows a half-hour for each interview. Most of
the interviews run over this allotment, but that is expected. The
first thing we begin to talk about is how the prospective counselor's schedule fits the schedule of our grief counseling routine:
time and dates for the training program, the ongoing training,
and the schedule at the Coroner's Office. If there is no fit, there
is no reason to continue the interview, except for suggesting that
when the applicant's schedule changes he can still telephone us
for another interview for a future training class. Time picked up
by not having to complete an entire interview allows certain of
the interviews to run over the half-hour with no one feeling
pushed or hurried.

Those present at the screening interview are the executive
director of the agency or an experienced grief counselor, and the
grief training and program coordinator. If the prospective counselor passes this interview, he is required to meet with two of the
agency's screening committee (these two people are professionals).
Every effort is made to make the applicant feel comfortable, relaxed, and feel that we are open and unthreatening.

Since grief counselors play an important role in assisting the
bereaved to express and to work through his grief, it is important
to have considerable knowledge about the prospective counselor
before he enrolls in the training class. The committee is looking
for information that indicates the applicant's strengths and weaknesses, ability to cope, and willingness to change some of his own

attitudes and habits.

A good deal of thought has gone into this process. These are some of the mental health criteria considered before accepting an applicant into our training program:

1. *Does the prospective counselor have a positive feeling toward himself?* Does he have a sense of safety, competence, mastery; an enjoyment of his own powers as a sensing, feeling, thinking being; an expectation that his own capacities will find appropriate fullfillment?

2. *Does the applicant have a realistic perception of himself and others?* Does he show a knowledge of self; a capacity to see others in terms of *their* motivations, opinions, and life-conditioning circumstances?

3. *How does the prospective counselor relate to people?* Is there a capacity to relate to others as individuals, relatively free from fixed or conventional patterns? Has he developed and sustained relations of depth and warmth? Has he found a balanced and flexible way of interacting (with ideas, activities, etc.) ? Can he sustain the core of his own individuality (opinion, style, values, etc.) ?

4. *How does he relate to his environment?* Has he a positive, motivated connectedness with the contemporary world of processes and ideas; the ability and drive to use his capacities and skills in effective new ways; the capacity to expand his activities beyond the realm of personal encounter?

5. *What about his independence?* Can he think independently? Is he free from compulsion to submit or conform, able to adapt to others' demands and goals? Does he have the capacity to accept help himself where he has insufficient knowledge, experience, or strength?

6. *Does he have curiosity and creativity?* Has he a sustained and deepened curiosity; a drive to penetrate the unknown and to work toward a directed search for resolution?

7. *How about his recovery and coping strength?* Has he shown his capacity to regain equilibrium in the face of trauma, frustration, and crisis? Can he pull together his available strength in the face of challenge and obstacle?

This list of seven mental health criteria for a prospective

counselor looks formidable and threatening. But we have found that we can fulfill our objectives and at the same time provide a warm, friendly atmosphere during the screening interview by weaving such questions as the following into our conversation:

How did you hear of our grief counseling program? What deaths have you had among your family or friends? How did you cope with them? Do you feel comfortable about your resolution of these deaths?

How does your family feel about your wanting to become a grief counselor? Comfortable? Puzzled? In the dark? Unsupportive? What about your children?

To your way of thinking, have you ever been seriously depressed? What did you do? What happened?

What do you generally do when you encounter the usual frustrations, disappointments, and failures we are all subject to?

In the course of our work we talk about or are with persons who have experienced traumatic deaths—often violent ones. These people are sad, depressed, angry, guilty, often suicidal. Do you think such a steady diet of talk and work with violence, depression, anger, death, etc., would disturb you? How do you think you would feel about that? How do you think you might behave?

What community resources do you habitually use (libraries, churches, theaters, recreational, etc.) ?

What do you do in your spare time? What do you do for fun?

What questions do you have about this service, the agency, or how we operate?

Some of these questions are never asked for they are answered in the process of explaining or talking about some life situation they have had and the way they coped with it. The goal of the entire interview is to conduct it so that the prospective counselor will progress from one subject to another in his own way and style without feeling pushed, hurried, or threatened.

It is important to realize that the applicant may feel threatened. For the first time, perhaps, the prospective counselor is free to talk about some important loss, separation, or grief. The applicant also wonders how you are going to respond to his life's dilemma and must decide whether you can be trusted with this information. How he decides to resolve this problem of trust is paramount both to the applicant and to the committee. Give the applicant permission to talk about what he wants to talk about. Much of the information that you feel is important to know about this person may be forthcoming if you allow him to determine the pace and content of the discussion.

Feel free yourself to ask questions about matters that come through a bit confused for you. Allow the applicant the same privilege. The interview is not intended as a time of drab questioning or probing but as an exchange between the committee and the applicant, a give-and-take, with time for humor and laughing.

Time is also spent explaining to the applicant the goals of the training program. We explain our belief that counselors are better prepared if they are given an opportunity to examine their own life problems, emotions, and behavior. By way of their questions about this approach, the applicants come to see that they and their families and friends will also benefit from their participation. They also see that by reexamining their own attitudes and behavior there is a need to share many aspects of themselves that perhaps they have never shared before. In short, efforts are made as early as this interview to foster the idea that the class will be one in which group trust is encouraged in the atmosphere of confidentiality of a "safe house."

In the process of such a discussion, it often happens that the applicant screens himself out of the program, either for the time being or for good. The applicant often recognizes that a reluctance to share, to be willing to be open and aware of himself, may be a stumbling block to his relationship with a client. He may also express doubts about his effectiveness or ability to handle the emotional load of frequent discussions of violence, guilt, anger, etc. If these doubts are voiced in different ways, the screening committee accepts the applicant's valuation of the situation and suggests that perhaps he is not yet ready for this class. He is told that if he later feels differently, he may ask for another appointment in a few months or even a year later. It is seldom beneficial for anyone to encourage persons to engage in an activity that seems completely beyond them or for which their family and friends are not supportive.

The committee looks for evidence of flexibility, nonjudgmental attitudes, willingness to learn something new, and a certain delight in the prospect of helping others in an entirely new way. At the conclusion of the interview, the spokesman for the committee explains that the committee will carefully consider his application and will inform him within a day whether or not he has been accepted for the class. When the spokesman for the committee telephones the applicant, he either arranges for him to participate in the next class or explains that the committee feels that he is not yet ready to begin the training. Where definite reasons for his rejection exist, the applicant is informed that at the present time he does not, in the committee's opinion, seem ready. Then the spokesman mentions the factors in the applicant's life that seem to the committee to interfere with his participation now. Some of the reasons that most commonly interfere with class participation are the applicant is looking for a job, getting a divorce, finishing school or his own grief, or that his children or his job presently need much of his time. We leave the door open for him to reapply at a later date when these personal pressures have lessened.

All applicants who are accepted for the class agree to serve as counselors for at least one year, barring such unforeseen circumstances as the onset of poor health, increased family responsibilities, or moving out of the area.

## Chapter 18

# THE GRIEF COUNSELING TRAINING
# CLASSES

### Introduction

THE TRAINING classes have changed greatly since the beginning of the project. At that time, there were no grief training models available. In the early 1970s, doctors, nurses, hospital administrators, and some social scientists were thinking of the dying patient rather than the grief of survivors of sudden, violent deaths. No one on our board or in our community had any knowledge or experience in conducting a counseling service such as the one proposed.

The first year, the training relied exclusively upon guest speakers as our principal informants. These speakers were local ministers, a funeral director, a psychiatrist, a psychologist, a medical doctor, a home economist, a probate attorney, and a juvenile hall chaplain. They informed the class of their experiences with the problems of the bereaved. There were also frequent consultations with the coroner's unit. Tapes were made of the significant presentations. In addition, the group attended Bay Area workshops and symposia conducted by the University of California, Berkeley YWCA, and the University of California, San Francisco Extension-Medical School. Participation in these local forums and our own guest speakers provided a wide exchange of opinion with as highly qualified professionals as were available to us. Materials obtained at these meetings were kept on file for further reference, along with the books, pamphlets, tapes, etc., that we were beginning to acquire.

It was soon evident, however, that grief counselors who do this kind of work day in and day out encounter problems in clients and in themselves that are not experienced by others who do grief work on an occasional basis. We realized that we needed much more than the theoretical approach to bereavement. We recognized that our clients were experiencing emotional upheavals that were normal components of the grieving process. We also sensed that unless we responded to them by acknowledging these upheavals, we were missing an important aspect of the whole process. Moreover, how could we offer clients counseling when they were experiencing such great change if the counselors had not themselves acquired knowledge of how grief reactions will affect them emotionally?

We began to introduce more and more experiential material, enabling the prospective counselors *to put themselves in the same situation* and to see how they would behave. From 1975 until 1977 this process grew and changed until the training program outlined in this chapter evolved. The response to this approach has been heartening. In examining their own emotional reactions, understanding their own feelings of guilt and anxiety, and learning more about their own normal expressions of depression, counselors have begun their counseling work with more calmness, assurance, and confidence than before.

We put considerable emphasis upon the importance of the first few sessions as experiential grounding. Great effort is made to incorporate what Dr. Pecci stresses in his introductory talk about self-awareness and being fully conscious. As the class progresses, members are encouraged to reread the Pecci material every week because originally they probably were not ready to hear what was in it. Later they are encouraged to reread it once a month or until they feel they have understood everything that he is suggesting. As their knowledge and practical experience of the subject grow, counselors find that they are *understanding and experiencing* more and more of their own emotional selves. This, in turn, often leads to a desire to change some attitudes, habits, and ways of thinking. This voluntary step toward a change in lifelong habits and attitudes is often mentioned by grief counselors as their true beginning in becoming counselors.

The trend of the discussions underlines the questions—conscious or subliminal—that undergird our lives: Who am I? Am I safe? Will I survive? The perennial question arises, "How can we—how dare we—help others in their grief if we are bothered by the same questions?" By holding to the Pecci model, it is possible to become actively involved in knowing one's own identity and purpose in life. In session after session, we soon find ourselves concerned with the questions and implications for counselors in helping agencies like ours: What is our role? What can we do to help our clients and to keep ourselves comfortable? (See Chapter 19 on How Counselors Can Take Care of Themselves.)

In addition to the material that is developed during the class sessions, the class members are expected to read and listen to tapes on these and other subjects. The additional topics covered by their reading and listening are as follows:

1. Sociological changes in our society, religious rituals practiced in our society, the role of the religious leader in death and grief.

2. Present-day funeral practices—the funeral, mortuary, cemetery, and cremation costs; laws affecting disposal of the body.

3. Probate law in California, insurance and pension programs, services and benefits offered by Social Security and Social Services.

4. Community resources for referral and for resocialization of the client.

5. Nutritional aids for the bereaved family, relief of depression by diet and exercise.

More and more relevant material is now available to us; our library of books, articles, and tapes has grown, and our training, in turn, has benefitted. Our role-playing experiences are greatly enriched by the ready access to our own abundant case material.

## THE TRAINING CLASSES

The training classes extend over an eleven-week period, meeting three hours once a week. The classes are informal. The group is arranged comfortably around a table or in a circle, with eye contact available for everyone and a good deal of space beyond the circle.

## *Session 1*

Brief explanations are given regarding the mechanics of the class: classes begin and end promptly; unavoidable absences are excused when arranged in advance in order for a tape to be made of the session; there is a ten-minute break during each session; how and where books are charged out and returned and class responsibility for signing the class attendance sheet are explained. The relationship of the grief counseling program and how it fits into the work of the Crisis Center is explained, with ample opportunity for questions. A mimeographed sheet is distributed which outlines the material covered in each session and the required reading.

Each class member introduces himself/herself and tells how he became interested in joining the class and any other information he wishes to share. The first Relaxation Exercise is introduced.

### RELAXATION EXERCISE

This exercise is used at the beginning of each session and may be repeated during any session when the going gets rough. It is recommended for use at any time of tension, confrontation, confusion, or frustration. Just take three deep breaths before any such situation or following one, and buy time and relaxation *to act originally* rather than to *react* or perform in a routine or cliché kind of way.

Sit upright in the chair, spine straight, with the head held erect, abdomen tucked in, both feet flat on the floor, eyes closed. (At other times this exercise may be performed while walking, sitting, riding in a car, etc.) With the arms dangling to the sides, take a deep breath and then slowly e-x-h-a-l-e. During this exhalation, concentrate on letting go of the frustration, anxiety, sense of being hurried or angered, or the "garbage" that has collected in the mind from the day's activities.

Just let go of these things and feel them slipping down the arms, through the fingertips, and onto the floor.

Take another deep breath—then e-x-h-a-l-e—letting go again of the built-up tension, being aware as it slips away of r-e-l-a-x-i-n-g the muscles around the eyes, and face and mouth, the throat. . . .

Take another deep breath—then e-x-h-a-l-e—letting go some more and being aware of the relaxation of the muscles of the chest, abdomen, back, and legs.

Sit quietly for a short while, enjoying the freedom from these tensions, then slowly open the eyes.

*Goals:* To learn of the work of the Crisis Center; to become familiar with the meaning of crisis and how to deal with it; to become familiar with the dynamics of suicide.

Presentation of material on crisis and how to counsel in a crisis situation, given by the Executive Director of the agency.

Presentation of material on the myths of suicide; the dynamics of suicide, epidemiology of suicide; assessment of suicide potentiality and lethality (see Chapter 9 on Suicide).

Discussion of questions raised by class members.

## Session 2

This session is devoted to the Art of Living by Ernest F. Pecci, M.D. (text follows). This tape is listened to and followed by reading a transcript of the tape. At the conclusion of the tape, there are questions, agreements, and disagreements.

*Goals:* To become familiar with Dr. Pecci's ideas about self-awareness and being fully conscious; to begin to practice experiencing the emotional self; to begin to examine personal attitudes, habits, and ways of thinking.

To practice relaxation both as a preparation for absorbing new material and for dealing with personal conflicts and confrontations.

## THE ART OF LIVING
### Ernest F. Pecci, M.D.

I want to discuss with you the art of living meaningfully. Art is one thing, to be alive is another. In this complex world we live in today to live life meaningfully really takes a lot of heart. It is my conviction that every life has a purpose, that everyone here has a destiny or purpose. The joy of living comes from the discovery of that purpose. Our natural state is to know what makes one happy—to be loving, to be creative. When this is blocked, we suffer. If you look around in the streets where people are going to and fro, you see a lot of suffering faces, people desperately trying to get some place, to do things, trying to survive, to live their life without finding what it is all about. We all have different talents, too, which we are meant to use. If we are obstructed from the expression of those talents and we do not use those talents and, in the use of those talents, discover ourselves, we then suffer from what might be called existential guilt, which is the guilt of a wasted life. We see that in people even in their 30s.

The greatest gift that we possess, that has any meaning whatsoever, is our consciousness and what we do with that consciousness. Because we are led to believe that we are at the mercy of unpredictable forces, we feel overwhelmed all the time; we compulsively try to retreat into unconsciousness. Our society is filled with all kinds of things that allow us to be unconscious most of the time: things that take up our time and our consciousness as an escape. A lot of people today go through life struggling as if they are trying to get to the other end, trying to get through somehow —like getting through school—without taking the time to sit back and *really* experience it and *really* enjoy it.

There are a number of reasons why this happens, why we cannot seem to experience life. First of all, we are caught up in a complex world that drains all our energies. We are trying to cope all the time and there is never enough time, never enough money, never enough energy, just never enough, always a struggle. What lies behind this is the belief that maybe *we* are not enough. If we stop even for a moment we will fall behind. If we are not enough is too much to cope with perhaps the solution is to try to stop trying to satisfy the endless series of wants. Then we can begin to enjoy where we have been and where we are and learn to sit back and enjoy it.

We of the western world believe that in order to enjoy material things we have to own them. We have a certain orientation in terms of what security is all about. We are driven to satisfy in symbolic meanings things we believe we must have in order to survive—position, power, money, and constant searching for security. We dream of the day when we have everything. Enlightened men from the East talk about the day they can detach themselves *totally* so they can have peace and have *nothing*. That is where you find your freedom to be free; to be able to live life having nothing.

It is hard for us to believe that the art of living involves the ability to do nothing except to be appreciative, being an appreciative recipient of life itself, just being here to enjoy it, just sitting *being*. There are so many barriers to that that it is difficult to believe that all you have to do is just *be*. Just as a child discovers himself through his play, we discover ourselves through just living, through the process of our living. But in this process we call "living" something happens and we get stuck, we lose sight of ourselves.

There are a number of ways in which our consciousness becomes stuck. I like to divide our consciousness into the intellectual aspect—that part which reasons—and the other part which is the emotional part—that part which feels. Both are ways of being conscious. Both parts, when they are harmoniously blended, make life worth living, make life real. But as we get older, especially in this society, we overdevelop our intellect, and more and more we put down our feelings. We begin to do things without feeling what we are doing. We go through the motion of emotion, we go through the motion of living.

Everything that we see we make judgments about and, depending upon these judgments, we become either energized or we become depressed. For example, we can look outside in the morning and say, "It's raining! Great! We finally have rain and, boy, I love the rain. It's fresh and makes me feel good!" Or you can look outside and be depressed and say, "Oh, it's raining." I want to emphasize that because, like everything you perceive, you make prior judgments that decide your state of mind, that decide whether you are experiencing something that makes you want to run away from life. It has to do with attitude. In other words, are we looking to every little experience with the anticipation of a child, with excitement, joy or, as it usually happens as we get older, to every new experience with a feeling of being overwhelmed, being apprehensive, hoping we can hide from it, what next? Do we go through life sideways, ducking blows, wincing?

One of the effects of this is that gradually we cut ourselves off from this external world which we ourselves are actually creating. By our own attitudes we create this external world and then we become a stranger to it. We cut ourselves off from it, we defend ourselves from it, and then we run from it. Then we feel so guilty, we feel lost trying to survive in a world where we feel strange. We fill out patterns where we are constantly running from our own nightmares. At the same time, we are not looking at our own inner world; we ignore our inner world. Because the outer world is telling us who we are, we let the outer world be our mirror and so we do not look at the inner world either, and we are lost. There are some very strange things that the average person does when that happens. He wants to hide, right? It is strange the way people hide. Believe it or not, we hide behind one thing, we hide behind negative emotions. Our negative emotions allow us to be unconscious. It is difficult to be negative and to be aware and perceptive of what is happening. I want you to get in touch with how you do this.

Everyone of us carries some power or space consciousness around us that could become dark as a cloud, if we let it. This cloud is full of upsets—things we keep to make us comfortably upset all the time—the old, familiar upset pattern. These are kinds of things that keep going over and over in our mind, over and over again, to keep us from looking at what is happening right now—from being lost. Some of this includes regrets about the past. We keep thinking about the past over and over, walking in a daze in the present, or worrying about the future, nursing old resentments, grievances, just nursing them over and over again. "I should have told them this, I should have told them that." Feeling guilty. Going around feeling guilty is a way of escaping; so is mulling over unfinished business. These are kinds of things you should not be doing since you purposely have not done them. How many of you have letters to write, things like that? We constantly hold an inner dialogue with ourselves. Sometimes we even talk aloud to ourselves. We are like an imaginary authority figure. An authority figure is anybody we give authority to have some control over us. We are always shifting blame, justifying our behavior, denying our responsibility—and the dialogue goes on and on. Finally, we find ourselves saying, "How did we get here, walking in a daze, not aware of what is going on?"

Everyone has a characteristic negative feeling stage. I want to see if you can get in touch with your own. Let me just give you a few suggestions to see which one fits you. Some of you feel overwhelmed, others are always feeling lonely, full of doubt; others feel defensive, apprehensive or worried about what is going to happen next; feeling defensive about it. Some go around always feeling guilty, being worried. There are any number of these. Look at it and see whether one of these fits the characteristic state you have. You always find some reason in a perfect world to justify feeling that way, but the truth is you cannot adapt the years and no matter what situation you get yourself into you will eventually set it up so you will justify having that feeling. It is like the beginning patterns of negative thinking, patterns of being unaware, of living a lie, of running from life. Because we cannot stand feeling overwhelmed, we like to lock our consciousness into reruns on television, on compulsive activities where we can be unconscious and get away with it. We want to go on vacation where no one can interfere with our being unconscious. What we really need is to stop fighting consciousness, to be feeling, aware, right down there, just being there.

What is it we all want? What does everyone want? Acceptance, communication, love, right? What did you want from your parents? Think about a scene in which your mother and father in a particularly receptive mood made you feel good because they were communicating, accepting, loving. When somebody gives you that it is just there. You do not have to do anything. To be able to receive that you have to be doing a lot of things too. You cannot be too busy and have no time to communicate or to be receptive. The thing that counts is being still, being quiet. It takes more willpower to still the mind from its frenetic rambling than to solve most problems of the world, and it seems like we feel we have a mandate to go about solving all the problems of the world. We make all kinds of judgments about things not being the way they should be. It is a certain attitude. To walk on the street when we can look at the sun coming through the trees, how can we focus on the journey instead of the houses that are not well painted? We have the tendency to look at all the things that are not the way we want them to be. That keeps us quite a bit upset and helps give us a certain kind of energy that keeps us from being totally conscious and totally aware.

One of the biggest reasons for the resistance to being totally conscious, totally alive, totally aware is the belief that we are not capable, not entitled to have more than we have, that we do not deserve it. Everyone in this world has exactly what they believe they deserve. You might complain about it and you might wish you had more. You might be jealous of people who do not deserve it but have it anyway, but if you think about it, like water that reaches the lowest point, you eventually settle down to being right where you believe you deserve to be. If something really great happens to you, if you win some money, you would blow it, so you do not deserve it. In your relationships also—you marry a person you are unhappy with, that is the person you deserve to have, good or bad. So we lose touch with our true being, our true nature. The real joy in life is discovering ourselves, who we are, and that we can never be totally defined. It is the process of continual discovery. We can get an idea, as I said, watching children at play, discovering themselves and their capacities through their toys, being aware, totally right there, alive. We can watch their parents taking them through Fairyland, through Safeway, through the parks or whatever—unconscious, anxious, worrying about getting home, apprehensive, what's next? The inner dialogue of negativity creates a different kind of energy between the child and all that happens to the child when he becomes an adult. It is the same with us. We stop rediscovering ourselves through what we do and that takes all the meaning out of life.

How many of you can say to yourself, "I really love you"? We are constantly running away from life because somehow we feel unlovable. Just as we judge others harshly, we judge ourselves harshly becaus ewe are not patient with ourselves, we do not realize we are growing. When we are growing we make mistakes, just as a child falls a number of times before he can walk. Everytime we make a mistake or do something we judge wrong we feel we are unlovable and, because we feel unlovable, then we are afraid to open our eyes to be alive. We are afraid to deserve total enjoyment of living the peak experiences of having our emotions, our feelings and our rational intellect all harmonized. We cannot create harmony and security in our own bodies until we have created it or restored it within ourselves. In fact, everything that we do affects our state of consciousness. Every feeling toward our fellowman is a reflection of our feelings toward ourselves. Every crime is a result of self-hate. So the way you feel about people—it could be the bitterest or meanest ways you feel about anyone—know that sometimes you have this feeling about aspects of yourself. It makes you feel you are all by yourself. Look now at all your fears, your state of mind, how you keep your house, your room, your office—in fact, everything represents what is going on in your mind, how orderly it is, how harmonized it is. The state of our mind creates what is out there and what is out there reflects the state of our mind. We forget what we have created out there; we forget that we created it, and we become upset about it. Then we tend to run from it. We must let go of our pain, let go of our resentments, let go of our decisions regarding right and wrong and alter that dialogue from a constant flow of negative thinking to positive thinking.

If we were to look at a movie and project a picture of a person in about 2000 A.D. in a beautiful spacecraft, cruising along a beautiful countryside, we might say, "Wow! It's wonderful to live in that time." Then look at a person in a horse-drawn cart going through some scenery and we might say, "That's beautiful, that's peace, that's nice." It looks beautiful because we do not realize that the person may be going through an inner dialogue which ruins the whole thing. That person may not be alive anymore. Look at a picture of yourself in a beautiful new car driving through the countryside—but you are not seeing the countryside, you are driving fast because you are always late. Or stand on any street corner and watch the people with desperation on their faces. They are desperately trying to get somewhere to make sure the world is running right and if someone hesitates or does not move along, the whole process slows down and "What's happening?"

The inner dialogue keeps us all tense, keeps us from living, from being totally aware of what is there. We keep striving and striving, trying to get some place where we will feel secure and happy, and we are totally unable to receive what is here right now. So the fact is—this is something I want you to get—that you are never going to be any happier than you are right now. You bring your state of mind with you wherever you go. You might temporarily feel great when you are in your office, on the football team, or something like that, but in terms of being happy, right now you are as totally capable of that as you will ever be. Happiness does not depend on what happens out there; it does not depend on what you are going to accomplish or what you want to accomplish. Right at this moment, people cannot feel any different about you regardless of what you accomplish. If you give them acceptance, communication and love they will like you now as much as they ever will when you have finally accomplished that very thing you think you need to accomplish.

The universe is always saying "yes." There is a whole big universal consciousness out there saying "yes" to us, saying "yes" to life, "yes" to enjoyment, "yes" to joy. Meanwhile, we are always saying "no" to ourselves, we are always belittling ourselves, bearing grudges and resentments. Everything we want is out there for the asking but we are too busy to receive it. There is no limit put on us; there is no limit of the proverbial three wishes. Some people think that if you are a little bit happy now it will be balanced by being miserable later. I have seen people who could not be happy unless they were totally miserable, then somehow, they were not accruing any debts which led them to believe that when you are happy you somehow have to pay for it later.

I want to say that to be most joyful is to be selfish because when you are joyful you are living a natural state and you are spreading it, you are radiating it and the people around you become joyful. To be less joyful means you are selfishly preoccupied with something that is harmful. Our natural state is to be creative, to enjoy life, to be appreciative. You see we are not being appreciative so we are being selfish. If we cannot appreciate what we have now we can never appreciate what we may have later. Our universe out there is constantly being created by what we expect to see out there. People say, "I blew it." Sure you blew it, you created it. It has always been created by your expectations, whether it is gratitude or whether it is fear. There is nobody out there to fight, nobody out there to resent, nobody that needs to change for our sake, nothing we have to prove. Look at all the energy we put in it—trying to survive, trying to prove things, trying to find love, trying to fight for things to satisfy people's needs—when the only thing we really have to learn is to appreciate what we receive so we can enjoy it. We must learn to love so we will be able to receive. Most of us feel guilty and do not love ourselves because we are too busy to love; we are not giving out enough love so we do not feel we deserve it.

One of the most powerful affirmations I know is this one. (An affirmation is something we should say every day, particularly one you say over and over to yourself, to program yourself positively, affirming in truth.)   The powerful one I know is, "I choose consciousness." You have the right to choose whether to be aware or asleep. You may think you do not have free will in this world, but you do. You do have free will in deciding how you are going to react to what you are perceiving. You decide whether you are going to be happy. It is a free will decision—to be aware or unaware.

I want to give you a little demonstration to help you to see that we control our own moods. What we accomplish has nothing to do with our state of happiness. Why postpone it, why not be happy right now?   How many times do you think, "Someday, when I get clear I'll be able to relax and live. When I finally reach that pinnacle when I am secure, retired or rested, then I can thank people—right now I'm too busy. I can give attention to people who deserve my attention, if they're still alive." Why do you keep postponing it, as if we had to get somewhere first? We can make people as happy to be with us now as if we had accomplished great things. We can be as happy right now as we will ever be regardless of what is there to be accomplished.   I want to put you in a little state of awareness to give you an idea of what I mean by that.

Let us relax and take a deep breath and close our eyes. I want to use your dream world to put yourself in a state of emotional happiness. Just sit there breathing and relaxing and realize that the world can right itself now. You do not have to deal with anything, you do not have to cope with anything, or react; no one is going to challenge you in any way. All you have to do is just *be*.

Picture a shaft of light like energy coming from the top of your head down your spine, and glowing. Get in touch with the inner energy in your spine. Let it radiate, just feel that inner energy. Now get in touch with what it must feel like to be happy, with what it would feel like to have written a bestseller. How would you feel? Get in touch with that. Get in touch with the feeling of knowing that all people who know you love you, that you are acceptable. How does that feel?

Get in touch with the feeling of having made it—whatever that means to you—that you did it! Great! You know you made it! How does that feel? How does it feel to know inside, deep in your heart, that you are lovable? To know it is going to be all right, everything is going to work out perfectly, just knowing everything is going to be perfect, how does that feel? Let your emotions keep expanding, let them radiate. Feel joy. Let it radiate out. It is ok to feel joyful. If you feel that, keep your eyes closed a moment longer. I want to say to those who got in touch with that, if you keep that all the time, the outside world will re-enforce it, that what happens outside will gradually change so that you feel justified feeling the way you feel right now—blissful, content, and joyful.

While you have your eyes closed, I want to give you one more little exercise. I want you to think of any person in your life whom you feel a little bit negative about. Now get in touch with that emotion. In front of you, floating in the air, is a bar about a meter long. One end is a beautiful gold, the other end is black. The black is negative emotion, hate and resentment and the gold is total love. When you think about this person a line appears on this bar which shows how you feel about this person, somewhere on the darker side, somewhere on the lighter side. Make a conscious effort to push that bar up toward the yellow. Start thinking positive things about that person instead of judging motives, instead of feeling hurt, or experiencing resentments or guilt. Just say, "OK, I forgive you. All my grievances are put aside." Now push that bar up slowly. As it gets toward the yellow, say what what you have to say to push it towards the yellow. See what feeling you get as you raise your level of vibration, how the way you feel about other people affects what is going on inside you. You find you have it within your capability to see that person in a much more lovable light. The important thing is that it does something for you. You are capable of raising your own moods.

I want to say again that you can work on getting rid of this negative space that surrounds you. I want you to get in touch with that, everyone has it. You are always overwhelmed, you make excuses, but you are always that way, but you can work to get rid of it, just like getting rid of a habit. If you work toward a change of perspective, a change in your attitude, you put yourself in a state of how you would like to feel if the world were only different. The state I am describing is one of being alive, radiating. It is the positive emotions radiating that make you alive. Another definition of negative emotions is being unconscious, or dead and not alive. The trick resembles an electric light bulb, nothing happens; electricity does not flow through the wire until the bulb goes on.

Whatever you want to receive you have to create. If you want acceptance, communication and love, you create it and then it is part of your whole world.

Living means being able to see everything fresh and new. Every experience you have you are not judging as an old one but as something fresh, something new, like a child, not just saying the same old thing. If we drive our car through some beautiful scenery where there are trees and clouds in the sky and we say, "So what else is new?" we do not see things especially new. Living means being in the process of continually seeking a sense of the inner self, continually trying to define yourself in the context of what you are doing—being fully aware of yourself and what you are doing, enjoying yourself. It is a process. It means listening to the song in your heart and knowing that it is there in the heart of your neighbor also. If your neighbor does not have a song in his heart it is because he is not listening to it. He needs to learn something more about the art of living.

Class members discuss how their own experiences have validated what they have just heard. The discussions are usually far-ranging, and the trainees are given wide latitude to speak freely and to question repeatedly. Some of the most frequent questions that arise are the following:

1. Does each life have a purpose?
2. What purpose would we place on such a list?
3. What are the barriers to "being" that exist in our lives?
4. Does our attitude affect our ability to experience what is available to us? How? Examples?
5. Do we have a "pattern" for accepting or rejecting life experiences?
6. What are some of our common patterns for "upsets"?
7. How does such a pattern fit into a feeling of guilt?
8. Do you think feeling unlovable contributes to our fears and other negative emotions? How? Examples?
9. What is your usual state of mind? What other states are present from time to time?
10. Do you think we all want acceptance, communication, and love? How has the lack of these affected our attitude toward life?
11. Do you feel being aware and conscious of what we feel, do, and think of ourselves affects our acceptance by others?
12. What are some of the negative patterns we recognize in ourselves? What ones would we like to rid ouselves of?
13. What are some of the positive emotions we would like to radiate?
14. Can these be built into our attitude toward life? How?

Following this discussion, a short list of rules, written by Dr. Pecci, is given the class. These rules are important adjuncts to the role the trainees are preparing themselves for—*a better, less stressful life for themselves and an open, self-awareness method of performing the work of a counselor without becoming either manipulative or judgmental.*

1. Be kind—in thought, word and action to everyone. Do not let pass an opportunity to be generous, to be charitable, to be loving and forgiving. Above all, be kind in your judgments and criticisms of others.
2. Be honest. Do nothing in the slightest way to incur the slightest guilt. Guilt accrues a debt that is paid off heavily by anxiety and compromised action. By your words, never distort truth in the slightest way. Do nothing, say

nothing, think nothing which you would not wish to be broadcast in the open streets. All persons pay too high a price for selfish thoughts and behavior.

3. Be responsible by doing day by day those things which are set before you to be done. Do not, out of pride, commit yourself to a burdensome yoke. A wise person has time for both work and play. A properly balanced schedule of time allowing for work, sleep, relaxation, and contemplative thinking is a responsibility of us all. Generally we pay too high a price for the worldly goods we accumulate and for the small satisfactions of our passions. We can accomplish nothing save what is set before us in very small packages day to day.

4. Don't fight back. It is hard to resist the impulses of defense and revenge. But all rage is negative and, generally, destructive. Provocations are meant to be testings, and a self-righteous response destroys what lessons might otherwise be learned. The guiltless person, the one who judges not, the contemplative one, does not fight back.

5. Take care of your body. Give thought to the proper care of the body, to the selection of proper foods, to the proper rest, to daily healthful activity and exercise in fresh air, and to proper elimination.

*Recommended Reading*\*
Benson, Herbert, *The Relaxation Response.*
Frankl, Viktor E., *Man's Search for Meaning.*
Koestenbaum, Peter, *Managing Anxiety.*
Mayeroff, Milton, *On Caring.*
Rogers, Carl, *On Becoming a Person.*

**Session 3**
Relaxation Exercise; questions that arose during week; additional questions regarding the Pecci material; presentation of material on loss and separation, and grief reactions (see Chapter 1

---

\*Unless indicated otherwise, recommended books are to be read in their entirety. These and more complete references related to the training program are fully cited in the Bibliography and Suggested Readings.

on Understanding Grief) ; presentation of the grief personalization Exercise.

*Goals:* To develop new insights from the Pecci material.

To seek new insights about personal attitudes and life patterns.

To share experiences resulting from the use of the relaxation exercise.

To become familiar with the importance of previous losses and separations in any grief situation.

To become familiar with common grief reactions.

### GRIEF PERSONALIZATION EXERCISE

Free your laps of papers and books. Make sure you are comfortably seated with the back held erect, abdomen tucked in. Close your eyes. Take a deep breath and force the exhalation of noisily pushing out the breath in two heavy puffs, mouth open. Hold the exhalation for a moment or two. Repeat twice. (The following is spoken in a slow, calm manner:)

With your right hand search for the pulse on your left wrist. Find the pulse and be aware of its rhythm. Now bring your heartbeat into your consciousness. Go with this beat for several moments, feeling its throb permeate your body, always there, constantly at work. . . .

Now be aware of your taut abdomen. Imagine you see its processes, the slow, steady movement of the assimilation of your last meal progressing to its inevitable end—the assimilation and feeding of those nutrients to the necessary parts of your body and the working and reworking of the residual materials into wastes that will be expelled at the appropriate time. Let your awareness inch slowly along with this process, visualizing in any way you wish the dispensing of this nourishment to your body and the sense of well-being and satisfaction that accompanies this ongoing routine of digestion and elimination that your body performs. . . .

Center your attention now upon your medulla oblongata, that elongated, balloonlike mass in the brain that is located at the back of your head. It is directly related to the spinal cord and its accompanying network of nerves, muscles, etc. See it as a kind of control board for the central nervous system. Visualize this mass at the back of your head and follow and be aware of your spinal column and the network of nerves that lies around it. Perhaps you see the control board as a clear white light with its signals running along the arterial routes of the nerves, which should be visualized as appearing in different colors. Stay with this visualization for a short period of time. . . .

Let the mind wander outside the body now. In your mind's eye, see the moon and the stars and a broad expanse of sky. Listen to the silence of the night. Now bring into your consciousness the feel of rain or snow and wind upon your face. Get the freshness of the smell of them. Discover the taste of salt in your mouth from the air blowing in from the sea. . . .

Let your mind wander again. This time look with your mind's eye at the faces of those who have been of significance to you and your life. See your parents, relatives, friends and neighbors, teachers, writers, artists and musicians, colleagues, and especially your loved ones. Let this parade of faces pass slowly in review. Catch each person's special beauty—the smile, the handclasp, the twinkle, the warmth of embrace, the humor—whatever characteristic is his or her special hallmark. Feel your joyousness as you respond to the beneficence of their gaze. Hold on to this feeling of community and comradeship. . . .

Now by an act of will, send a message from the control board to your arms that you wish to raise them high above your head. (Raise your arms now.) Send a message to your voice box to speak words that you have learned, miraculously, as an infant or a small child. Say these words in your native language, "Oh, how wonderful it all is!" Repeat these words once more. (Long pause.) Now lower your arms and rest your hands in your lap. Sit quietly. . . .

You have just experienced some of the obvious support systems you have for living. Most of these systems are so automatic you hardly give a thought to them. Others are so taken for granted you neglect to avail yourself of them, even though they are always available; many of the words you can say are never spoken. . . . Now open your eyes.

(Continue speaking in a calm and assured manner.)

Take your notebooks and write down some notes on what I want you to do during the coming week: Choose one of the persons who passed in review before your eyes. Fantasize this person whom you love, respect, and cherish as dead; all of his support systems for being alive have failed.

During the week, I want you to work with this fantasy. Select a time and a place for this activity, which will probably take the better part of a half-day. Choose a time when you will be uninterrupted, quiet, and free to express your emotions. Write down whether this death was natural, accidental, suicidal or homicidal; write down the cause of death also. Did this person die in infancy, childhood, youth, adulthood, or in advanced age?  Were you taken by surprise by this death?

Write down what you *feel* upon learning of this death.  How are you reacting to this feeling?  What emotions are uppermost in your consciousness?  What words do you find yourself saying?  What unfinished business do you have with the deceased?  What social support systems do you have now that this person is gone from your life?

I want you to know that this exercise is safe for you to do.  No harm can come to you or to the person whom you fantasize as being dead.  If you feel any anxiety during the week, just take three deep breaths and relax; let go of your anxiety, and begin the exercise again.  You will have strong feelings, perhaps, that you do not wish to do this exercise.  The stronger the feelings you have against doing the exercise, the more apparent it is that you *need* to do it.  The purpose of the exercise is to simulate the emotions that arise when a loved one has died; this exercise can also relieve you of previous anxieties about old losses and separations.  You may be very angry with me for suggesting that you do this.  That's all right.  Go ahead and get angry with me.  I give you permission to be as angry with me as you need be.  I can handle your anger; dump it on me.

There are likely to be other side effects of this exercise in addition to becoming angry with me.  You may be irritable and petulant with your friends and family; you may cry unexpectedly or have nightmares or wake up crying.  These are normal and should not upset you because you are expecting them to happen.  However unpleasant the exercise is, stick with it.  You will be glad at the end that you did.

Next session, and perhaps part of the following one, will be devoted to your account of what happened, what you felt, how you handled it, what it means to you now that it is over.  Your account to the class may either be written, put on tape, or given orally.  Your account is private and confidential, neither your tape nor your written notes will ever leave your hands.  We are all in this together, and we trust each other to respect our privacy, our sorrow, anger, whatever.

Now take three deep breaths and relaxxxxxxxxxxx.  Let the anxiety of this assignment slip away from you.  Now, relaxxxxxxxxxxxxx.  Everything is going to be all right. . . .

Questions about the assignment are answered at this time. Each one is given thought and careful reply.  The class is adjourned when the questions subside.

Some of the most frequent questions asked about loss and separation and grief reactions are the following:

1. What other common losses and separations come readily to your mind?
2. What losses and separations have given you trouble or still give you trouble?
3. What can one do to help grieving persons who are depressed or disoriented?
4. How do people *react* to medications at the time of a traumatic experience? What can a counselor do if the client has already been given medications for sedation?
5. How can one deal with the problems of "resocialization" of a client without seeming to take charge of his life?
6. Has anticipatory grief ever affected you? How?
7. What does a counselor do when it is apparent that the grieving style of "mummification" is taking place?
8. How does a counselor deal with denial of suicide, grief, need to grieve?
9. Are there differences in degree of grief if the deceased is a spouse, child, relative, or friend?
10. Is there such a thing as "unhealthy" grief?

## Recommended Reading*

Gorer, Geoffrey, *Death, Grief and Mourning.*
Grollman, Earl, *Talking About Death.*
———, *Living When a Loved One Has Died.*
Parkes, C. Murray, *Bereavement.*
Schiff, Harriet S., *The Bereaved Parent.*
Switzer, David K., *The Dynamics of Grief.*

## Session 4

Relaxation Exercise—with concentration upon being aware of what we shall be hearing, maintaining an attitude of quiet listening, empathy, and encouragement for allowing tears to be shed and the expression of whatever emotions stir the one presenting his account of the Grief Personalization Exercise (see Session 3); response to the Grief Personalization Exercise. This session is de-

---

*These references are listed completely in the Bibliography and Suggested Readings.

voted entirely to experiential material.

*Goals:* To simulate the emotions that arise when a loved one has died.

To reactivate old losses and separations and to experience the fear, anger, or other trauma of this loss.

To experience the anxiety of dependency.

To express the emotions this personalization evokes.

To share these private emotions with the class.

Allow the Grief Personalization presentations to be given on a voluntary basis. There will be some persons who feel that they must be among the first to do this, others will prefer to come on later. Allow them to arrange the sequence in which the accounts are given. A box of tissues is a handy item to have on hand.

Each person needs to feel that there is plenty of time. When long silences occur, let them happen without interruption. This can be a heavy experience for the trainees, so allow time for each to relate the experience at his own pace and with intervals in which to recover poise before moving into another phase of the experience. Only when it is clear that the speaker is completely finished with either one phase or the whole presentation—depending upon his acknowledgment that there is no more to follow —is the class encouraged to ask questions, to console, or make other overtures of comfort and friendship.

The discussion that follows each presentation is likewise unhurried. The flow of discussion among the trainees and the person involved is often a uniquely valuable teaching and learning aid for everyone. If the discussion occasionally drifts away from the one who made the presentation, that is all right, for it permits him to pull himself together again.

This pattern is followed, sometimes, with breaks for relaxation exercise, for coffee, or a bit of walking about, until all the reports for that session have been heard. Some may need to be heard in the following session, particularly if some trainees had a hard time getting into the exercise and do not feel satisfied with what they have done. Allowing them to rework their presentation during the coming week is an important concession to make.

This exercise is *the most important* personalization *exercise of the entire training session.* The trainees are impressed by the number and kinds of things they "got into" during this experience and their ability to share such personal matters with others. Moreover, the atmosphere of the entire class is changed. From here on there is much more sharing, caring, and trusting. As a result of sharing this experience with the group, the trainees now *know what confidentiality is all about.* Now they are released from any previous doubts they had and can talk about anything; they *know* they are in a "safe house," which is the ambience we also want to create for our clients.

This is a time of considerable anxiety for the leader. There is no way one can predict what will take place in these sessions, so varied are the experiences of the trainees. Their grief reactions are often acute and intense. As they relive their experiences, they are caught up in fresh attacks of guilt, anxiety, and fear that did not occur when they fantasized this at home. Consequently, it is important for the leader to remain calm, accepting, sympathetic. It is a time for the leader to put *his* humanity on the line.

Questions frequently asked at this time are
1. What were some of the reasons you gave yourself for *not* doing this exercise?
2. Did you feel this exercise would harm the person you chose? How did this affect you?
3. You have mentioned different kinds of guilt you experienced. How did this guilt affect you?
4. Do you think your guilt feelings were helpful to you?
5. Was it easier for you to recognize someone else's guilt than to recognize your own?
6. How did you deal with your guilt feelings?
7. At what point did you cry the most?
8. Do you know what you were crying about? For whom?
9. Were you angry with me for laying this assignment on you?
10. Where else did you direct your anger?
11. How did you express your anger?
12. What response did you hope your anger would have? For yourself, for others?

*Recommended Reading\**

    Gibney, Harriet H., *"What Death Means to Children."*
    Grollman, Earl, *Explaining Death to Children.*
    ———, *Talking About Death.*
    Kastenbaum, Robert, "The Kingdom Where Nobody Dies."
    ———, *"Time and Death in Adolescence."*
    Laing, R. D., *The Politics of the Family.*
    LeShan, Eda, *Learning to Say Good-By.*
    Satir, Virginia, *Conjoint Family Therapy.*

The Meditation Fantasy (see Session 8) may be used follow-ing the Grief Personalization Exercise if the instructor feels it would be useful in reducing unusual stress encountered at this time. If the topics of funerals, wills, and how to attend to one's own unfinished emotional business arise, be flexible enough to allow these topics to be introduced (See Chapter 15, Funerals).

### Session 5

Relaxation Exercise; conclusion of presentations on Grief Personalization; presentation of didactic material on children and grief (see Chapter 2, Children and Grief); presentation of didac-tic material on guilt and anxiety and aggression (see tapes listed in Recommended Reading); discussion. Hand out mimeo-graphed material on anger (see Appendix for questions on anger).

    *Goals:* To become familiar with the theoretical material deal-ing with children and grief; how children grieve, how they react to grief; the importance of the grieving process for children and adolescents.

          To become familiar with the theoretical material re-garding guilt and anxiety and aggression. To be-come familiar with the roles these emotions take in grief for adults and children. To see how we handle these emotions ourselves.

    *Questions:* The reader is probably wondering by now how these questions are responded to in the classes. If the question

---

\*These references are listed more completely in the Bibliography and Suggested Readings.

deals with a *personal* experience or emotion of the trainee, the discussion centers on alternative ways of dealing with the question, based on our present knowledge of the didactic material. If the question deals with a *client's* experience and emotion, these alternatives are summarized and fleshed out by additional case material from our files which illustrate how the client reacted, difficulties encountered by the counselor, and the final resolution of the question.

Often these questions come up *before* the presentation of the didactic material. If they do, the trainee is either asked to wait for the basic presentation when most of the problem areas, including the one he raises, will be discussed, or if the question is sparked by the trainee's *personal need,* it is answered briefly at the time it is asked, with a mental asterisk placed on it for further discussion when the topic is regularly scheduled for presentation. No trainee's question regarding some personal experience or emotional reaction is ever disregarded or left dangling. Relating the trainee's problem to those of the clients confirms and strengthens the "new spirit" of motivating the prospective counselors to understand themselves in order to work honestly and understandingly with the client.

1. How has this personalization exercise affected you?
2. Did you share it with anyone at home, elsewhere? What was the reaction?
3. How can you deal with your own emotional unfinished business?
4. What plans or ideas do you have for your funeral, memorial service, etc.?
5. What change do you now see needs to be made in your own life?
6. How does one find out what a client has told his children about death?
7. How does one go about suggesting another way for parents to present this death to children?
8. If guilt is something we wish to rid clients of, how do we do that?
9. What fears did you have about death as a child?

10. What are your strongest fears about death now?
11. Why is guilt such an important factor in children's grief?
12. How can you tell if a child is feeling guilty?
13. How can a young child express his feelings when a family member has died?
14. What behavior does one look or ask for that indicates a child is upset or disturbed?
15. Is there an age where death is harsher for children?
16. Do parents resent being told what to do for their children at the time of a death?
17. What does one do if parents do not want to be helped and you feel the children need help?

*Recommended Reading\**

Crammer, Leonard, *Up From Depression.*
DeRosis, Helen A., *How Women Can Overcome Depression.*
Engel, George, *"Emotional Stress and Sudden Death."*
Mitchell, Ross, *Depression.*
*Newsweek,* "Coping With Depression."
Rubin, Theodore, *The Angry Book.*
Seligman, Martin, *"Fall Into Helplessness."*

*Tapes*

The Thin Edge, *Depression.*
——, *Aggression.*
——, *Anxiety, the Endless Crisis.*
——, *Guilt.*
American Association of Suicidology Symposium, "Understanding and Treating Depression." Two tapes from the New Orleans Meeting, 1978.

**Session 6**

Relaxation Exercise; discussion of questions on anger (see Appendix) ; presentation of didactic material on depression (see Chapter 4, Depression) ; discussion of depression chart (see Ap-

---

*These references are listed more completely in the Bibliography and Suggested Readings.

pendix B) ; Depression Fantasy (following) .

> *Goals:*  To learn how we express and manage our own anger.
> To become familiar with differences between endog-
> enous, reactive, and neurotic types of depression.
> To learn basic steps counselors can use to relieve de-
> pression, such as diet, exercise, resocialization.
> To fantasize/relive a depressive situation.

*Questions:*

1. How does one "gently provoke" anger?
2. Can a client express too much anger?
3. What can be done when the anger goes on and on?
4. How can you sometimes determine over the telephone whether the client is depressed?
5. What can be done about this depression?
6. Do we continue to see clients who are seeing a therapist?
7. Do anger and depression go together?

The purpose of the fantasy which is given below is to provide the trainee with a means of imagining, experiencing, reliving a depressive situation.

### GUIDED FANTASY ON DEPRESSION*

We are going to take a trip together, a guided fantasy trip. I hope that at its conclusion we'll all have something to share from this trip together. Before we begin, however, I want each of you to know that if at any time along the way you do not wish to continue the trip, please open your eyes and just relax until the rest of us join you.

Please find a comfortable position now. Close your eyes and relax. Take a deep breath, hold it, let it out slowly, and relaxxxx. Another deep breath; hold it . . . now let it out slowly and re-laxxxxxxxxxx. . . . Feel all your tensions just flow away; let go of the tightness in your scalp, the little muscles around your eyes and eye-lids—just let go and relaaaaxxxxx. . . . Loosen the tension in your neck and those knots there in your back, at the center of your shoulder blades. Just reeeeelaxxxxxxxxxx all over.

I want you to visualize yourself going to a carnival. There is noise all about—difficult games of chance, a shooting gallery, ohhhh! and

---

*This personalization exercise was written by Julia Beard, a former grief coun-selor.

there's a sword swallower.  Up ahead there is a building that catches your eye.  It's advertised as the House of Illusion—seeing is not always believing.  Do come in and see what surprises are in store.  Step right up.

You decide you'll go in and see what there is to be seen.  You take out a coin and pay the entry fee, and then you step through the door.  Inside is a dimly lit hallway and as you walk along it veers to the left and you enter a room.  The room is full of mirrors, only they are mirrors such as you have never viewed yourself in before.  As you look into one mirror, you seem to dissolve around the edges; you are solid in the middle but all fuzzy in outline.  You turn and look into another mirror.  On this one, your body remains as you are accustomed to seeing it reflected back to you, only your head has become waaaay stretched out and thin, almost two feet in height.  Another mirror reflects back an image in which your head seems to disappear into your body, and your body is shaped like a triangle.  Now you seem to catch your reflection in one more mirror, only when you take a closer look, there is no reflection at all.  With a sense of having enough of such distorted reflections, you are glad to see a doorway leading from the room, and you go through it.

Following the hallway further along, you enter another room.  As soon as you enter  this room, you feel as if you have stepped into some sticky, gluey substance.  It is very hard to lift your foot from the floor and to take another step forward.  You do take another step, and again your foot sticks in this gluey substance.  At the same time, you feel an invisible pressure all around you.  It is not heavy; yet you feel weighted.  Your movements are slowed to the speed of a slow motion film.  There is no way you can hurry across the room.  You must continue at this very slow and weighted pace, your feet kept from any rapid movement by the sticky substance all over the floor.  You continue across the room to another doorway.  Once through, your feet move with ease and the pressure weighing your body is gone.  With a sense of freedom, you continue down the hallway.  Only now, instead of leading you into another room, the hallway begins to go up.

You find yourself climbing a rather steep incline, and just when you feel that you'll make it over the top, you slip and slide back toward the bottom.  You stand up and start climbing again, and again you slip back.  It seems as if the hallway at this steep point conspires against you, and you are unable to reach the top.  You try again and again.  A feeling of hopelessness begins to come over you, for you feel you will never progress over the top, and you are unable to turn around and return the way you came for the doors are shut to any other rooms. One more time you begin your climb up the steep hallway, once more you slip and feel yourself sliding backwards. Only this time there is a difference. Instead of sliding directly back you slant off to the side and find yourself in an entirely different room. You have never before seen a room like this one.

All around this room, on every wall, are small TV screens. Each one is in operation, and you find that you recognize what is on each screen. On one you see your husband/wife or a dear companion. Another shows your children, while yet another shows special friends who mean much to you. Happily you recognize that another screen shows scenes from a relaxing vacation, still another shows your home, your place of work. Another, family member. You realize that you are surrounded by images of all you hold dear; these are the persons who bring meaning and richness into your life. Just as you settle down to enjoy the flickering scenes that surround you, one goes dark, and then another, yet another. Soon all screens are dark and you are alone, in the dark, cut off from everyone and everything.

The blackness of the room seems much darker, and you begin to feel a sense of isolation. Certainly there must be a door out of this room. But you do not find one. For a moment you begin to feel trapped, and you lean against the wall. Unwittingly you touched a hidden release button, and the four walls disappear and you are out, outside!

At first, after that darkness, you are uncertain of what you are seeing and feeling. You seem to be surrounded by green, a deep blue green color. As your eyes adjust, you realize that you are in the midst of a redwood forest, and you sense a deep stillness all about you. The sunlight filters down through the trees. There is a feeling of deep stillness and peacefulness in the green of the redwood trees reaching high over your head like a cathedral. Your nerves relax. All your anxieties, nervous tensions, and self-doubts just melt away and disappear. You sit down at the base of one of the giant trees, feeling the quiet and peacefulness, along with the soothing coolness of the color green. You are filled with a healing feeling of self-worth as a human being. You notice a tiny green seedling of a redwood tree at the base of the giant tree that rises above you. While it seems small at this moment, it too has the capacity for growth and one day will give forth through its green beauty and giant strength the same feelings of peace, quiet, strength, and security that you now feel as you sit here in the midst of the redwood forest.

When you feel like opening your eyes and rejoining us in the room, you may do so. No hurry. Just relax and open your eyes when you are ready.

*Recommended Reading**

Belz, M., *"Is There Treatment for Terror?"*
Cain, Albert, *The Survivors of Suicide.*
Farberow and Shneidman, *Cry for Help.*
Klagsbrun, F., *Too Young to Die.*
Kubler-Ross, E., *"Questions and Answers About Death."*
Lunde, Donald, *"Our Murder Boom."*
Seiden, Richard, *The Campus Suicide.*
Seyle, Hans, *Stress Without Distress.*
Wolfenstein, M., *Disaster.*

**Session 7**

Relaxation Exercise; presentation of didactic material on sudden death; presentation of material on the role of the coroner's unit and the autopsy (see Chapter 13, The Coroner's Role in Grief Counseling and Chapter 14, The Autopsy) ; the need for accuracy and confidentiality in filling out our forms used in reporting all forms of sudden death; the Epidemiology of Homicide (see tapes listed) . Hand out mimeographed material on homicide and sudden death. Availability of material from Chapter 15, Funerals.

Goals: To learn the dynamics of sudden death, its modes, and how it complicates grief.

To relate modes of sudden death to functions in the coroner's unit.

To become familiar with state laws regarding what kinds of deaths become coroner's cases; the state law regarding autopsies; the purpose of the autopsy; what we can learn from it; how to use this material with our clients.

To become familiar with the responsibilities of confidentiality vis-à-vis our clients, the coroner's unit, and our agency.

To become familiar with laws, provisions, and costs of funerals.

---

*These references are listed more completely in the Bibliography and Suggested Readings.

*Questions:*

1. How does sudden death affect grief?
2. Does one try to shorten a prolonged grief?
3. What is meant by abnormal grief?
4. What is the role of the counselor in a sudden death?
5. Why is an autopsy performed? Who performs it? What can we learn from it?
6. Does our client have access to the information we have?
7. Do we tell him things in the file he seems not to know about?
8. What do we do if the client keeps asking for information we do not have?
9. What do we do if the client wants information we should have but do not?
10. What abbreviations and codings do we use?
11. What different kinds of traffic fatalities do we categorize?
12. What special information regarding lab tests is important for us to know?
13. What can we learn from the photographs?
14. What are some of the important things to know about denial?
15. What is special about the anger displayed by those bereaved by suicide and homicide?

*Recommended Reading**

Weisman, Avery D., *On Dying and Denying,* Chapters 3 and 5. Complete readings already recommended.

*Tapes*

Allen, Nancy, *The Epidemiology of Homicide.* Two tapes from the American Association of Suicidology Meetings, New Orleans, 1978.

Shneidman, E., *Death the Enemy.*

---

*These references are listed more completely in the Bibliography and Selected Readings.

### Session 8

Relaxation Exercise; presentation of didactic material on stress (see Chapter 3, Stress) ; use of the stress rating scale; presentation of didactic material on suicide among the young, teenagers, and the elderly (see Chapter 10) ; the Meditation Fantasy. (See Appendix C for the Holmes-Masuda Stress Rating Scale.)

*Goals:* To become familiar with the basic material about stress.

To rate our own stress level and discuss how it can be lowered (if it is high) ; application of this rating scale to client stress and how to help clients.

To become familiar with the dynamics of suicide among the young, teenagers, and the elderly.

To experience the Meditation Fantasy; to see how it can be used as a tool for lessening stress and for coming to grips with other personal problems.

*Questions:*

1. How does one help a client who is undergoing a great deal of stress?
2. What does one do if the client is an alcoholic?
3. What kinds of psychosomatic diseases or illnesses do the bereaved have?
4. What kinds of symptoms do they have that can become serious, if overlooked?
5. What is meant by "resocialization" of the bereaved?
6. What are some commonly used referrals each counselor should know?
7. Why do we not give a referral right away?
8. How do we determine whether a client is suicidal?
9. What steps do we take with suicidal clients?
10. What is the most important thing we can do for suicidal clients?
11. What special precautions do we take with the elderly to alert us to their suicidal feelings?

## THE MEDITATION FANTASY

(The Meditation Fantasy is presented to trainees as one way to lessen their own stress. It helps relieve tensions due to negative confrontation, anger, anxiety, or fear. This fantasy is not intended to be used with clients except in situations where the counselor has had more experience with the fantasy than this class exposure.

This fantasy may be presented following the Grief Personalization Exercise if the instructor feels it would be helpful in reducing unusual stress encountered at that time.)

Sit quietly for a few moments. Close your eyes and take three deep breaths. . . . With your eyes still closed, I want you to think of a quiet, beautiful place where you feel comfortable. This can be a place you know, have visited, or it may be an entirely imaginary place. This place needs to have visible a broad expanse of sky and the presence of water—either a stream, lake, the sea, or some other body of water.

Look around at the place you have selected. Notice its beauty, feel its serenity and quietness begin to envelop you. Let your eyes sweep across the sky, across the water; then let your eyes notice what is nearer at hand—the trees, shrubs, vegetation.

*This place,* which you have selected and which you are now viewing with new interest, *is your sanctuary.* This is a place that is known only to you. It is your own private place where no one can interrupt you or come to without your permission. This is a place where you can come as often as you like to obtain peace, quiet, serenity, and to regather yourself, to recharge yourself, to see and experience the events in your life in a new perspective.

In this place of yours is also your guide. This guide is unique: he is the only person you know who has your best interests at heart. Sit quietly now while your guide makes himself known to you. This guide may be a man or a woman and may be dressed in an unfamiliar way. Sometimes you may have more than one, or from time to time these persons may be interchangeable. Sharing this sanctuary with a guide may come as a surprise to you. Actually, you have had this guide since early childhood, and he has been always with you, helping, guiding, watching, and getting to know you. Some people call this guide by different names: a guardian angel, an imaginary friend, we just call him our guide.

Don't be alarmed if you do not see his face or if he does not at first speak to you. Just be aware of his presence and leave the rest up to him.

Now your guide is moving toward you and taking you by the hand. He leads you to the body of water in your sanctuary where you remove your clothing and slip quietly into the water. Feel how cool and refreshing the water is, how relaxed it makes you feel. You smile at your guide. He motions you to come out of the water; you dry yourself and put on the white garments that he holds out to you. Both of you return to the central part of your sanctuary.

Here the guide asks you to put on the ground before you all the anger, resentments, grudges, fears, and anxieties you have brought with you to this place. Think about this for awhile and begin to unload these negative thoughts and attitudes on the ground before you. Your guide sweeps them into a pile and ignites them. They burn until they are completely consumed, leaving only a small bit of ashes that the light breeze begins to blow away. Then you see that wherever these ashes blow to the ground, a small, white flower springs up.

You have now a sense of well-being and relaxation that is new to you. Get in touch with how good it feels. You are relaxed; you are no longer anxious about anything; you don't feel hurried; you seem to have all the time in the world. You can experience this feeling any time you wish by coming here to this place you have selected as your sanctuary.

Here no one can come without your permission. Your guide will see to that and protect your privacy. But you may invite anybody you wish to share this place with you; just inform your guide whom you have asked. Here you can bring your friends and loved ones, or you can bring persons with whom you are having difficulties. Here you can experience their reactions in a safe place and perhaps gain new insights into their attitudes and behavior that you need to know.

You can come here when you are troubled or in doubt about whatever it is in your life that makes you feel upset, disturbed, uncomfortable. Here in this quiet place you may find new approaches to your life, new sources of strength, new understanding about the people and events in your life.

No harm can come to you in your sanctuary. It is perfectly safe to come to as often as you wish. Using this place you have selected in no way interferes with any religion or philosophy you may have. Your guide is in your sanctuary to help you maintain your integrity.

Whenever you wish to leave this place, just announce to your guide that you are leaving. Mentally surround yourself in a luminous white light, then slowly count to ten and slowly open your eyes, and you will be back in this place of reality again.

Return now by saying farewell to your guide. Feel the warmth of the white light as you wrap yourself in it. Count slowly to ten. Now open your eyes, and here we are again.

*Recommended Reading\**

Lester and Brockopp, *Crisis and Counseling by Telephone.*
Complete readings already recommended.
Complete tapes already recommended.

**Session 9**

Relaxation Exercise; grief counseling paper work and forms (see Appendix) ; review of specific of grief counseling (see Chapter 11, How to Counsel the Bereaved) and how to care for oneself (see Chapter 19, How Counselors Can Take Care of Themselves) ; role playing the initial call, based on actual cases (see cases following) .

*Goals:* To become familiar with the forms used in our office for reporting sudden deaths, reaching the next-of-kin, and reports for subsequent client sessions (telephone or home visits) .

To review the specifics of how to counsel the bereaved and how to care for oneself during these sessions.

To learn, by role playing, how to make the initial telephone call; develop rapport with client, answer his questions, and make an appointment for a home visit.

*Important Steps to be Included in Initial Telephone Call:*
1. Identify yourself and the agency.
2. Did you receive our letter?
3. Answer their questions.
4. May I help?
5. Assess willingness for seeking help.
6. Are there children, etc.?
7. Arrange to call again or to make visit; be specific, when and where.
8. Obtain permission to follow up.
9. Obtain information on directions to their home.
10. Be sure they have our telephone number and know our availability.

---

*This reference is listed more completely in the Bibliography and Selected Readings.

## BE FRIENDLY, PLEASANT — LISTEN

Samples of cases for role playing to learn the basics of the telephone call and the home visit:

1. Mrs. Jones is a middle-aged, divorced, employed woman whose aged mother was killed when struck by an automobile. She was walking down a country road after 10 PM. The autopsy report showed the alcohol content of her body to be 0.09.

2. Mr. and Mrs. Jones are the parents of a fourteen-year-old girl who was killed while driving their truck into town. She swerved to avoid a bump and overreacted. The truck crushed her and slightly injured her sister.

3. Mr. Jones is the husband of a woman who suicided by overdose. One of the young children discovered her body. She had never made an attempt before, but she had a long history of depression.

4. Mrs. Jones is a young black woman whose infant was stabbed to death by the person who broke into her house and raped her. Mrs. Jones lives alone; the father of her child assumed all responsibilities for the burial needs of the child.

5. Mr. and Mrs. Jones are the parents of a toddler who drowned in their swimming pool. One of the older children found the body.

6. Mrs. Jones is the mother of a four-year-old child who was killed by an automobile while playing on the street adjacent to the roadway. She and her husband are separated. This was their only child.

7. Mrs. Jone's father shot himself after his wife overdosed. There are four grandchildren under the age of fourteen.

8. Mrs. Jones is the young wife of a man who drowned in a boating accident while fishing with friends. His blood analysis showed an alcohol content of 0.2. Mrs. Jones has two small children and is five months pregnant.

*Recommended Reading*

Complete readings and tapes already recommended.

Review notes on counseling the bereaved and taking care of oneself.

### Sessions 10 and 11

Relaxation Exercise; use of agency file of community resources for referral and resocialization of the client; role playing the initial telephone call and the first visit (using cases just mentioned).

*Goals:* To become familiar with the agency's file of community resources for referral and resocialization of the client.

To learn the use of the resource book the agency provides counselors for home use.

To learn how to obtain additional community information for the client.

To learn through role playing how to conduct a counseling session, the importance of listening, asking questions.

The material presented in these eleven sessions is sufficient for counselors to begin work with clients. Additional skills, techniques, and theories are discussed in the ongoing training classes which meet for two hours twice a month. Ongoing training also provides opportunities for counselors to seek additional help, criticism, and suggestions for dealing with their clients, as well as an opportunity to work through any anxieties they are experiencing.

The recommended reading for the class sessions is just a beginning. Grief counselors continue to read widely and to discuss books and journal articles pertinent to this field. Our library of books and tapes is actively used and continuously growing. (When recommended readings have been completed, continue to read books from the library. Donations of books to the library are gratefully received.)

*Chapter 19*

# HOW COUNSELORS CAN TAKE CARE
# OF THEMSELVES

IT HAS BEEN said elsewhere in this book that persons who do grief counseling day in and day out encounter problems in clients and in themselves that are not experienced by others who do grief work on an occasional basis. The training program has been designed to prepare counselors for meeting hundreds more grieving persons than are ordinarily seen in any individual practice. This training program enables counselors to develop *within themselves* qualities that surpass a knowledge of the theory and practice of counseling the bereaved. Every effort has been made to allow counselors to realize this goal by emphasizing the following:

1. Our role as a helper is not to *do* things for the client one is helping but to *be* things; not to try to train and change *his* actions but to take responsibility for ourselves and to train and change our reactions.

2. Each person needs to open himself to continued growth. As a counselor changes his negatives to positives, his fears to faith, his contempt for the client to respect for the client's potential, his rejection of the client to release with love, his dominance to encouragement, his panic to serenity, his false hope (self-centered) to real hope (other-centered), his rebellion of despair to the energy of personal revolution, his driving to guidance, and his self-gratification to self-understanding—as one changes in such ways as these, he can change the world about him and all the people in his world for the better. *If we change, all the others seem to change also.*

3. We need to continue to work on the art of listening. Listening requires more than just hearing, the heart is involved also. It is an act of kindness and of love. More is required than just being compassionate. Many compassionate people make poor listeners. They are too eager to solve problems, to give advice and solutions before they have the whole story. We must learn to listen in silent sympathy. In this way, one can show he cares and accepts the client for what he is (Mayeroff, 1971).

4. We need to develop the ability to suspend moral judgment. Morality does not enter into the picture of grief at all.

5. Since death and dying happen to all of us, we begin to think of our own death without becoming upset about it. Thinking about how one wants to die is another way of saying, "I think about how I want to live." It was Leonardo da Vinci who said at the end of an exciting, creative, and turbulent life, "I thought I was learning to live, but all the time I was learning to die."

6. Since the preponderance of survivors of death are children, we begin to learn to explain death to a child. *Become* as a little child by imagining you are a child who has experienced a sudden death. Unless you become as a little child, you will not grasp the basic emotional trauma of death or be effective with your client. This approach uses a great deal of role-playing.

In spite of the efforts made in the training program to prepare counselors for the intensive kind of counseling they do, there are times when the counselors encounter situations in their own lives or with their clients that make it imperative that they be given special consideration. At times like these, counselors are given either lightened case loads or are put on a three-week to three-month leave. Persons experiencing a marriage dissolution or a death are given a year's leave. No counselor is encouraged to visit a client unless he is in both good health and good spirits.

Various parts of the training program deal with both theoretical material regarding the stressful emotions (anger, anxiety, depression, fear, etc.) and experiential exercises dealing with them. The role-playing sessions are replete with experiential situations involving stressful emotions. To make the role playing even more informative to prospective counselors, the summary that follows is presented *before* the first role-playing session. The summary is also given at intervals during the ongoing training sessions to remind experienced counselors of what they have previously learned about helping themselves cope with the stressful emotions.

## NEGATIVE EMOTIONS

The material that follows is based on Dr. Pecci's *The Art of Living* (See Chapter 18). This article is given a prominent part in the training program, is read and re-read by the trainees, and is re-examined in many discussions of class topics related to grief work.

The negative emotions are the one set of factors which keep one from feeling good about the performance of *any* task. Let us take anger, for example. Anger can destroy good feelings whether it is expressed or not. Anger drains strength and energy from the body. (A good energy field is important for the performance of any task.) When the energy field is drained by anger it produces a low energy state which exposes one to thoughts of despair and helplessness or depression.

Anger is *unreal* for it is an imitation of a state we have adapted, copied or identified with by long association with our parents or other role models in our lives. We have practiced this anger-role since childhood: We did not get what we wanted as a child, so we got angry. We found that our anger—

1. gave us physical pleasure, hence it was an indulgence;
2. could be used as a defense against fear, and in the process of using it defensively it greatly inhibited our use of free will;
3. relieved us from guilt and depression, and we used it also to mask other emotions we could not handle, such as grief and love.

## What Can Be Done About Anger

What can we do to pull ourselves out of this angry morass of bad feelings? By a daily examination of a renewed approach to life we can perform what has to be done. We need to write down in detail our angry *reactions* and thoughts and then read them the following day. Perhaps this reading will tell us what we need to know about ourselves, such as

   a. What produced this susceptibility to anger?

   b. Do we recognize that every miserable state is one we cause in order to rework our miserable states of childhood? Can we wean ourselves from this immature game?

   c. Can we throw away this childish script in order to reach a level of being where everything seems ordered, progressive, and where it ought to be? Try to become free enough to perform daily responsibilities and tasks as though participating in a slow dance. In this way, we can attune ourselves to the flow of events. We will not be *trying* to do something, *we will be doing it.*

Make an honest effort to examine anger by using the following suggestions:

1. Do not bury the anger. Face it and face honestly your reaction to it. Spend enough time examining it so that you realize what you have to learn from your angry reaction.

2. Examine your attitude today toward life. What is your disposition? Are you irritable, grouchy, cheerful? Are you affable, congenial, benevolent with others?

3. Are you making a conscious effort to keep out anger, jealousy, competition, pride, etc.? These reactions are characteristic of the ego that needs reworking. These characteristics lead only to a dead end.

### Upsets in Our Lives

Let us look at some of the patterns of upsets in our lives that produce anger:

1. Something of momentary irritation ("The damn flies are bad this year," "It's too hot, it's too cold," "Why does she *always* come barging in just when I'm settling down to do something really productive?") is interfering with our routine. This interference triggers us in a way that makes us feel deprived of our free will. We feel "put down," threatened. This loss of self-esteem is accompanied by a *body feeling*—a gut reaction—that this is something we cannot handle, we are going to be defeated

by it.

2. We begin to have the fear of survival; that is, we worry about money, our job, about moving or changing jobs, or losing a significant other by divorce or death. In short, we anticipate that someone in our lives is not going to fulfill our needs or expectations (a broken contract in marriage, loss of a big business account, or a prolonged strike with which we do not identify).

3. We find ourselves at odds with our world, not playing the role we had anticipated, and being humiliated in the process. We look for others to blame for this state of affairs. These targets for our anger are easy to find because they are already the candidates toward whom we direct our personal grudges and resentments. It gives us pleasure to allow these grudges and resentments to accumulate now because they underscore our belief that "They won't listen; I'm right and they won't listen."

Are you minimizing the upsets in your life or feeding them? The upsets listed below affect our disposition:

1. Worry about people.
2. Unfinished business keeps one busy and gives a sense of self-importance. A backlog of unfinished business drains the body's energy level.
3. Survival worries—money, fear of physical harm or real violence, worry about the future or any of our unmet needs and expectations. Survival worries can also lead to cop-outs, such as alcohol, drugs, acting out, emotional blocking, escaping from it all, dismissing the whole thing. When there is a strong compulsion to eat, drink, use drugs, act out or escape into work, suspect it is likely that you are *trying to escape from the basic upsets in your life.*

You can deal with the upset patterns in your life by convincing yourself that

1. The timing is right to experience what you are experiencing.
2. You can get trapped in preconceived ideas about reactions to these upsets. Do something different; react in a new, fresh, original way.

3. You can take responsibility for those who helped trigger your anger. Make them feel considered and important. You do not have to fill their needs, but you do have to acknowledge them. There is no way that getting rid of the person who triggered this upset can help you. Accept that person, try to understand him better, even acknowledge that you need to validate *his* anger or complaint.

4. Set limits to the behavior of others ("Wait a minute" or "That's too much"). Allow them to blow off steam, but let them know you are allowing it. Refuse to settle for a masochistic solution. Such a solution may relieve your guilt, but it leads to additional upsets.

5. What you reject in someone else is generally put back on you.

6. It is important to examine your suffering. By looking at it and the whole pattern of your present state, you can end by changing it and using it for attaining a new level of personal development and spiritual growth. The challenge comes always from the outside, but the battle to resolve it takes place within.

7. You can be an example of emotional maturity and responsiveness. If you do not show fear, hurt, pain, or rejection, the person you resent will respond in kind. Adjust your attitude to one of understanding rather than anger.

8. You can practice giving without manipulation or placating. *They are hurting,* so give!

9. You do not need to give reasons for not being upset. Give reassurance and raise the client-person to a higher emotional level. What you say is unimportant. What is important is your attitude and reassurance. Ease the wound, calm him down.

There are two important tools that counselors have been given to take care of themselves: the use of the Meditation Fantasy (Chapter 18, pp. 245-246) and Dr. Pecci's short list of rules: Be kind; be honest; be responsible; don't fight back; and take care of your body (Chapter 18, p. 228).

Consistent and repeated reviews of this material can be useful for counselors, both prospective and experienced. If counselors can feel comfortable with themselves, they can do much to give comfort and assurance to their clients. Working to change ourselves is a job that is never completed.

## REFERENCE

Mayeroff, Milton, *On Caring*. New York: Perennial Library, 1971.

*Appendix A*

# HOW YOU FEEL ABOUT ANGER*

PERHAPS a good beginning in discovering how to deal with anger in your clients is to find some clarity on your own attitudes about anger in yourself. The following questions, some of which come from Theodore Rubin's *The Angry Book,* may help you learn more about your personal response to anger.

Try spending a couple of hours in a quiet, relaxed environment where you will not be disturbed. Work through this list. Each class member will be given time to comment on his pattern of anger and his reactions to his pattern.

1. What lessons about anger did you learn from your mother? Your father? Verbal messages? Nonverbal messages? What *statements* were made about anger to you as a child?
2. What was the proper response from you? When your parents were angry? When you were angry?
3. What values about anger that you learned as a child do you now, as an adult, accept? Which ones do you reject?
4. How do you respond to normal anger? Your own? Others? Are you controlling?
5. Do you think there is justified anger? Unjustified? What is your response? Are you defensive?
6. When was the last time you got *very* angry? Did the world fall apart?
7. Do you become angry easily?
8. Do you have friends with whom you can get angry, or are your friendships based on a "don't make waves" approach?
9. Do you lump all anger together or do you know the differences in intensity and kinds of anger?

---

*To be used with Session 6, Chapter 18, pp. 238-239.

10. Do you sometimes use anger as a mask for fear?
11. Are you aware that healthy anger functions in the service of real closeness?
12. Do you always rationalize your anger?  Do you rationalize your joy, your love?
13. Are you afraid of loud voices?  Your own?  Others?
14. When you feel angry, do you *talk about* being angry without affect, or do you *get angry*?
15. What is your time lapse between feeling angry and showing anger?
16. Do you show anger when you feel it or do you save up until you have a garbage bag full?
17. How do you show your anger?  Do you make ample use of your voice, gestures, strong language?  Are you aware of the purpose of strong language?
18. Can you "think standing on your feet" when angry?  Do you always think of what to say later, when it's too late?  Why?
19. When you get angry do you smile and laugh it off or go to another room to cry?  If so, why?
20. When angry, do you sulk and give others the silent treatment?
21. Do you save anger for your enemies only?
22. Do you avoid controversial discussions because you are afraid that strong feelings may slip out?
23. Do you see a difference between animated discussions involving disagreement over issues—politics or religion—and heated arguments over personal matters?
24. How do you react when a friend talks angrily about someone or something related to you?  Do you try to relate the anger to yourself?  Do you assume your friend, because he is angry, is really angry with you?
25. Are you afraid to speak up because you may "hurt" the other person?  Do you want to hurt him?  Are you afraid he will hurt you?  Do you think you could survive?  Could the relationship survive?
26. Do you resent others because you feel you cannot be honest with them?  Have you tried?

27. Are you a perpetual peacemaker, forcing people directly or through manipulation to shake hands when they are not ready to?
28. Do you think there is such a thing as anger that cannot be resolved because of problems that cannot be solved? What do you do about it?
29. How are you at forgiving and forgetting?
30. When you are angry, do you break things? Throw things? Yell?
31. Can you apologize when you realize after an argument that you were disproportionately angry? Do you take responsibility for your own anger, or is it always the other person's fault?
32. Do you carry grudges? Often? For how long?
33. Do you insist that others, particularly children, have more control than you yourself are capable of?
34. Do your jaw and face hurt because you keep your teeth clenched?
35. Are you overly drawn to sadistic people? Fights? Violent books or movies? What is the state of your regular anger outlets?
36. Do you listen as closely to others when they are delivering angry messages as when they are delivering loving ones? Why not?
37. Do you force others to yell and scream to get your attention or do you listen carefully when a problem is discussed in matter-of-fact tones?
38. Are all your conversations in calm, cool, intellectual terms? Are they ever warm, dramatic, voluble?
39. Have you honestly not been angry for years?
40. Are you aware that sympathy and empathy for a person do not preclude anger at him?
41. Are you aware that the biggest dangers are not feeling and not knowing what you feel?
42. Are you afraid of the pain behind anger? Do you always attempt to diffuse it? Do you always make jokes to distract people who are angry? What do you think would happen if you didn't?

43. Do you usually know when you feel angry?
44. Do you often fall into the "compassion trap"? Do you suppress anger with understanding?
45. How do you estimate the depth of your reservoir of anger?
46. Are you chronically depressed? Fatigued? Accident prone? Have you frequent headaches? Do you think these could be the result of anger turned inward?
47. Are you vindictive towards people who have hurt you?
48. Do you feel that being universally loved is the only way to be safe in the world?
49. Do you feel that any show of anger will alienate someone else?
50. How do you feel about taking risks other than getting angry?
51. What kinds of situations always make you irritated? Furious?
52. Can you remember the time in your life when you felt most angry? What was it about? How did you show it?
53. Do you attempt to deny angry feelings while attempting to make the other person feel guilty?
54. Are you familiar with healthy, nonviolent methods to release the tension of anger from your body?
55. Do you know that when you allow yourself to feel angry and to express it, you then have the choice of doing so when it is appropriate, and with whomever you choose?

Anger and hatred are not the opposites of love, but indifference is.

*To be used with Session 6, Chapter 18, pp. 238-239.

# COMPARISON OF DIFFERENT TYPES OF DEPRESSION*

| | *ENDOGENOUS DEPRESSION* | *REACTIVE DEPRESSION (GRIEF)* | *NEUROTIC DEPRESSION* |
|---|---|---|---|
| Cause | A primary disturbance in the structure and function of brain and nervous system; also toxicity, infection, injury. | A specific, meaningful loss of a loved one, of material things, or of an opportunity; displacement; loneliness. | Exhaustion of adaptation; severe prolonged stress; inadequacy; personal strivings; unresolved conflicts; chronic anxiety, in anger. |
| History of depression in family | Common, other family members have had depressions. | No relationship to depression in family. | Illness can sometimes be related to depression in the family. |
| Onset | Fairly rapid (1–4 weeks) and seems to come from nowhere. | Sudden, and specifically related to a loss. | Gradual, over several weeks. Seems to build up slowly. |
| Nature of depression | Usually of agitated type with restlessness and "nervousness." | Tends to be retarded and slowed down. | Mixed: sometimes slowed, other times agitated. |
| Intensity of depression | Most often severe and with time gets worse. | Mild to moderate but occasionally severe. Tends to remain steady. | Fluctuates from mild to severe. |
| Duration of depression | If untreated, may last 3–24 months then improve, but can remain chronic indefinitely. | If untreated, may last 3–12 months. Improves with time, but may remain chronic. | Varies, depending on personality. Many remain chronic with periods of improvement. |
| Tendency to recurrence | Common, with varied periods of remission. | Only with a new loss. | Frequent relapses and remissions. |
| Mood | Worse in the morning and tends to be better in the evening. | Constant feeling of sadness. Little variation in intensity. | Unpredictable; person blows "hot and cold." Usually optimistic in morning and depressed toward evening. |

|  | ENDOGENOUS DEPRESSION | REACTIVE DEPRESSION (GRIEF) | NEUROTIC DEPRESSION |
|---|---|---|---|
| Sleep | Falls asleep easily but awakens at 4 to 5 AM and cannot fall asleep again. | Difficulty in falling asleep but then sleeps through. | Fitful. Awakens readily, sleeps, reawakens. Morning sleep is deep. |
| Arising | Awakens tired and jittery, with no sense of rest. Feels miserable in the morning. | Awakens with some feeling of repose and refreshment. | Awakens with a heavy head but hopes for a good day. |
| Eating | Little interest in food, and rapid weight loss. | Sluggish appetite but can be coaxed to eat something. Mild weight loss. | Varies. Some show loss of appetite; others are compulsive eaters and gain weight. |
| Crying | Intense, spontaneous, and agitated crying spells. | Steady tearfulness and quiet sobbing associated with ruminations over the loss. | Some crying spells, or the person may say, "If I could cry I'd feel better." |
| Emotional control | Generally, none. Person needs to be managed at all times. | Person retains enough control to manage self. | Varies from well-controlled to unmanageable. |
| Self-esteem | Completely lost. Feeling of emptiness in the self. | No loss of self-esteem. Feeling of emptiness in environment. | Fluctuates between high and low. |
| Anxiety | Present and tends to increase as illness progresses. | Present, but tends to diminish with time. | Constantly present and may rise to panic states. |
| Expressions of fear | Usually intense; mostly fear of being alone. | Occasional mild fears about "what will happen." | Multiple fears about present and future constantly voiced. |
| Ability to make decisions | Absent. Almost totally indecisive. | Retains ability to decide on important issues. | Indecisive on important matters. Positive decisions on minor matters. |

| | | | |
|---|---|---|---|
| Ability to concentrate | None, especially when agitated. | Can concentrate some when distracted from loss. | Varies, but mostly poor. |
| Memory | Poor. | Poor. | Variable and unreliable. |
| Sense of responsibility | Mostly lost. | Retained. | Usually diffused. |
| Contact with reality and the surroundings | Usually poor. Distorted judgment, lack of orientation, and inadequate perceptions are common. | Good. Oriented to environment and reality situations. | Varies. Judgment colored by level of hysteria and perceptual distortions. |
| Delusions | Very common. Mostly paranoidal; ideas of poverty, self-depreciation, unworthiness. | Uncommon. If appear, usually as feeling of remorse or guilt about contributing to the loss. | Varies. If present, usually of persecution, oppression, or guilt; occasionally, of unworthiness. |
| Tendency to alcoholism | Strong, especially if illness is prolonged. | Some tendency, which disappears when mourning stops. | Strong tendency to drown sorrows in drink. |
| Fatigue | Chemically tired but shows some energy when agitated. | Constant weariness is present. | Feelings of "no pep" but occasional bursts of energy. |
| Attitude to fatigue | Does not care. | Accepts the weary feeling. | Feels shame; embarrassed at failure to mobilize self. |
| Reserve of strength | Little to none. | Can be mobilized and person pulls self together for periods of time. | Very little, but person may "push" for brief intervals. |
| Physical symptoms | Many complaints about stomach, bowel function, chest pains, headache. | Few complaints. If present, mostly about stomach and chest. | Innumerable vague complaints, such as headache, tightness in chest, indigestion, cramps. |

|  | ENDOGENOUS DEPRESSION | REACTIVE DEPRESSION (GRIEF) | NEUROTIC DEPRESSION |
|---|---|---|---|
| Sexual interest | Complete loss. | Usually diminished, but in some instances may be aroused. | Fluctuates. Generally diminished, but person may try to "prove" sexual competence. |
| Interpersonal relationships | Disturbed; the person withdraws. | Usually greater feelings of closeness and dependence. | Often destroyed; relationships probably poor all along. |
| Family attitudes to patient | Removed; treat patient as a nuisance and problem. | Empathetic, warm, and protective. | Mixed feelings; family quarrels with patient. |
| Suicidal thoughts | Present and intense; also expressions of fear of death. | May be present and intense. | Frequently present but covered up by desire to live. |
| Suicide attempts | Common and should be anticipated. Determined suicidal attempts relate to desire for relief from mental pain. | Occasional but meaningful suicidal attempts to relate to loss of hope. | Frequent suicidal attempts appear to be attention gathering, but person hopes to be rescued. |

*To be used with Session 6, Chapter 18, pp. 238-239.
From Leonard Crammer, *Up From Depression*, 1971. Courtesy of Simon and Schuster, New York.

# *Appendix C*

# LIFE EVENTS RATING*

| | Life Event | Point Value | Your Score |
|---|---|---|---|
| 1. | Death of a spouse | 100 | _____ |
| 2. | Divorce | 73 | _____ |
| 3. | Marital separation | 65 | _____ |
| 4. | Jail term | 63 | _____ |
| 5. | Death of close family member | 63 | _____ |
| 6. | Personal injury or illness | 53 | _____ |
| 7. | Marriage | 50 | _____ |
| 8. | Fired at work | 47 | _____ |
| 9. | Marital reconciliation | 45 | _____ |
| 10. | Retirement | 45 | _____ |
| 11. | Change in health of family member | 44 | _____ |
| 12. | Pregnancy | 40 | _____ |
| 13. | Sex difficulties | 39 | _____ |
| 14. | Gain of a new family member | 39 | _____ |
| 15. | Business readjustment | 39 | _____ |
| 16. | Change in financial state | 38 | _____ |
| 17. | Death of a close friend | 37 | _____ |
| 18. | Change to different line of work | 36 | _____ |
| 19. | Change in number of arguments with spouse | 35 | _____ |
| 20. | Mortgage over $10,000 | 31 | _____ |
| 21. | Foreclosure of mortgage or loan | 30 | _____ |
| 22. | Change in responsibilities at work | 29 | _____ |
| 23. | Son or daughter leaving home | 29 | _____ |
| 24. | Trouble with in-laws | 29 | _____ |
| 25. | Outstanding personal achievement | 28 | _____ |
| 26. | Wife begins or stops work | 26 | _____ |
| 27. | Change in living conditions | 25 | _____ |
| 28. | Revision of personal habits | 24 | _____ |
| 29. | Trouble with boss | 23 | _____ |
| 30. | Change in work hours or conditions | 20 | _____ |
| 31. | Change in residence | 20 | _____ |
| 32. | Change in recreation | 19 | _____ |
| 33. | Change in church activities | 19 | _____ |

## Appendix C (Continued)

| Life Event | Point Value | Your Score |
|---|---|---|
| 34. Change in social activities | 18 | _____ |
| 35. Mortgages or loans less than $10,000 | 17 | _____ |
| 36. Change in sleeping habits | 16 | _____ |
| 37. Change in number of family get-togethers | 15 | _____ |
| 38. Change in eating habits | 15 | _____ |
| 39. Vacation | 13 | _____ |
| 40. Christmas | 12 | _____ |
| 41. Minor violations of the law | 11 | _____ |
| Your Total | | _____ |

*To be used with Session 8, Chapter 18, pp. 244-247.

From Thomas H. Holmes and Mineru Masuda, Psychomatic Syndrome, *Psychology Today*, April, 1972.

# FORM USED TO REPORT DATA
# GATHERED AT CORONER'S OFFICE

---

A    Hom.
Auto   Indus. Ac.
C-V   Suicide      GRIEF COUNSELING OF CONTRA COSTA
Drn   Special (over)           COUNTY
SD    Indeter.

Found by:

Name_____    Spouse_____
      Last            First           Initial    Family_____

Address_____    Friend_____

Profess._____

Day, Mo, Date, Year_____ Time_____A/P    Cleric_____

Neighbor_____

Hospital Duration_____ Place of Death_____    Other_____

Sex_____ Age_____ Race_____ Educa._____ Religion_____

(NO P C J M O)

Marital Status  U  M  D  S  W  CL     How long suicidal this time?_____

Current Behavior  NO  SA  ST  SB  SI     *Stress, Anger, Depression, Medication, Other*

Current Method NO  OD  GSS  C  H  U     Type gun_____ Location_____

Type and amt of Drugs_____    Amt. Alcohol_____ Amt. CO Saturation_____

                _____
                _____
                _____
                _____

Autopsy_____ Limited examination & why_____ Photos, drawings, etc.

_____

Previously suicidal_____ Prior attempt  0  1  2    Prior most Lethal

                                  NO  DO  GS  C  H  J  U

Current Therapy_____ Previous Therapy_____ Multiple Therapy_____

267

**High Risk Syndrome:**

| | |
|---|---|
| Alcoholic | Stress |
| Med. Illness | Anger |
| Depression | Depression |
| Homicidal Comp. | Medication |
| Living Alone | Other |
| Marital Diff. | |
| Multiple Marriages | |
| Drugs | |
| Others (Specify) | |

Suicide Potential   Low_____   Medium_____   High_____

Occupation_____ Welfare_____ Unempl._____ Income $L$   $M$   $H$

*Grief & Mourning Info:*

    Children in home & ages_____

    Children away from home & ages_____

    Previous suicides in family or group_____

    Other_____

Coroner's File #_____

Census Tract #_____

Volunteer_____ Date_____ Use reverse side for additional info.

*Appendix E*

# SAMPLE OF LETTER SENT TO NEXT-OF-KIN, ETC.

Dear

Please accept the sincere condolences of the Contra Costa Crisis and Suicide Intervention Center on the loss of your

In a few days one of our Grief Counseling members will phone to make an appointment for a visit. It is our hope that we can be of help and comfort to you at this difficult time.

Grief Counseling for families where a death has occurred is part of this Center's community service. Both services are free of charge for Contra Costa residents.

If you feel an immediate need, please call our Crisis Line, 939-3232, and ask for a Grief Counselor. We are here to help you.

Sincerely

Grief Counseling Committee

PD:bbm

*Appendix F*

# FORM USED TO REPORT TELEPHONE COUNSELING

Ac      Homi                                                                         7/1/76
Auto    Ind. Ac
C-V     Suic        GRIEF COUNSELING OF CONTRA COSTA COUNTY
Drn     Indeter.
SD

Client's Name_____     Date_____ CR File #_____

Address_____     Deceased_____

Phone_____                    Date of Death_____

# Children at home, ages, sex_____     Resources:
                                                Religion_____
_____        Associations_____

Length of call_____        Friends_____

Suicide in Family_____        Relatives_____

_____        Employment_____

                                                Other_____

Volunteer's Name_____

*Comments:*

## Appendix G

# FORM USED TO REPORT HOME VISITS

Ac    Hom.                                                            7/1/76
Auto  Ind. Ac
C-V   Suic          GRIEF COUNSELING OF CONTRA COSTA COUNTY
Drn   Indeter.
SD

Date_____

Client's name:_____         Family Resources:
                                              Religion_____

Address_____                Associations_____

Phone_____                  Friends_____

No. of children in home, ages:_____

_____           Relatives_____

No. of children out of home, ages:_____ Employment_____

_____           Special Abilities_____

CR File #_____              _____

Relationship to deceased:_____      Other_____

Deceased_____

Date of Death_____

Suicide in Family_____

Date of First Visit_____

Mileage_____

Revisit Requested_____

Client:  Symptoms of stress, depression, anxiety, medication:_____

Deceased:  Symptoms of stress, depression, anxiety, medication:_____

Clue Words:_____

Legal Status or Other Complications:_____

Comments:_____

**Use Reverse Side for Additional Comments**          Visitor:_____

## *Appendix H*

# FORM USED TO REPORT ANNIVERSARY INTERVIEW

12/5/77

The Anniversary Appointment

Client_____ CR#_____

Phone Call, Visit, Mileage_____

Date_____

Counselor_____

1. How have the children in the family reacted during the year?

2. Do the children and the adults speak naturally and comfortably about the deceased?

3. Does the client feel there are any problems with any particular child?

4. Is the client in good health? The children?

5. Is the client satisfied with his own grief progress during the year?

6. What is the client doing now? New job, relocated, new friends, remarried, etc.

7. What does the client think was the hardest thing he had to do during the year?

8. What does the client think was the most help to him during this time?

9. Are there other persons — children, friends, or neighbors — who could have benefitted from our service but who were unknown to us?

10. What suggestions has the client concerning how we could have been more helpful? What did we do that "bugged" you?

## *Appendix I*

*SUMMARY SHEET USED FOR ALL CLIENTS*

GRIEF COUNSELING        YEAR:_____

| VICTIM: | CORONER # | NEXT OF KIN (CLIENT) |
|---|---|---|
| TYPE: | VOLUNTEER CALL: | ADDRESS: |
| AGE: | REFERRED BY: | |
| DATE OF DEATH: | | PHONE: (R)_____ (B)_____ |
| LETTER SENT: | ASSIGNED TO: | |
| RELATION: | RE-ASSIGNED: | RELATION: |
| OTHER: | | OTHER: |

| DATE | FIRST PHONE VISIT | SUBSEQUENT PHONE VISITS | FIRST HOME VISIT | MILEAGE | SUBSEQUENT HOME VISITS | MILEAGE | NO. OF CHILDREN | CONTAGION | ANNIVERSARY | REPORT RESPONSE |
|---|---|---|---|---|---|---|---|---|---|---|
| | | | | | | | | | | |
| | | | | | | | | | | |
| | | | | | | | | | | |
| | | | | | | | | | | |
| | | | | | | | | | | |
| | | | | | | | | | | |
| | | | | | | | | | | |
| | | | | | | | | | | |
| | | | | | | | | | | |

# BIBLIOGRAPHY AND SELECTED READINGS

## AGED

Burgess, E. W., *Aging in Western Societies*. Chicago: U Chicago Pr, 1960.

Carp, F. M. (Ed), *The Retirement Process*. Public Health Service Publication No. 1778. Bethesda: National Inst Child Health and Human Development, 1968.

Cumming, E. and W. E. Henry, *Growing Old: The Process of Disengagement*. New York: Basic, 1961.

Dangott, Lillian R. and Richard A. Kalish, *A Time to Enjoy, The Pleasures of Aging*. Englewood Cliffs, New Jersey: P-H, 1979.

Downs, Hugh, *Thirty Dirty Lies About Old*. Niles, Illinois: Argus Comm, 1979.

Kimmel, D. C., *Adulthood and Aging*. New York: Wiley, 1974.

Studies and case histories in man's adulthood, with good sections on aging, retirement, death, and bereavement. Illustrations. Very good.

Lipman, A. and K. J. Smith, "Functionality of Disengagement in Old Age," *J Gerontol*, 1968, p. 23.

Schoenberg, B., A. C. Carr, D. Peretz, and A.H. Kutscher, *Psychosocial Aspects of Terminal Care*. New York: Columbia U Pr, 1972.

Scoggins, W. F., "Growing Old: Death by Installment Plan," *Life-Threatening Behavior, 1*:2, Summer, 1971.

An examination of the disengagement theory of aging of Cumming and Henry, 1961 and Lipman and Smith, 1968.

Sinick, Daniel, *Counseling Older Persons*. New York: Human Sci Pr, 1977.

Good sections on dying from terminal illness, taking one's life, bereavement, and trends and issues.

Worcester, A., *The Care of the Aged, the Dying, and the Dead*. Springfield: Thomas, 1961.

## AUTOPSY

Casey, Thomas M., Donald Niswander, Donald E. Sanborn, and Barnard Segal, "Psychological Autopsy, The Life History of Kip," *Bulletin of Suicidology*, No. 8, Fall, 1971, pp. 85–89.

Deikel, Stuart M., "The Life and Death of Lenny Bruce: A Psychological Autopsy," *Life-Threatening Behavior, 4:3,* Fall, 1974.

A student paper in a Death and Suicide class at the University of California, Los Angeles, 1973.

Shneidman, Edwin S., *Deaths of Man.* New York: Penguin, 1974.

Excellent chapters on the medicolegal aspects of death and the psychological autopsy.

Ungerleider, J. Thomas, "Psychological Autopsy: A Case Commentary," *Bull Suicidology, 8:*90–91, Fall, 1971.

Weisman, Avery, *The Realization of Death.* New York: Aronson, 1974.

A fine book on the psychological autopsy; not for the general reader.

Weisman, A., and R. Kastenbaum, *The Psychological Autopsy.* New York: Behavioral Pubns (Community Health Journal Monograph 4), 1968.

Good. Not for the general reader.

## BOOKS FOR CHILDREN

The Amazing Life Games Company, *Good Cents — Every Kid's Guide to Making Money.* New York: Houghton Mifflin, 1974.

Fascinating for children. Excellent layout, typography, and illustrations. How-to-do-it details for forty-four ideas; based on actual experiences.

Anderson, Phoebe M., *Mr. Red Ears.* Philadelphia: United Church, 1960.

Suitable for three-year-olds. The story of the death of a pet turtle.

Aradine, Carolyn, "Books for Children About Death," *Pediatrics, 57,* No. 3, March, 1976.

Bartoli, Jennifer, *Nonna.* Chippewa Falls, Wisconsin: Harvey, 1975.

After Nonna's funeral her family bakes cookies from one of her recipes. There are laughter and tears while they share memories of her. Ages seven to nine.

Brown, Margaret W., *The Dead Bird.* Reading, Massachusetts: A-W, 1958.

Little children find a dead bird and bury it. Much later they return to bring flowers and sing. Ages four to seven.

Carrick, Carol, *The Accident.* New York: Seabury, 1976.

Christopher's dog is hit by a truck. His grief is quick and strong. Beautiful illustrations. Ages five to ten.

Cleaver, Vera and Bill Cleaver, *Grover.* New York: Lippincott, 1970.

Grover's mother died when he was ten. He learns to share his good and bad emotions with his friends. Ages eight to twelve.

DePaola, Tomie, *Nana Upstairs and Nana Downstairs.* New York: Putnam, 1973.

Parents share a loving experience with their little boy about his two grandmothers in their nineties. Beautiful and compelling illustrations. Ages five to eight.

Farley, Carol, *The Garden is Doing Fine.* New York: Atheneum, 1975.

A high school girl makes an effort to lead a normal life while her father is dying from cancer. The living garden is the children of dead parents. The agony of slow sickness, guilt, and sadness and the happiness in between. Ages ten to fifteen.

Fassler, Joan, *My Grandpa Died Today.* New York: Human Sci Pr, 1977.

This is one of a series of illustrated books for small children on psychologically relevant themes. Grandpa told David that he could not live forever, but was not afraid to die. One day he did die. David's loss is great, but the author emphasizes the richness of the relationship, and that gives him happy memories of Grandpa. Ages four to eight.

Greene, Constance, *Beat the Turtle Drum.* New York: Viking Pr, 1976.

A description of Kate's painful adjustment to her sister's sudden accidental death. Done with care and skill. Ages ten to fifteen .

"I and the Others" Writers' Collective, *It's Scary Sometimes.* New York: Human Sci Pr, 1978. Illustrated by the children themselves.

A delightful and insightful description of the how's and why's of children's fears. Helps young children recognize those situations in which it is perfectly reasonable or even useful to feel afraid and those where fears are really unnecessary. Illustrated by the children themselves. Ages four to eight; parents and teachers.

Kennedy, Richard, *Oliver Hyde's Dishcloth Concert.* Boston: Little, 1977.

When Oliver's wife died, he could only sit in a corner with a dishcloth over his head. Later he is able to play his fiddle at a wedding. The pictures clearly depict his loss and anger. Ages six to ten.

Klein, Stanley, *The Final Mystery.* New York: Doubleday, 1974.

Good sections on death, ancient beliefs, death and religion, and medical progress. Ages eight through the teens.

Lee, Virginia, *The Magic Moth.* New York: Seabury, 1976.

Maryanne is ill and dying from heart disease. A caring family share openly, the parents one way, the siblings another.

Lichtman, Wendy, *Blew and the Death of the Mag.* Berkeley: Freestone Pub Co, 1975.

A sensitive and knowledgeable book about a young girl's experience with the death of her imaginative friend. Blew asks good questions, and her feelings come up front in a moving and inspiring way. Suitable for children of all ages.

Miles, Miska, *Annie and the Old One.* Boston: Little, 1971.

An eleven-year-old girl's experience with her grandmother.

Peck, Robert Newton, *A Day No Pigs Would Die.* New York: Dell, 1974. Novel of a Shaker family in New England. Narrates a boy's struggle to accept death and how his father influenced him. Excellent. Paperback.

Rock, Gail, *The Thanksgiving Treasure.* New York: Knopf, 1974.

A growing-up tale set in Nebraska of a young girl and her horses and an old man who dies. Ages eight to twelve.

Skorpen, Liesel Moak, *Old Arthur.* New York: Har-Row, 1972.

About an old dog that needs special care and love and a child who fills his need. Good.

Slote, Alfred, *Hang Tough, Paul Mather.* New York: Lippincott, 1973.

With the help of his doctor, Paul finishes a season of baseball, even though he is in and out of the hospital with an incurable disease. Ages ten to twelve.

Smith, Doris, *A Taste of Blackberries.* New York: Crowell, 1973. Little Little Jamie dies from a bee sting. His best friend is shocked by this, and his adjustment is described. He finally becomes good friends with Jamie's mother. Ages eight to twelve.

Viorst, Judith, *The Tenth Good Thing About Barney.* New York: Antheneum, 1971.

During his cat's funeral, a little boy decides on nine good things to say about his cat. He and his sister later discuss whether the cat is in heaven or in the earth. Ages five to ten.

Warburg, Sandol, *Growing Time.* New York: Houghton Mifflin, 1969.

A little boy of five reacts with anger and hurt to the death of the dog that has helped him learn to walk. Ages seven to nine.

White, E. B., *Charlotte's Web.* New York: Har-Row, 1952.

A classic. A young farmgirl's fantasy about her animal friends. A beautiful presentation of life cycles, friendship, loyalty, and death. From six to sixty.

Zolotow, Charlotte, *My Grandson Lew.* New York: Har-Row, 1974.

Lew, age six, shares his recollections of his grandfather with his mother. Suitable for children from four to eight. Readable for younger children. Wonderful illustrations.

## CHILDREN AND GRIEF

Anthony, Sylvia, *The Discovery of Death in Childhood and After.* Harmondsworth, Middlesex, England and New York, Penguin, 1973.

A classic. How children learn about death and what they do with this knowledge.

Axline, Virginia, *Play Therapy.* Boston: Houghton Mifflin, 1947.

Baran, Annette, Reuben Pannor, and Arthur D. Sorosky, "The Lingering

Pain of Surrendering a Child," *Psychology Today,* June, 1977, pp. 58–60, 88.

Parents who gave up their children for adoption for the best of reasons now wonder, how are their children doing?

Baran, Annette, Arthur D. Sorosky, and Reuben Pannor, "Secret Adoption Records: The Dilemma of Our Adoptees," *Psychology Today,* December, 1975.

When an adult adoptee looks for his or her natural parents, it is a search for identity, not a hunt for love. But sealed records keep the searcher dangling in a void.

Barnes, Marion J., "Reactions to the Death of a Mother," in *The Psychoanalytic Study of the Child,* New York: Intl Univs Pr, 1964, pp. 334–57.

Bender, Louretta, *Aggression, Hostility, and Anxiety in Children.* Springfield, Thomas, 1953.

Bernstein, Joanne, *Loss and How to Cope with It.* New York: Seabury, 1977.

The author suggests how young children can be aware of and cope with their fear, anger, lack of concentration, loss of appetite, and odd behavior following a death. Ages ten through the teens.

Best, Pauline, "An Experience in Interpreting Death to Children," *J Pastoral Care, 2*:29–34, Spring, 1948.

Bowlby, J., "Grief and Mourning in Infancy and Early Childhood," *Psychoanal Study Child, 15*:9, 1960.

――― "Childhood Mourning and Its Implications for Psychiatry," The Adolf Meyer Lecture, *Am J Psychiatry, 119*:481, 1961.

Bro, Marguerite H., *When Children Ask.* New York: Har-Row, 1956.

See Chapter 6, "What of Death?" Good.

Brown, Catherine Caldwell, "It Changed My Life," *Psychology Today,* November, 1976, pp. 47–58.

A consumer's guide to the four major parent-training programs.

Burton, Lindy, *Care of the Child Facing Death.* London and Boston: Routledge & Kegan, 1974.

Cain, A. C. and J. Fast, "Children's Disturbed Reactions to Parent Suicide," *Am J Orthopsychiatry, 36*:873–80, October, 1966.

Childers, Perry and Mary Wimmer, "Concept of Death in Early Childhood," *Child Dev, 42,* October, 1971.

Doyle, Polly, "Grief Counseling for Children," in Danto, Bruce and A.H. Kutscher (Eds.), *Suicide and Bereavement,* New York: Arno, 1977.

An account of the early years of a program designed for the counseling of the survivors of suicide.

Easson, William M., *The Dying Child: The Management of the Child or*

*Adolescent Who is Dying.* Springfield, Thomas, 1972.

Erikson, Erik H., *Childhood and Society,* Revised ed. New York: Norton, 1963.

A classic in every way. In the grieving context, his discussion of the development of "basic trust" is a paramount contribution.

Fine, Louis L., *After All We've Done for Them: Understanding Adolescent Behavior.* New York: P-H, 1977.

A direct, open book by a specialist in adolescent medicine. The progression of adolescent behavior from early teens to late adolescence; delineation of what is normal, what is not; excellent guidelines for parents and others who work with this segment of our population.

Fischhoff, J. and N. O'Brien, "After the Child Dies," *J Pediatr, 88:*140–46, No. 1.

This excellent article deals with numerous topics, such as parental reactions before and after  death, how to help the spouse and siblings; God and the clergy.  Examples and discussions.

Furman, Erna, *A Child's Parent Dies: Studies in Childhood Bereavement.* New Haven, Connecticut and London: Yale U Pr, 1974.

An excellent study of childhood bereavement, complete with some case studies and a review of the literature.

Galen, Harlene, "A Matter of Life and Death," *Young Children,* August, 1972.

For preschool teachers. Death education.

Gardner, Richard A., *The Boys' and Girls' Book About Divorce.* New York: Bantam, 1971.

The author says this book "is to help children get along better with their divorced parents."  Printed in large type, with cartoon illustrations. Offers kids loving, straight-from-the-shoulder advice.

Gibney, Harriet, H., "What Death Means to Children," *Parents' Magazine* March, 1965.

Ginott, Haim G., *Between Parent and Child.* New York: Macmillan, 1965.

The first of his books about how to communicate and to understand your child.  Very readable and useful.  It and its companion book, *Between Parent and Teenager,* are must reading for parents.

———, *Between Parent and Teenager.* New York: Macmillan, 1967.

Excellent presentation, with specific suggestions for the opening-up of communication between parents and teenagers.

Goleman, Daniel, "The Child Will Always be There:  Real Love Doesn't Die," *Psychology Today,* September, 1976.

An interview with Elisabeth Kübler-Ross about sudden death of children. For all adults, especially parents.

Grollman, Earl (Ed.), *Explaining Death to Children.* Boston: Beacon Pr, 1967.

An excellent presentation of different aspects of death education for children—how they view death, how to talk about it with different ages, and religious and cultural differences of approach. Splendid bibliographies, by ages, fiction, myths, pictures. Introduction by Louise Bates Ames.

———, *Talking About Death, A Dialogue Between Parent and Child.* Boston: Beacon Pr, 1970.

Grollman at his best. Beautiful illustrations.

Gurmond, Joyce, "We Knew Our Child Was Dying," *Am J Nurs,* February, 1974.

When the tragedy of a child's death is about to strike a family, how social talk and false cheer compound the parents' anguish.

Hagan, Joan, "Infant Death: Nursing Interaction and Intervention With Grieving Families," *Nurs Forum, 13* (14), 1974.

Hartley, Ruth E. and Robert M. Goldenson, *The Complete Book of Children's Play.* New York: Crowell, 1963.

A child learns best in a situation where he is nearly whole, self-directed, open, and creative—spontaneous interaction between his mind and heart. A wonderful book. Divided into chapters by age, from year one to the teens. "We All Need a Hobby," "They All Want Pets," "The Doctor Prescribes Play," "Fun on the Town," "Play That Develops the Mind." Lists household items to save for use in play, equipment to build; books and records.

Hogan, Robert A., "Adolescent Views of Death," *Adolescence, 5,* 1970.

Jackson, Edgar N., *Telling a Child About Death.* New York: Channel Pr, 1965.

Old but good.

Johnson, Leonard and Marc Miller, *Shannon, A Book for Parents of Children with Leukemia.* New York: Hawthorn, 1975.

Kane, Fred, "The Development of Concepts of Death," *Proceedings,* 6th International Conference on Suicide Prevention, Mexico City, 1967. Ann Arbor, Michigan: Edward Brothers, Inc., 1968.

How young children develop a sense of death as a result of maturation and parental response to death.

Kastenbaum, Robert, "Time and Death in Adolescence," in Feifel, Herman (Ed.), *The Meaning of Death.* New York: McGraw, 1959.

How adolescents think about death and aging.

———, "The Kingdom Where Nobody Dies," *Saturday Review of Science,* December 23, 1972.

A beautiful and moving article about many things—how a child responds to death, children and death during the Great Plague, etc.

———, "We Covered Death Today." *Death Education,* Spring, 1977.
Death education programs and practices.   (Hemisphere Publishing Corp.,
    1025 Vermont Avenue, NW, Washington, D.C. 20005.)
Klaber, Florence, *When Children Ask About Death.*   New York:   Society
    for Ethical Culture.

A liberal's approach, available from the Society for Ethical Culture, 2 West
64th Streett, New York, 10023.

Koocher, Gerald, "Talking with Children about Death," *Am J Orthopsy-*
    *chiatry, 44:3,* April, 1974.
Koop, C. Everett, "What I Tell a Dying Child's Parents," *Readers, Digest,*
    *92,* February, 1968.
Kübler-Ross, Elisabeth, "The Child Will Always Be There.   Real Love
    Doesn't Die," *Psychology Today,* September, 1976.
Kübler-Ross, Elisabeth and Jeanne Quint Benoliel, "Death and Children,"
    delivered before Symposium on Confrontation With Dying, Gerontology
    Center, University of Southern California, December 10–11, 1971.
Laing, R. D., *The Politics of the Family.*   New York:   Random, 1972.

An excellent description of the highly complicated relationships in the
family.   Case examples.   One of the most significant books in the field by a
British psychiatrist whose writings and theories are revolutionary.

LeShan, Eda, *Learning to Say Good-By.*   New York:   Macmillan, 1976.

An excellent book.   How a child copes with his questions, fantasies, and
fears when a parent dies.   The stages of mourning children and adults pass
through and the painful feelings involved.   Must reading for parents also.
Ages eight through the teens.

Liebman, Joshua L., *Peace of Mind.*   New York:   S & S, 1946.
See Chapter 6, "Grief's Slow Wisdom."

This author deals with the importance of honesty with children.

Mahler, Margaret S., "On Sadness and Grief in Infancy and Childhood:
    Loss and Restoration of the Symbiotic Love Object," in *Psychoanalytic*
    *Study of the Child,* vol. 16, pp. 332–51.   New York:   Intl Univs Pr, 1961.
Martin, Mildred Crowl, "Helping Children Cope with Sorrow," *Parents'*
    *Magazine,* 45, August, 1970.
Maurer, Adah, "Adolescent Attitudes Toward Death," *J Genet Psychol, 105:*
    75–90, 1964.
Miller, Jill B., "Children's Reactions to Death," *J Am Psychoanal Assoc, 19,*
    October, 1971.
Nagy, Maria, "The Child's Theories Concerning Death," *J Genet Psychol,*
    73, 1948.
———, "The Child's View of Death," in Feifel, Herman, in *Meaning of*
    *Death,* New York:   McGraw, 1959.

A presentation of research findings. Excellent.

*Newsweek,* "Kids With Cancer," August 15, 1977, pp. 57–58.

An account of clinical work being done at St. Jude Children's Research Hospital in Memphis, Tennessee and an interview with Dr. Stephen Sallan of Boston's Sidney Farver Cancer Institute.

Parness, Estelle, "Effects of Experiences with Loss and Death Among Preschool Children," *Child Today,* November-December, 1975.

Ramos, Suzanne, "Learning About Death," *New York Times Magazine,* December, 1972.

Rochlin, Gregory, "The Dread of Abandonment: A Contribution to the Etiology of the Loss Complex and to Depression," in *Psychoanalytic Study of the Child,* vol. 16, pp. 451–70. New York: Intl Univs Pr, 1961.

Rogers, Rita R., "Paradoxes of Children," *Proceedings,* World Congress of Psychiatrists, Honolulu, 1977.

The paradoxes and ambiguities of present-day children and how these messages affect their behavior.

Rudolph, Marguerita, *Should the Children Know?* New York: Dell, 1974.

Sahler, Ollie Jane Z. (Ed.), *The Child and Death.* St. Louis: Mosby, 1978.

Satir, Virginia, *Conjoint Family Therapy.* Palo Alto, California: Sci and Behavior, 1967.

*Sci Digest,* "Scientific Frontiers: Children View Death in Many Ways," *73,* May, 1973.

Sherill, Helen H., "Answering the Child's Questions About Death," *Child Guidance,* April, 1961.

Excellent.

Shoor, Mervyn and Mary H. Speed, "Delinquency as a Manifestation of the Mourning Process, *Psychiatric Quarterly, 37:*540–58, 1967.

Troup, Stanley and William A. Greene (Eds.), *The Patient, Death and the Family.* New York: Scribners, 1974.

Viorst, Judith, "The Hospital that has Patience for its Patients: A Look at Children's Hospital, in Washington, D.C.," *Redbook Magazine,* February, 1977, pp. 50–54.

Vogel, Linda Jane, *Helping a Child Understand Death.* Philadelphia: Fortress, 1976.

A small book dealing with basic questions that children ask: "Why?" "Understanding a Child's Understanding;" "Pitfalls to Avoid;" "When Pets Die;" "Helping a Child;" "Sharing Our Faith;" "Where Do We Go From Here?" Readable. Suitable for parents, teachers, clergy, and prospective counselors.

Wolf, A.W.M., *Helping Your Child to Understand Death.* New York: Child Study Assn of America, 1958.

A pamphlet. Deals with the psychological perspective; also has section on

Jewish, Roman Catholic, and Protestant approaches.

Zim, Herbert and Sonia Bleeker, *Life and Death.* New York: Morrow, 1970.

Good presentation of the aging process, funeral practices, body decomposition, and other topics. Ages eight through the teens.

## DISASTER

Belz, Mary, Ellen Zlotnick Parker, Lawrence Sank, Carolyn Shaffer, Joan Shapiro, and Linda Shriber, "Is There a Treatment for Terror?" *Psychology, Today,* October, 1977, p. 54.

Six therapists report on their work with hostages held by the Hanafis.

Defoe, Daniel, *A Journal of the Plague Year.* New York: New American Library, 1969.

London during the Great Plague of 1665; gives good presentation of how people respond to epidemic death.

Dynes, Russell R. and E. L. Quarantelli, "Effects of Distaster on Community Life," *Proceedings,* Seminar on Family Agencies' Role in Disaster (in English and French), November 14–17, 1966. Canadian Department of Health and Welfare.

———, "Function of an Organization Under Stress," *Proceedings,* Seminar on Family Agencies' Role in Disaster (in English and French), November 14–17, 1966. Canadian Department of Health and Welfare.

———, "Group Behavior Under Stress: A Required Convergence of Organizational and Collective Behavior Perspectives." *Sociology and Social Research,* 52, July, 1968.

———, "The Absence of Community Conflict in Early Phase of National Disaster," in Smith, Clagett G. (Ed.), *Conflict Resolution: Contributions of the Behavioral Sciences.* Notre Dame, Indiana: U of Notre Dame Pr, 1971.

———, "The Family and Community Context of Individual Reactions to Disaster," in Parad, Howard, H. L. F. Resnik, and Libby G. Parad (Eds.), *Emergency and Disaster Management: A Mental Health Sourcebook.* Bowie, Maryland: Charles, 1976.

Dynes, Russell R. and Daniel Yutzy, "The Religious Interpretation of Disaster," *Topic 10: A Journal of the Liberal Arts,* Fall, 1965.

Fenyvesi, Charles, "Six Months Later: Living with a Fearful Memory," *Psychology Today,* October, 1977, pp. 61 ff.

One of the hostages of the Hanafi talks with other victims.

Frederick, Calvin, "Disaster Crises and the Federal Response," *Proceedings,* 8th Annual Meeting American Association of Suicidology, St. Louis. Houston, Texas: *Am Assn Suicidology,* 1976, pp. 65–68.

Dr. Frederick asks important questions about the reactions to natural disasters: who is affected, age groups, when—during the crises or after, do disadvantaged groups react differently from advantaged ones, how do we intervene, kind of training needed, and critical issues in research and service.

Grosser, George H. Wechsler, and Greenblatt (Eds.), *The Threat of Impending Disaster: Contributions to the Psychology of Stress.* Cambridge, Massachusetts: MIT Pr, 1965.

Primary concern that of stress, but includes material on cultural variations towards death and disease and some of Lifton's work reporting the effects of the bomb in Hiroshima.

Harshbarger, Dwight, "Picking up the Pieces: Disaster Intervention and Human Ecology," *Omega, 5,* 1974.

The aftermath needs of a disaster—shelter and survival and the psychosocial needs of the survivors that may persist for months or years.

Hoehling, Adolph A., *Disaster: Major American Catastrophes.* New York: Hawthorn, 1973.

A popular book with some pictures of the main United States disasters from 1863 on but not including the Coconut Grove Fire.

Johnston, Moira, "The Last 77 Seconds of Flight 981," *Psychology Today,* November, 1976, pp. 58–66.

A reconstruction of a DC-10 crash that killed 346 people.

Lifton, Robert Jay, *Death in Life.* New York: Random, 1967.

A penetrating analysis of the long-term effects of the bomb upon survivors in Hiroshima. Makes wide and effective use of recorded interviews and analyzes the survivors' reactions. A National Book Award book.

Mershiser, Marvin R. and E. L. Quarantelli, "The Handling of the Dead in a Disaster," *Omega, 7*(3), 1976.

How the dead are treated by the living, a case study of the handling of 273 victims of a flash flood disaster.

Pine, Vanderlyn R., "Grief Work and Dirty Work: The Aftermath of an Aircrash," *Omega, 5*(4), 1974.

This paper describes the activities of and the organizations responsible for the handling of the dead after a major airplane crash in which 32 people were killed.

Quarantelli, E. L., "A Selected Annotated Bibliography of Social Science Studies on Disasters," *American Behavioral Scientist, 13*(3):452–56, January-February, 1970.
———, "Human Behavior in Disaster," *Proceedings,* Conference to Survive Disaster. Chicago: IIT Research Institute, 1973, pp. 53–74.
———, "Human Response in Stress Situations," in Halpin, B.M. (Ed.), Proceedings, First Conference and Workshop on Fire Casualties. Laurel,

Maryland: Applied Physics Laboratory, Johns Hopkins U, 1976, pp. 99–112.

Quarantelli, E. L. and Russell R. Dynes, "When Disaster Strikes (It Isn't Much Like You've Heard and Read About)," *Psychology Today*, 5(9):66–70, February, 1972.

Roth, Robert, "Cross-cultural Perspectives on Disaster Response," *Am Behavioral Scientist*, 13(3):440–51, January-February, 1970.

Taylor Verta, G., Alexander Ross, and E. L. Quarantelli, *Delivery of Mental Health Services in Disasters: The Xenia Tornado and Some Implications*. Columbus, Ohio: Ohio St U Pr, 1976.

Taylor Verta, "Good News About Disaster," *Psychology Today*, October, 1977, pp. 93 ff.

Natural disasters don't always increase mental illness; they may even have positive effects.

Tauber, Erwin B., "Emergence and Change of Human Relations Groups," *American Behavioral Scientist*, 16(3):391–401, January-February, 1973.

US, "That Devastating Nightclub Fire: How Ordinary People Became Unsung Heroes," July 12, 1977.

An article and photographs of the Beverly Hills Supper Club in Southgate, Kentucky which burned the last weekend in May, 1977, and in which 162 persons died.

Wolfenstein, Martha, *Disaster, A Psychological Essay*. New York: Arno, 1957.

An excellent book resulting from a study undertaken for the Committee on Disaster Studies of the National Academy of Sciences and the National Research Council. A big book, difficult to read because the important things she writes of are condensed to a minimum of wordage.

## FUNERALS

Bayly, Joe, *View From a Hearse*. Elgin, Illinois: Cook, 1969.

Blackwood, A., *The Funeral*. Philadelphia: Westminster, 1942.

Bowman, L., *The American Funeral: A Way of Death*. Washington, D.C.: Public Aff Pr, 1959.

A classic study of the subject by the first president of the Continental Association of Funeral and Memorial Societies.

Coriolis, *Death—Here Is Thy Sting*. Toronto: McClelland, 1967.

A funeral director, disillusioned, tells what is going on in the Canadian funeral industry.

Habenstein, Robert W. and William M. Lamers, *The History of American Funeral Directing*. Milwaukee: Bulfin Printers Inc., 1962.

———, *Funeral Customs the World Over*. Milwaukee: Bulfin Printers, Inc. 1974.

Harmer, Ruth Mulvey, *The High Cost of Dying.* New York: Macmillan, 1963.

Another of the early fusilades upon the funeral industry. Well documented. Proponent of burial societies.

Irion, Paul, *The Funeral: Vestige or Value.* Nashville: Abingdon, 1966.

Irion, *A Humanist Funeral Service, A Manual and Guide.* Baltimore: Waverly Pr, 1971.

Klein, Stanley, *The Final Mystery.* New York: Doubleday, 1974.

Mitford, Jessica, *The American Way of Death.* New York: Fawcett World, 1963.

A serious criticism of the customs that have become almost universal in the United States regarding the role of the funeral director, costly funerals, and burial rites.

Morgan, Ernest, *A Manual of Death Education and Simple Burial.* Burnsville, North Carolina: Celo Pr, 1973.

An early pamphlet on the memorial societies. Not much on death education.

Neilson, W. A. and C. G. Watkins, *Proposals for Legislative Reform Aiding the Consumer of Funeral Industry Products and Services.* Burnsville, North Carolina: Celo Pr, 1973.

A study commissioned by North American Funeral and Memorial Societies of the funeral industry. Good details and coverage on both proposals and legislation for reform of the industry. Not for the general reader.

Shaffer, Thomas L., *Death, Property, and Lawyers.* New York: Dunellen, 1970.

Van der Zee, James, Owen Dodson, and Camille Billions, *The Harlem Book of the Dead.* Dobbs Ferry, New York: Morgan & Morgan, 1978.

Photographs (taken in mortuaries), poems, and text reflecting the mourning rites of Harlem Blacks in a time now past. "The rituals presented in this book are as universal as death—and there are Harlems everywhere."

Waugh, Evelyn, *The Loved One: An American Tragedy.* New York: Grosset and Dunlap, 1949.

## GENERAL
## DEATH, DYING, ETC.

Becker, Ernest, *The Denial of Death.* New York: Free Pr, 1973.

A dying writer ponders his own death, the nature of man, and his fear of death. This essay or inquiry is too inconclusive, to say the least.

Bowers, Margaret, Edgar Jackson, Knight and Lawrence LeShan, *Counseling the Dying.* New York: Aronson, 1975.

Brim, Orville G., Howard E. Freeman, Sol Levine, and Norman A. Scotch,

*The Dying Patient.* New York: Russell Sage, 1970.

Brown, Norman O., *Life Against Death.* Middletown, Connecticut: Wesleyan U Pr, 1959.

*Death and Dying: Attitudes of Patient and Doctor,* Symposium, Group for the Advancement of Psychiatry, Nov. 11, 1965. New York, Group for Advancement of Psychiatry, 1972.

Five studies on attitudes toward death; a stunning essay by Herman Feifel on the function of such attitudes.

Eliot, Gil, *The Twentieth Century Book of the Dead.* New York: Random, 1972.

This book is a shocker. Presents the statistics of *this* century: 110 million persons killed by legal state action, mostly war. He itemizes the death toll, gives localities, methods.

Feifel, H., (Ed.), *The Meaning of Death.* New York: McGraw, 1959.

A classic. Feifel and his contributors cut a broad swathe, for the first time, across a field that has since burgeoned—thanks to this beginning. Excellent.

———, "Death" in Farberow, N. L. (Ed.), *Taboo Topics.* New York: Atherton Pr, 1963.

———, *New Meanings of Death.* New York: McGraw, 1977.

Glaser, Barney G. and Anselm L. Strauss, *Awareness of the Dying.* Chicago: Aldine, 1965.

Goleman, Daniel, "We Are Breaking the Silence About Death," *Psychology Today,* September, 1976, pp. 44ff.

Author feels a new candor about the final human adventure is emerging.

Gordon, David Cole, *Overcoming the Fear of Death.* New York: Macmillan, 1970.

The loss of self as related to the fears and anxieties regarding death.

Grollman, Earl A. (Ed.), *Concerning Death: A Practical Guide for the Living.* Boston: Beacon Pr, 1974.

Twenty contributors write on everyday problems connected with death— the different ways of different religions, the law and legal aspects, aspects of the funeral, the survivors, now to express our sympathy, suicide, and death education. Very good.

Gutherie, George P., "The Meaning of Death," *Voices: The Art and Science of Psychotherapy,* 5(1), 1969.

A teacher and counselor writes of death as a pervasive human problem, not just as a fact of life but the paradoxical qualities of our modes of relating to it. He recognizes the widespread need to talk of it.

Hendin, D., *Death as a Fact of Life.* New York: Norton, 1973.

Deals with aspects of death, euthanasia, cryonics, etc. Florid writing.

Hinton, John, *Death.* New York: Penguin, 1967.

Hinton, John, *Dying.* New York: Penguin, 1967.

Huston, Ted L., Gilbert Geis, and Richard Wright, "The Angry Samaritans," *Psychology Today,* June, 1976, pp. 61–66.

People who risk personal injury to help others are not merely angels of mercy. They are confident, assertive risk takers who know violence and love the limelight.

Kalish, R. A., *Death and Dying: A Briefly Annotated Bibliography.* New York: Russell Sage, 1970.

Quite good coverage, personal annotations with feeling.

Kalish, Richard A. and David K. Reynolds, *Death and Ethnicity: A Psychocultural Study.* Los Angeles: U of S Cal Pr, 1976.

Kastenbaum, Robert and Ruth Aisenberg, *The Psychology of Death.* New York: Springer Pub, 1972.

An almost encyclopedic book. An excellent reference book. No library on the subject is complete without it. Over 500 pages of tightly written material we all need to know.

Kavanaugh, Robert E., *Facing Death.* New York: Penguin, 1974.

Good popular treatment of basic topics.

Keleman, Stanley, *Living Your Dying.* New York: Random, 1974.

Highly recommended for adults.

Kluge, Eike-Hebber W., *The Practice of Death.* New Haven, Conneticutt: Yale U Pr, 1975.

An analytic view of serious bioethical problems confronting the medical profession, such as abortion, suicide, euthanasia, infanticide, and senicide. For a very special reading group only.

Kübler-Ross, Elisabeth, *On Death and Dying.* New York: Macmillan,

Her first book on the subject. Contains her controversial "Stages of . . ." which she has modified in later writings.

———, *Questions and Answers on Death and Dying.* New York: Macmillan, 1974.

Full of important material if you can stick with it to the end.

———, *Death the Final Stage of Growth.* Englewood Cliffs, New Jersey: P-H, 1975.

Essays of some dozen writers on different views and approaches to death and dying. Contains references and index.

Kutscher, A. H. (Ed.), *A Bibliography on Books on Death, Bereavement, Loss and Grief: 1935–1968.* New York: Health Sci Pubns, 1969.

Unannotated, unselective, uncritical.

Langone, John, *Vital Signs: The Way We Die in America.* Boston: Little, 1974.

Excellent. Includes a vivid account of the experience of human dissection and some outstanding interviews.

Lifton, Robert Jay, *Home From the War.* New York: S & S, 1973.

Lifton, Robert J. and Eric Olson, *Living and Dying.* New York: Praeger, 1974.

A wide-ranging book dealing with both the political as well as the psychological dimensions of death. Broad, philosophical, relevant.

Mack, Arien (Ed.), *Death in American Experience.* New York: Schocken, 1973.

Essays on death in America, written from such points of view as religion, society, medicine; also deals with attitudes toward dying.

Mannes, Marya, *Last Rights.* New York: Morrow, 1974.

How the dying in America fare today; ranges from existing laws through the labyrinth of the family, the church, and our attitudes toward death.

Mayeroff, Milton, *On Caring.* New York: Har-Row, 1972.

A classic. A *must* book for all professionals.

Mills, Liston A. (Ed.), *Perspective on Death.* Nashville: Abingdon, 1969.

Pattison, E. M., "Help the Dying Process," *Voices: The Art and Science of Psychotherapy,* Spring/Summer, 1969.

Pearson, Leonard (Ed.), *Death and Dying.* Cleveland: Case Western Res Pr, 1969.

Five essays on this subject by Robert Kastenbaum, Lawrence LeShan, Richard Kalish, Cicely Saunders and Anselm Strauss. Good readable material.

*Psychology Today,* August, 1970. Entire magazine on death articles.

Reeves, R. B., R. E. Neale, and A. H. Kutscher, *Pastoral Care of the Dying and Bereaved: Selected Readings.* New York: Health Sci Pubns, 1973.

A collection of articles from *Pastoral Psychology* and the *Journal of Religion and Health.*

Ruitenbeek, H. M., *Death: Interpretations.* New York: Dell, 1969.

Seligman, Martin E. P., "Submissive Death: Giving Up on Life," *Psychology Today,* May, 1974, pp. 80–86.

Animals and people who learn that they are helpless become highly vulnerable. In a marginal situation, that can mean death.

Shneidman, Edwin, "Orientation Towards Death," from White, Robert W. (Ed.), *The Study of Lives.* New York: P-H, 1963.

———, "You and Death," *Psychology Today,* June 1971.

———, *Death and the College Student.* New York: Behavioral Pubns, 1972.

———, *Deaths of Man.* New York: Quadrangle, 1973.

The author explains the work of the clinical thanatologist, the need to prepare the loved ones to be survivors, the dilemma of the dying person in a modern hospital, the different dimensions of death (intention, ambivalence, death taxonomies, and equivocal death), the medicolegal aspects of death, and the partial deaths of psychological and social withdrawal and our reality vis-à-vis the nuclear bomb. Not a book for everybody; special appeal to people working with the dying or survivors.

Siggins, Lorraine, "Mourning: A Critical Survey of the Literature," *Int J Psychiatry, 3*:418–32, May, 1967.

Simpson, Michael A., *Death and Dying and Terminal Care, An Annotated, Critical Bibliography.* 2nd ed., 1975.

Circulated privately.

Sudnow, David, *Passing On.* New York: P-H, 1967.

A sociological study of death in a county hospital. This is how we do it? A shocker. Very good.

Weisman, Avery, *On Dying and Denying.* New York: Behavioral Pubns, 1970.

An important book about the aspect of denial during both the dying process and on the part of the bereft. Slow reading, but there are many good examples. This is a book one keeps coming back to, finding more each time.

———, "Psychosocial Death," *Psychology Today,* November, 1972.

———, *The Realization of Death.* New York: Aronson, 1974.

Wordon, J. William and William Proctor, *Personal Death Awareness.* Englewood, New Jersey: P-H, 1976.

The psychological aspects of death awareness. Includes bibliographical references and index.

## GRIEF

Anderson, Marianne S. and Louis M. Savary, *Passages: A Guide for Pilgrims of the Mind.* New York: Har-Row, 1972.

Bachmann, C., *Ministering to the Grief Sufferer.* Englewood Cliffs, New Jersey: P-H, 1964.

Baker, A., and J. Golde, "Conjugal Bereavement: A Strategic Area of Research in Preventive Psychiatry," *Working Papers in Community Mental Health.* Cambridge, Massachusetts: Harvard U Pr, 1967.

Beachy, William N., "Assisting the Family in Time of Grief," *JAMA, 202:* 559–70, November 6, 1976.

Beck, F., *The Diary of a Widow: Rebuilding a Family after the Funeral.* Boston: Beacon Pr, 1966.

Benfield, Gary D., Susan A. Leib, and Jeanette Reuter, "Grief Responses of Parents After Referral of the Critically Ill Newborn to a Regional Center," *New Engl J Med, 294*(18):975–78, April 29, 1976.

Bowlby, J., "Processes of Mourning," *Int J Psychoanal, 44*:317, 1961.

Claypool, John, *Tracks of a Fellow Struggler, How to Handle Grief.* Waco, Texas: Word Bks, 1976.

A minister shares his thoughts about his grief when his young daughter dies of leukemia. Does Christian faith make any real difference? What actually helps?

Clayton, P., L. Demarais, and G. Winokur, "A Study of Normal Bereavement," *Am J Psychiatry, 125:*168, 1968.

Cochrane, A. L., "A Little Widow is a Dangerous Thing," *Int J Psychoanal, 17:*494, 1936.

Colgrave, Bloomfield and McWilliams, *How to Survive the Loss of a Love, 58 Things to do When There is Nothing to be Done.* New York: S&S, 1976.

A small book of readings, poetry, exercises, etc., done up in an attractive way. Here the loss of a love also means separation and/or divorce as well as death.

Danto, Bruce L. and Austin H. Kutscher (Eds.), *Suicide and Bereavement.* New York: Arno, 1977.

A compilation of papers read at the 1973 Foundation of Thanatology conference held at Columbia University. Persons experienced in different fields have commented in areas the editors divide into these sections:  Loss and Bereavement; The Act of Self-Destruction; Crisis and Death Intervention.

Edgar, N., *When Someone Dies.* Philadelphia: Fortress, 1971.

A small book that is used as a handout by the clergy.

Eliot, T. D., "Bereavement:  Inevitable but Not Insurmountable."  In Becker, H. and R. Hill (Eds.), *Family, Marriage and Parenthood,* Boston: Heath, 1948.

Engel, George, "Grief and Grieving," *Am J Nurs, 64*(9):93–98, September, 1964.

Freese, Arthur, *Help For Your Grief.* New York: Schocken, 1977.

A journalist looks at the grief and mourning process in order to use that process for growth and maturity of the individual.

Fulton, Robert, "Death, Grief and Social Recuperation," *Omega, 1:*23–28, 1970.

Futterman, E. H. and Hoffman and Sabshin, "Parental Anticipatory Mourning," in *Care of the Family of the Patient,*

Excellent presentation.

Gerber, Irwin, "Bereavement and the Acceptance of Professional Service," *Community Ment Health J, 5*(6):487–95, 1969.

Gordon, D. C., *Overcoming the Fear of Death.* New York:  Macmillan, 1970.

Gordon, Thomas, *P.E.T., Parent Effectiveness Training.* New York and London: Wyden, 1970.

An excellent handbook for parents and others involved with children.

Gorer, Geoffrey, *Death, Grief, and Mourning.* New York: Doubleday, 1965.

An excellent book by a British social anthropologist. Covers a large range of subjects, including a fine study of grief in children as well as an examination of funerals, cross-cultural approaches, symptoms of grief, styles of mourning, etc. Interesting reading, lively style.

Grollman, Earl A., *Talking About Death.* Boston: Beacon Pr, 1970.

All Grollman's books are good.

———, *Living When a Loved One Has Died.* Boston: Beacon Pr, 1977.

A beautiful small book. Captures the essence of grief. Simple, direct language.

Insel, Shepard A., *Confronting a Death in the Family* (A Guidebook to Crisis Management). Burlingame, California: Research, Training, Education Services, Inc., 1974.

This book begins at the moment of learning of a death in the family. There are discussions of funeral arrangements, costs, death benefits, crisis management, and how to organize a family information resource file for a survivor's personal information.

Jackson, Edgar N., *You and Your Grief.* New York: Hawthorn, 1961.

———, *When Someone Dies.* Philadelphia: Fortress, 1971.

A pamphlet, but it covers the situation well.

Kohn, June Burgess and Willard K. Kohn, *The Widower.* Boston: Beacon Pr, 1978.

Kassorla, Irene, *Putting It All Together.* New York: Warner Bks, 1973.

Psychological self-help; a combination of age-old wisdom and modern common sense.

Kübler-Ross, Elisabeth, *To Live Until We Say Good-bye.* Englewood Cliffs, New Jersey: P-H, 1978.

Photographs by Mal Warshaw.

Kutscher, Austin H., "The Moment of Grief," in Kutscher, Austin H. (Ed.), *Death and Bereavement.* Springfield, Thomas, 1969.

Metaphysical questions about death and immortality.

Lewis, H. R. and H. Streitfeld, *Growth Games.* New York: HarBraceJ, 1971.

Maddison, D. C. and W. L. Walker, "Factors Affecting the Outcome of Conjugal Bereavement," *Br J Psychiatry, 113*:1057, 1967.

How the health of conjugal pairs is affected by death and bereavement.

Marshall, John, "Helping the Grief-Stricken," *Postgrad Med, 45*:138–43, February, 1969.

Morris, Sarah, *Grief and How to Live With It*. New York: Grosset and Dunlap, 1972.

A widow's account of her grief and how she handled it; works in a good deal of the grief literature and cases whose origin she does not identify. Concerned primarily with widowhood; does not cover children's grief.

Nolfi, Mary W., "Families in Grief: The Question of Casework Intervention," *Soc Work*, *12*(4):40–46, 1967.

Parad, Howard and Gerald Caplan, "A Framework for Studying Families in Crisis," *Soc Work*, 5:3–15, July 1960.

Park, C. C. and L. N. Shapire, *You Are Not Alone*. Boston: Little, 1976.

Parkes, C. Murray, "Bereavement and Mental Illness," *Br J Med Psychol*, *38*:13–26, 1965.

——, "The Nature of Grief," *Int J Psychiatry*, *3*:435–38, May, 1967.

——, *Bereavement Studies of Grief in Adult Life*. Intl Univs Pr. 1972.

One of the few books solidly based on research studies, written by a British physician and psychiatrist, the book is concerned solely with the *adult* experience of grief. It deals thoroughly with the various facets of grief, how to help the bereaved, reactions to other loses, and a typical grief. A classic: readable.

Paul, Norman, "The Use of Empathy in the Resolution of Grief," *Perspect Biol Med*, Autumn, 1967, pp. 153–68.

Pincus, Lily, *Death and the Family, The Importance of Mourning*. New York: Pantheon, 1974.

This Tavistock Institute writer came to grief by way of marriage counseling. She has important things to say about the effect of grief on young married persons, as well as the entire family.

Rochlin, G., *Griefs and Discontents: The Forces of Change*. Boston: Little, 1965.

Rose, A. C., *Acquainted with Grief*. Philadelphia: Westminster, 1967.

Rosenfeld, Stephen S., *The Time of Their Dying*. New York: Norton, 1977.

A journalist's account of his passage through the time of his parents' illnesses and deaths. A moving account of a son's exploration of the new frontiers that opened in his life with them and his own family and in himself.

Schiff, Harriet S., *The Bereaved Parent*. New York: Crown, 1976.

An excellent presentation of the subject by a parent whose child died.

Schoenberg, Bernard, Arthur Carr, David Peretz, Austin Kutscher, and Ivan Goldberg (Eds.), *Anticipatory Grief*. New York: Columbia Pr, 1974.

Schoenberg, Bernard and Irwin Gerber (Eds.), *Bereavement: Its Psychological Aspects*. New York: Columbia U Pr, 1975.

Shepard, Martin, *Someone You Love is Dying, A Guide for Helping and Coping*. New York: Crown, 1975.

Silverman, Phyllis, "Services for the Widowed: First Steps in a Programme of Preventive Intervention," *Community Ment Health J, 3:*37, 1967.

———, "Grief is Not an Illness," *Life-Threatening Behavior, 3*(4):307, Winter, 1973.

A review of Murray Parke's book *Bereavement, Studies of Grief in Adult Life.*

Sulzberger, Cyrus, *My Brother Death.* New York: Har-Row, 1961.

Switzer, David, *Dynamics of Grief.* Nashville: Abingdon, 1970.

Troup, S. B. and W. A. Green, *The Patient, Death and the Family.* New York: Scribner, 1974.

Volkart, E. H., and S. T. Michael, "Bereavement and Mental Health," in Fulton, R. L. (Ed.), *Death and Identity.* New York: Wiley, 1965.

Welu, T. C., "Pathological Bereavement: A Plan for its Prevention," in Schoenberg, Bernard and Irwin Gerber (Eds.), *Bereavement: It's Psychosocial Aspects,* New York: Columbia U Pr, 1975, pp. 139–49.

Westberg, Granger E., *Good Grief.* Philadelphia: Fortress, 1971.

An excellent pamphlet-size presentation of the stages of grief and how to cope; commonly presented to parishioners by the clergy.

## LOSS AND SEPARATION

Bowlby, J., *Attachment and Loss,* Vol. 1, *Attachment.* London: Hogarth; New York: Basic, 1969.

A lengthy discussion of the evolution of attachment behavior by an emminent British researcher, one of the greats from the "gold mine" known as the Tavistock Institute of Human Relations.

———, *Attachment and Loss,* Vol. II, *Separation.* New York: Basic, 1969.

Encyclopedic; full of empirical data; review of separation studies and much ethological material. Heavy reading. Bowlby is of one of the Tavistock Clinic research groups that turns out first-rate books.

Fried, M., "Grieving for a Lost Home," in Duhl, L. F. (Ed.), *The Environment of the Metropolis.* New York: Basic, 1962.

A good presentation of an example of another kind of grieving, that of the loss and separation of a place.

*Health Headlines, The Care and Feeding of Single Parents.* Contra Costa, California: Contra Costa Health Department, March, 1978.

Heinicke, C. and I. Westheimer, *Brief Separations.* New York: Intl Univs Pr, 1966.

Rochlin, Gregory, "The Loss Complex: A Contribution to the Etiology of Depression," *J Am Psychoanal Assoc, 7:*299–316, 1959.

Schoenberg, B., A. C. Carr, D. Peretz, and A. H. Kutscher (Eds.), *Loss and Grief: Psychological Management in Medical Practice.* New York: Columbia U Pr, 1970.

## MEDICAL ASPECTS

Anderson, C., "Aspects of Pathological Grief and Mourning," *Int J Psychoanal, 30:*48, 149.

Bermann, E., *Scapegoat: The Impact of Death-Fear on an American Family.* Ann Arbor: U of Mich Pr, 1973.

The detailed study of a family caught up in the illness of the father. A young son becomes the scapegoat for the family problems and as a result becomes aggressive. Of interest to clinicians.

Bowlby, J., "Pathological Mourning and Childhood Mourning," *J Am Psychoanal Assoc, 11:*500, 1963.

Caplan, G., *Principles of Preventive Psychiatry.* New York: Basic, 1964.

Caplan, Marion G. and Douglass, "Incidence of Parental Loss in Children with Depressed Mood," *J Child Psychol Psychiatry, 10,* 1969.

Research paper on parental loss and depression in children. Good.

Cartwright, Hockey and Anderson, *Life Before Death.* Boston: Routledge and Kegan, 1973.

An excellent study of the last year of life — from the "why me?" through symptoms — and who gives the care in the home, hospital or community. We all need to know what this book can tell.

Clark, Margie B., "A Therapeutic Approach to Treating a Grieving Two-and-a-Half-Year Old," *J Am Acad Child Psychiatry, 11,* Oct., 1972.

*Consumer Reports,* "Laetrile," August, 1977.

A history of the use of laetrile and an account of the recent political success of what the author calls "a scientific failure."

*Death and Dying: Attitudes of Patient and Doctor,* Symposium, New York: Group for the Advancement of Psychiatry, 1965–1972.

Engel, George, "Is Grief a Disease?", *Psychosom. Med, 23*(1):18–22, 1961.

Freud, Sigmund, *Mourning and Melancholia.* Standard ed., Vol. 14, 1917.

A discussion of melancholia as a pathological form of grief and the ambivalence the patient expresses towards both himself and his grief object.

Goldberg, Malitz and A. H. Kutscher (Eds.), *Psychopharmacologic Agents for the Terminally Ill and Bereaved.* New York: Columbia U Pr, 1973.

Uses for drugs with the care of the ill and bereaved, including chlorpromazine, heroin, LSD. Some on grief and pain. Very long and involved.

*Harper's Magazine,* "The Anti-Social Cell," June, 1975.

Hodge, J., "Help Your Patients to Mourn Better," *Med Times, 99:*53–64, June, 1971.

Jackson, Pat Lunner, "Chronic Grief," *Am J Nurs, 74:*1288–93, July, 1974.

Keen, Sam, "Medicine is a Major Threat to Health," *Psychology Today,* May, 1976, pp. 66–78.

A conversation with Ivan Illich in which Illich charges that physicians make us sick and take the dignity and meaning out of death. Followed by a sketch of Illich.

Kushner, Rose, *Breast Cancer.* A Personal History and an Investigative Report. New York: Har-Brace, 1975.

Lindemann, E., The Symptomatology and Management of Acute Grief," *Am J Psychiatry, 101*:141, 1944.

One of the earliest American treatments of this subject. A classic presentation and still worthy of close reading.

Lynch, James J., *The Broken Heart.* New York: Basic, 1977.

A specialist in psychosomatic disease at the University of Maryland's Medical School has written a moving book on the consequences of loneliness and how it can actually kill. In many diseases the single, widowed, and divorced have significantly higher mortality rates than married people. Contains bibliographical references and index.

Patterson, R.P., Denning, and A.H. Kutscher (Eds.), *Psychosocial Aspects of Cystic Fibrosis.* New York: Columbia U Pr, 1973.

Covers also other kinds of death in children and adolescents; chronic diseases.

*The Right to Die: Decision and Decision Makers,* Symposium No. 12, New York: Group for the Advancement of Psychiatry, 1973.

Schoenberg, B., A.C. Carr, D. Peretz and A.H. Kutscher, *Loss and Grief: Psychological Management in Medical Practice.* Columbia U Pr, 1970.

Volkan, Vamik, "Typical Findings in Pathological Grief," *Psychiatric Quarterly, 44*:231–50, 1970.

Volkan, Vamik, "Normal and Pathological Grief Reactions, A Guide for the Family Physician," *Virgin Med Monthly, 93*:651–56,

## NUTRITION

Lappe, Frances Moore, *Diet for a Small Planet.* New York: Random, 1971.

An excellent book on nutrition with explanations of the structure and interaction of the various chemical and nutrient elements of our diet. Illustrations, graphs, charts, lists, recipes.

## PAIN

Freese, Arthur S., *Pain, The New Help for Your Pain.* New York: Putnam, 1974.

Hilgard, Ernest R., "Weapon Against Pain: Hypnosis Is No Mirage," *Psychology Today,* November, 1974, pp. 120–26.

Hypnosis has come a long way from the days of parlor magic. It is effective against the pain of cancer, dentistry, and childbirth, but we still do not know just how it works.

Lewis, C. S., *The Problem of Pain.* New York: Macmillan, 1962.

Melzack, Ronald, *The Puzzle of Pain.* New York: Basic, 1973.

An examination of the facts and theories about pain and how to control it.

Wang, Julie, "Breaking Out of the Pain Trap," *Psychology Today,* July, 1977, pp. 78–86.

How effective are the new versus the traditional treatments for chronic pain? Surprisingly effective, according to this survey.

## PERSONAL ACCOUNTS, FICTION

Adler, C. A., G. Stanford, and S. M. Alder, *We Are But a Moment's Sunlight, Understanding Death.* New York: WSP, 1976.

Excerpts from many essays, poems, novels, plays, etc. that relate to different kinds of deaths and different feelings of grief.

Agee, James, *A Death in the Family.* New York: Bantam, 1970.

How a sudden death affected a family. Pulitzer Prize book.

Alsop, Stewart, *Stay of Execution.* Philadelphia: Lippincott, 1973.

A journalist's account of his life with a prognosis of an early death.

Alvarez, A., *The Savage God.* New York: Bantam, 1973.

Society's attitudes toward death as seen through history and literature; author's relationship to Sylvia Plath; an account of her suicide and his own attempt.

Caine, Lynn, *Widow.* New York: Morrow, 1974.

A widow's own account of her grief and how she managed it.

Camus, A., *The Stranger.* New York: Random, 1942.

Camus, A., *A Happy Death.* New York: Knopf, 1972.

Craven, Margaret, *I Heard the Owl Call My Name.* New York: Dell, 1973.

The story of one man's discovery of the ultimate truths of life and love, courage and dignity, among the proud Indians of the Northwest.

de Beauvoir, Simone, *A Very Easy Death.* Harmondsworth, Middlesex, England, Penguin, 1969.

A daughter's account of her mother's difficult death in France. The daughter's love and anger flame around the dying mother. Excellent.

Defoe, Daniel, *A Journal of the Plague Year.* New York: NAL, 1960.

DeVries, P., *The Blood of the Lamb.* Boston: Little, 1961.

Faulkner, William, *As I Lay Dying.* New York: Modern Lib, 1946.

Glasser, Ronald, *Ward 402.* San Diego, New York: Braziller, 1973.

Gunther, John, *Death Be Not Proud.* New York: Har-Row, 1949.

The author's account of the illness and death of his teenage son.

Jury, Mark and Dan Jury, "Gramp," *Psychology Today,* February, 1976.

A tough old man faced the fact that he was growing senile and took death with his own hands. With the loving knowledge of his family, he stopped eating and his grandsons documented his last weeks. Remarkable photographs.

Lewis, Clive Staples, *A Grief Observed*. New York: Seabury, 1961.

A tender and moving account of the loss of his wife. A classic.

Lowenstein, Prince Leopold of, *A Time to Live . . . A Time to Die*. New York: Doubleday, 1971.

Lund, Doris, *Eric*. Philadelphia: Lippincott, 1974.

An effective and good account by a mother whose teenage son had leukemia; *his* creativity and grace in meeting death.

Odell, Mary Clemens, *Our Little Child Faces Life*. Nashville: Abingdon, 1939.

See Chapter 8, "The Problem of Death." A mother tells of her experiences with her son.

Plath, Sylvia, *The Bell Jar*. New York: Har-Row, 1971.

Presumably autobiographical. An account of a young woman's despair with life and her attempt at suicide. Excellent.

Rosenthal, Ted, *How Could I Not Be Among You?* San Diego, New York: Braziller, 1973.

Dying at age 30, this young poet sings his lamentations. Beautiful and moving illustrations from the film of the same name. Excellent.

Shuman, Ron, "In the Presence of Death, A Determined Fight for Life," *Psychology Today*, September, 1976, pp. 57ff.

Ron Shuman's photographs show what happens at a children's clinic when doctors, parents, and small patients decide that cancer need not be fatal.

Tolstoy, Leo, *The Death of Ivan Illych*. New York: NAL, 1948.

Trumbo, Dalton, *Johnny Got His Gun*. Seacaucus, New Jersey: Lyle Stuart, 1970.

Valens, E. G., *The Other Side of the Mountain*. New York: Warner Bks, 1975.

An account of Jill Kinmont's crash in a qualifying race before the Olympic ski tryout and her long climb back from total helplessness to a useful, meaningful way of life.

Waugh, Evelyn, *The Loved One*. London: Hinneman, 1948.

A brilliant account of the wild funeral and burial customs of Hollywood. One wants to say "sick, sick, sick!" but it must be read to be believed.

Wechsler, James A., *In A Darkness*. New York: Norton, 1972.

West, Jessamyn, *A Matter of Time*. New York: Har-Brace, 1966.

## RELIGIOUS AND PHILOSOPHICAL INTERPRETATIONS

Choron, Jacques, *Death and Western Thought*. New York: Macmillan, 1963.

What western philosophers from Socrates to the mid-sixties have thought about death. Excellent.

———, *Modern Man and Mortality*. New York: Macmillan, 1964.

Clark, Elmer T., *The Small Sects in America*. New York: Abingdon, 1949.

A study of almost 300 little-known religious groups. Indispensable as a reference book.

Eakin, Mildred Moody and Frank Eakin. *Your Child's Religion*. New York: Macmillan, 1956.

See Chapter 4, "Death."

Good liberal Protestant approach.

Fairly, John L. and Arleene Fairly, *Using the Bible To Answer Questions Children Ask*. Atlanta, Georgia: John Knox, 1959.

See Chapter 14, "What Does It Mean to be Dead?"

Conservative Protestant approach.

Finklestein, Louis, *The Jewish Religion — Its Belief and Practices*. New York: Har-Row, 1949.

A Jewish Rabbi gives an adult approach to death.

Frankl, Viktor, *The Doctor and the Soul*. New York: Knopf, 1955.

———, *Man's Search for Meaning*. New York: WSP, 1959.

———, *The Unheard Cry for Meaning, Psychotherapy and Humanism*. New York: S & S, 1978.

Fromme, Allan, *Our Troubled Selves*. New York: Pocketbooks, 1968.

Fromm, Erich, *The Revolution of Hope*. New York: Bantam, 1968.

Gaylin, Willard, "Caring Makes the Difference," *Psychology Today,* August, 1976, pp. 34–41.

Our national despair is unwarranted; humanity's loving nature is a good guide for the future as its tendencies toward violence.

Geissler, Eugene S. (Ed.), *You and Your Children*. Chicago: Fides Publishers Association, 1969.

A Roman Catholic interpretation; detailed.

Godin, A. (Ed.), *Death and Presence: The Psychology of Death and the After-life*. Lumen Vitae, 1972.

Green, Betty R. and Donald P. Irish, *Death Education: Preparation for Living*. Gen Lern Pr, 1971.

Hall, Elizabeth and Paul Cameron, "Our Failing Reverence for Life," *Psychology Today,* April, 1976, pp. 104–113.

Americans are changing their attitudes toward death. Euthanasia, suicide, abortion, and capital punishment have become respectable. If population problems become unbearable, we may solve them in a final fashion.

Huxley, Aldous, *Perennial Philosophy*. New York: Har-Row, 1945.

The first two sections of this anthology are based largely on the writing of Eastern mystics. The author seeks to establish the essentials, recognized by all great religious systems. His is an attempt to find the "highest common factor" of religion by studying them and comparing them. Also sections on prayer, silence, mortification, self-knowledge, and spiritual exercises. A far-reaching and perennial source for those who wish to take this sweeping turn through the world's great religions.

James, William, *Varieties of Religious Experience*. New York: Longman, 1958.

A classic and still going strong. James studies and reports on the behavior pattern of those who seek religion. An excellent book. Read it in conjunction with Huxley's *Perennial Philosophy*.

*J Thanatology*, January-February, 1971.

Available, Foundation of Thanatology, 630 W. 168th St., New York, New York.

Keen, Sam, "The Heroics of Everyday Life: A Theorist of Death Confronts His Own End," *Psychology Today*, April, 1974, pp. 70–80.

A conversation with Ernest Becker. With his own death clearly in sight, the author of *The Denial of Death* discusses his theories, his belief in God, and his conclusion that mankind is abandoned on this planet. Concludes with a sketch of Ernest Becker.

Manwell, Elizabeth M. and Sophia L. Fahs, *Consider the Children: How They Grow*. Boston: Beacon Pr, 1960.

See Chapter 12, "When Death Comes."

A Unitarian approach.

Newland, Mary Reed, *We and Our Children*. New York: Macmillan, A Roman Catholic interpretation.

Nouwen, Henri J. M., *The Wounded Healer, Ministry in Contemporary Society*. Garden City, New York: Doubleday, 1972.

A moving book about the healing attempts made in our societies toward those suffering from the major anxieties of our time. Numerous, concrete examples. Finally, how these efforts affect the minister himself, "wounded so that he can help others."

Reik, Theodor, *Listening with the Third Ear*. New York: FS&G, 1948.

Russell, O. Ruth, *Freedom to Die, Moral and Legal Aspects of Euthanasia*. New York: Human Sci Pr, 1977.

Second edition which includes material on the Karen Quinlan case. Given an award in 1977 by the American Humanist Association.

Seabury, David, *The Art of Selfishness*. New York: S&S, 1971.

Sherill, Helen H. and J. Lewis, "Interpreting Death to Children," *Int J Religious Education*, October, 1951.

Smith, Huston, *The Religions of Man*. New York: Har-Row, 1965.

A clear and objective description of the great religions. Highly readable, highly recommended.

Thielicke, Helmut, *Death and Life*. Philadelphia: Fortress, 1970.

Toynbee, Arnold, and others, *Man's Concern with Death*. New York: Mc-Graw, 1968.

Contributors have written chapters on death and dying, concepts of death, dying and the doctor, death and the young. Another section deals with attitudes toward death, written mostly by Toynbee and Smart, including those attitudes found in Eastern religion, changing attitudes, inadequacies of Christian thought, and the decline of religion in the West.

Wuthnow, Robert and Charles Y. Glock, "A Survey Report: The Shifting Focus of Faith, God in the Gut," *Psychology Today*, November, 1974,pp. 131-36.

*Psychology Today's* Religion Questionnaire moved 40,000 readers to answer. God is alive, but their search is turning hard away from a Supreme Being out in space toward the inward and personal mysteries. Eastern insight, ESP, and the Occult are but part of a deeper, broader move to find the spiritual in the living self.

## THE STRESSFUL EMOTIONS:
## ANGER, ANXIETY, DEPRESSION, FEAR, ETC.

Abram, H. S. (Ed.), *Psychological Aspects of Stress*, Proceedings of a symposium sponsored by the University of Virginia School of Medicine and Medical Education for National Defense. Springfield, Thomas, 1970.

Seven specialists discuss psychological and physiological reactions in such stressful situations as disasters, life-threatening illness, combat, concentration camp, outer space.

Arieti, Silvano and Jules Bemporad, *Severe and Mild Depression*. New York: Basic, 1978.

Destined to become one of the classics in the field. Key concepts explored here are "Dominant Other" and the "Dominant Goal," both seen as part of the depressive personality's lifelong quest to recover a profound childhood loss. Also there is the concept of "Sorrow Work" which these authors believe is essential for preventing or relieving depression.

Baron, R. A., *The Tyranny of Noise*. New York: Har-Row, 1971.

The stress effects of various types of noise in our society, with special attention to noise in urban life, abuses of our technology and aviation, satistics in terms of health and dollars, means to avoid or minimize noise.

Bartley, S. H. and E. Chute, *Fatigue and Impairment in Man*. New York: McGraw, 1947.

Description of various types of specific organ system impairments and general fatigue. A great deal of empirical information.

Basowitz, H., H. Persky, S. J. Horchin, and R. R. Grinker, *Anxiety and Stress*. New York: McGraw, 1954.

Much documentation on anxiety in relation to stress.

Beier, Ernst G., "Nonverbal Communication: How We Send Emotional Messages," *Psychology Today,* October, 1974, pp. 52–60.

Actions do speak louder than words. Our faces, our intonations, the ways we hold our bodies often send emotional messages we do not intend — at least consciously.

Benson, Herbert, *The Relaxation Response.* New York: Morrow, 1975.

A medical doctor advocates combatting stress and pressure by relaxation through meditation.

Berman, E., *Scapegoat: The Impact of Death-Fear on an American Family.* Ann Arbor: U of Mich Pr, 1973.

Detailed account of a family faced with the father's illness and how the family uses the young son as a scapegoat for its problems until he becomes aggressive and unmanageable. Not for the general reader.

Cannon, W. B., *Bodily Changes in Pain, Hunger, Fear and Rage.* Newton Centre, Massachusetts: Bradford, 1953.

Classic observations of the manifestations of acute emotions upon the sympathetic nervous system and adrenaline secretion.

Casady, Margie, "Character Lasts But If You're Active and Savvy at 30, You'll be Warm and Witty at 70," *Psychology Today,* November, 1975, pp. 138.

We have our rocky years, but a 40-year study of several dozen people shows how healthy personalities adapt from youth to prime to the mellow years. But elderly agony often has roots in youth.

Cherry, Laurence, "On the Real Benefits of Eu-stress," *Psychology Today,* March, 1978, pp 60–63, 69–70.

An interview with Dr. Hans Selye of the International Institute of Stress, University of Montreal, who says we can use stress to our advantage.

Cohen, B. M., and M. Z. Cooper, *A Follow-up Study of World War II Prisoners of War.* Washington, D.C.: Veterans Administration Medical Monograph, 1954.

A statistical analysis of the survivors of Japanese and German prisons during World War II. Special attention to aftereffects following release or escape. Suggests lasting aftereffects.

Crammer, Leonard, *Up From Depression.* New York: S&S ,1971.

A very good presentation of what depression is, how it develops, different kinds, and how to cope with it.

Crary, William G. and Gerald G. Crary, "Depression," *J Nurs,* March, 1973, p. 475.

Notable for what the authors say about the use of tranquilizers and depressants during grief.

Danto, Bruce L., "Lecture National BBI National Academy," Quantico, Virginia, August, 1977.

Available from 466 Fisher Building, Detroit, Michigan.

Darwin, Charles, *The Expression of the Emotions in Man and Animals.* London: Murray, 1872.

DeRosis, Helen A. and Victoria Y. Pellegrino, *The Book of Hope, How Women Can Overcome Depression.* New York: Macmillan, 1976.

Not only a good book describing depression in women, but an excellent set of exercises for pulling one's self together, making decisions, using assertiveness, and increasing one's optimism.

Elkind, David and J. Herbert Hamsher, "The Anatomy of Melancholy," *Saturday Review,* September 30, 1972.

A good, short resume of depression and how it affects both young and old.

Engel, George, "Emotional Stress and Sudden Death,' *Psychology Today,* November 1977, pp. 114–20.

Farber, Leslie H., "Merchandising Depression," *Psychology Today,* April, 1979, pp. 63–64.

Does the cure contribute to the disease? A psychiatrist says that depression may be achieving celebrity status precisely because more remedies for it have come on the market.

Farber, S. M., P. Mustacchi and R. H. L. Wilson (Eds.), *Man Under Stress.* Berkeley: U of Cal Pr, 1964.

A University of California symposium (including Brock Chisholm, Rene Dubos, Seymour Farber, Stanley Sarnoff, Hans Seyle, Paul Dudley White) with discussions of aspects of stress in relation to the philosophy of life, social environment, cardiovascular disease, and space medicine. Not highly technical.

Fromm, Erich, *The Anatomy of Human Destructiveness.* New York: Fawcett World, 1973.

A classic discussion of aggressiveness and violence.

Gaylin, Willard (Ed.), *The Meaning of Despair.* New York: Aronson, 1968.

A good collection of articles on depression and despair.

Glass, David C., "Stress, Competition and Heart Attacks," *Psychology Today,* December, 1976, pp. 54–58.

Impatient, hard-driving men may control their environment and lives, but they win at the cost of risking heart disease.

Glass, D. C. and J. E. Singer, *Urban Stress: Experiments on Noise and Social Stressors.* New York and London: Acad Pr, 1972.

Socio-Psychological Prize of the American Association for the Advancement of Science. The effect of noise, mainly as a function of predictability and subject control.

Goleman, Daniel, "Meditation Helps Break the Stress Spiral," *Psychology Today*, Feburary, 1976, pp. 82–86, 93.

Stress is a disagreeable side effect of an active life. It is unavoidable and creates tension from one situation to another. Through a review of the work of Thomas H. Holmes, Hans Selye, and people who meditate, the author concludes that meditation (any brand) helps one to cope serenely.

Green, Hannah, *I Never Promised You a Rose Garden*. New York: HR &W, 1964.

A classic. Intimate account of the relationship between a knowledgeable therapist and a young girl who is schizophrenic.

Harris, T. George and Barbara B. Brown, "New Mind, New Body," *Psychology Today*, August, 1974, pp. 45-56, 74–112.

Condensation of Brown's new book on new field uses of biofeedback in the areas of moods, muscles, heartbeat and blood pressure, alpha waves.

Hill, R., "Generic Features of Families Under Stress," I. Social Stresses on Family, *Social Casework, 39:*139–50, 1958.

A conference on the behavior of families under stress sponsored by the Family Service Association of America and the Elizabeth McCormick Memorial Fund. An examination of stressor agents, hereditary predisposition, and interpersonal relationships which may affect adjustments to crises. Emphasis on advice to social agencies regarding policy and practice.

Hoff, Lee Ann, *People in Crisis*. Menlo Park, California: A-W, 1978.

Holmes, Thomas H. and Masuda, Mineru, "Psychosomatic Syndrome," *Psychology Today*, April, 1972.

Horn, Jack, "Bored to Sickness," *Psychology Today*, November, 1975.

High-pressure jobs can cause stress, but new research indicates that boring jobs can steal appetites, keep us awake, and lead to depression.

Huxley, Laura, *You Are Not the Target*. New York: FS&G, 1963.

Jacobi, Jerome H., "Reducing Police Stress: A Psychiatrist's Point of View," in U.S. Dept. of H.E.W., *Job Stress and the Police Officer*. December, 1975, p. 91.

Kempe, Ruth S. and C. Henry Kempe, *Child Abuse*. Cambridge, Massachusetts: Harvard U Pr, 1978.

Kennedy, J. A., *Relax and Live*. Englewood Cliffs, New Jersey: P-H, 1953.

A layman's approach to how to relax and avoid illness; good section on aging and the general adaptation syndrome.

Kirkham, George L., "The Metamorphosis," in U.S. Dept. of H.E.W., *Job Stress and the Police Officer*. December, 1975.

Klerman, Gerald L., "The Age of Melancholy," *Psychology Today*, April, 1979, pp. 36–42, 88.

Melancholy — ranging from ordinary sadness to severe depression — may be the most common psychological complaint of our times. The author is the nation's highest ranking mental health officer.

Kline, Nathan S., *From Sad to Glad*. New York: Random, 1975.

Koestenbaum, Peter, *Managing Anxiety*. New York: P-H, 1974.

Excellent.

Kraus, H., *Backache, Stress and Tension: Their Cause, Prevention and Treatment*. New York: S&S, 1965.

A popular book on the role of stress in causing backache; advice on physical therapy and exercise; illustrations.

Kroes, William H. and Joseph Hurrell (Eds.), "Job Stress and the Police Officer, Identifying Stress Reduction Techniques," Proceedings, Cincinnati, Ohio symposium, May, 1975. Washington, D. C.: U.S. Dept. of H.E.W., December, 1975.

Lande, Nathaniel, *Mindstyles/Lifestyles*. Los Angeles: Price Stern, 1976.

A comprehensive overview of today's life-changing philosophies. Introduction by Hans Seyle, conclusion by Buckminster Fuller, color illustrations by Corita Kent. A reference book for what is going on *now;* colorful thumbnail sketches of things you have heard about but are not sure what they are or what they do.

Lazarus, R. S., *Psychological Stress and the Coping Process*. New York and London: McGraw, 1966.

Very good discussion of stress, with special emphasis on coping with threatening situations.

Levi, L., *Stress: Sources, Management, and Prevention*. New York: Norton, 1967.

Exceptionally readable. Foreword by Hans Selye.

Levi, L. (Ed.), *Society, Stress and Disease*. New York and London: Oxford U Pr, 1971.

An international interdisciplinary symposium sponsored by the University of Uppsala and the WHO. An excellent review of recent ideas on the various somatic and psychic manifestations of stress. An unusual source for references.

Levine, S., "Stress and Behavior," *Scientific American, 224,* 1971.

Popular reading on role of pituitary and adrenal hormones in the regulation of behavior during the general adaptation syndrome.

Liebman, S. (Ed.), *Stress Situations*. Philadelphia: Lippincott, 1955. An Anthology of publications for laymen on the emotional reactions to stress of frustration, illness, catastrophes, marriage, fertility and sterility, divorce, death, and suicide.

Lindsey, Robert, *"Police Stress: Cause, Effect and Solution," Vita* (International Association for Suicide Prevention), December, 1977.

Deals with the awareness that concerns itself with the concept of the postkilling syndrome; defines the syndrome, outlines its effects on the officer, and supplies some practical remedies. A studied look at an important social problem.

Madow, Leo, *Anger.* London: Allen and Urwin, 1972.

Maslach, Christina, *Burnout,* Shanti Symposium, Second Annual Conference for physicians on Death and Dying, Berkeley, California, 1977.

May, Rollo, *The Meaning of Anxiety.* New York: Ronald, 1950.

A classic work dealing with the major approaches to the definition of anxiety. Excellent for professionals and/or investigators but probably too heavy going for the ordinary reader.

McKenna, M., *Revitalize Yourself! The Techniques of Staying Youthful.* New York: Hawthorn, 1972.

A popular book of practical advice on how to stay fit; section on Stress and Its Aging Effects; well illustrated; special attention to exercises.

Mehrabian, Albert, "The Three Dimensions of Emotional Reaction," *Psychology Today,* August, 1976, pp. 57–62.

Every feeling — anger, boredom, etc. — is some combination of arousal, pleasure, and dominance.

Minderman, John, "Traumatic Incident Reaction in Law Enforcement Officers," Behavioral Science Unit, FBI National Academy, Quantico, Virginia, 1977.

Mitchell, Ross, *Depression.* Harmondsworth, Middlesex, England: Penguin, 1975.

One of the best small books available.

Moskin, J. Robert, "Calling Dr. Stress," *Psychology Today,* September, 1977, pp. 93–105.

An interview with Dr. Louis Miller, chief national psychiatrist of Israel who relates how tensions affect a people's character.

*Newsweek,* "Coping with Depression," January 8, 1973.

O'Neill, Nena and George O'Neill, *Shifting Gears.* New York: Avon, 1975.

Paige, Karen E., "Women Learn to Sing the Menstrual Blues," *Psychology Today,* September, 1973.

An account of how not only a woman's biological clock tells of her discomfort, but society and religion pitch in taboos to make her feel restive, cramped, embarrassed, and unclean.

Roberts, Michael D., "Job Stress in Law Enforcement: A Treatment and Prevention Program," in U.S. Dept. of H.E.W., *Job Stress and the Police Officer,* Washington, D.C.: U.S. Dept. H.E.W., December, 1975, p. 228.

Rubin, Theodore Isaac, *The Angry Book.* New York: Macmillan, 1969.

The author of *David and Lisa* has written at length about anger, its origins, and where it leads. Don't miss reading this book.

Scarf, Maggie, "The More Sorrowful Sex," *Psychology Today,* April, 1979, pp. 45–52, 89–90.

The cultural reasons that two to five times as many women as men are likely to be diagnosed as depressed are those that relate to what "being feminine" requires. The author thinks the problem may be reaching epidemic proportions.

Seligman, Martin E. P., "Fall Into Helplessness," *Psychology Today,* June, 1973.

An explanation of how depression affects a person and pitches him into helplessness when he believes his actions make no difference.

Seyle, Hans, *Stress Without Distress.* Philadelphia: Lippincott, 1974.

A fine book about how to use stress as a positive force for personal achievement and happiness. His research in the physiology of stress has led him to a humane philosophy that allows one to be selfish as Nature intended and at the same time be altruistic and "earn our neighbor's love."

Singer, Jerome L., "Fantasy: The Foundation of Serenity," *Psychology Today,* July, 1976, pp. 32–38.

Fantasy does more than make life interesting, it may save us from violence, obesity, and dangerous drugs.

*Stress,* Blue Cross Plan Report, Vol. 25, no. 1. Oakland, California: Blue Cross, 1974.

Available from Blue Cross, 1950 Franklin Street, Oakland, California.

Suin, Richard M., "How to Break the Vicious Cycle of Stress," *Psychology Today,* December, 1976, pp. 59–60.

Four steps to breaking out of the Type-A rut, including detailed instructions in deep relaxation and in meditation. Tapes $7.95 each from PT Consumer Service Division, 595 Broadway, NY, NY 10012.

*Symposium on Stress.* Washington, D. C.: Army Medical Service Graduate School, 1958.

The hormonal and nervous regulation of stress responses in situations relating to combat, interpersonal relationships, nutrition, and catastrophic events.

Tanner, Ira J., *Loneliness: The Fear of Love.* New York: Har-Row, 1973.

Toffler, A., *Future Shock.* New York: Random, 1970.

A popular book dealing with the stressor effect of the continuous changes in our society and the way we either adapt or fail to adapt to the future. Several hundred references.

Tony 1277, London, "Take a Break," *Vita* (International Association for Suicide Prevention), December, 1977.

A personal account of the effects of burn-out in a volunteer in the Samaritans; his reactions, what he did, and how he adapted. Important reading for volunteers in continuing positions of "heavy" work with people in crisis.

Vaillant, George E., *Adaptation to Life.* New York: Little, 1977.

A study of the lives of young men from several successive classes of a liberal arts college from 1937 until the present. A mental health study to determine, by tests, questionnaires, dossiers, interviews, etc., how these most-likely-to-succeed young men cope with life. His thesis is that the difference between emotional health and some degree of emotional unhealthiness is the way individuals react to challenges, defeats, and sorrows. Precise accounts and life histories of promising men. Great stuff; too bad no women were included.

Viscott, David, *The Language of Feelings.* New York: Pocket Books, 1976.

How to understand your feelings of hurt and loss, anxiety, anger, guilt and depression. A readable simplistic book.

Visotsky, H. M., D. A. Hamburg, M. E. Goss and B. Z. Lebovits, "Coping Behavior Under Extreme Stress," *Arch Gen Psychiatry, 5:*423–48, 1961.

Observations on how patients with severe poliomyelitis adopt or fail to adapt.

Wolff, H. G. (Ed.), *Life Stress and Bodily Disease, Proceedings,* Association for Research in Nervous and Mental Diseases. Baltimore: Williams & Wilkins, 1950.

Papers on life stress; headaches; disorders of growth, development, and metabolism; diseases of the eye, respiratory passages, gastrointestinal tract, locomotor apparatus, cardiovascular system, skin, and genital organs.

———, *Stress and Disease,* 2nd ed., revised and edited by S. Wolf and H. Goodell. Springfield: Thomas, 1968.

The decisive role adaptive reactions play in man's resistance to common stressors in modern life; part played by stress in headache, migraine, respiratory, cardiovascular, and digestive diseases; role of social adjustment and a philosophy of life.

## SUDDEN DEATH

Allen, Nancy H., "Epidemiology and Prevention of Homicide," an unpublished paper presented at the American Association of Suicidology, Annual Meeting, New Orleans, 1978.

Bergman, Abraham, Margaret Pomeroy, and Bruce Beckwith, "The Psychiatric Toll of the Sudden Infant Death Syndrome," *GP, 50*(6), 99–105, December, 1969.

Casady, Margie, "The Sleepy Murderers," *Psychology Today,* January, 1976, pp. 79–80.

Sufferers of a rare condition (dysomnia) called sleep drunkenness can kill without knowing what they are doing. Roused suddenly from deep sleep, they erupt into violence.

Dahlberg, Charles Clay, "Stroke," *Psychology Today,* June, 1977, pp. 121–128.

A psychiatrist who has had the personal experience describes the effects of his own stroke and how it changed his life.

Friedman, Stanford, "Psychological Aspects of Sudden Unexpected Death in Infants and Children," *Pediatr Clin North Am, 21*(1), 113–114, 1974.

Green, Morris, "Psychological Aspects of Sudden Unexpected Death in Infants and Children, Review and Commentary," *Pediatr Clin North Am, 21*(1), 113–114, 1974.

Halpern, Werner, "Some Psychiatric Sequelae to Crib Death," *Am J Psychiatry, 129*(4), 398–402, October, 1972.

Kaplan, David M. and Edward A. Mason, "Maternal Reactions to Premature Birth Viewed as an Acute Emotional Disorder," in Parad, Howard (Ed.), *Crisis Intervention: Selected Readings.* Family Service Association of America, 1965.

Lee, Melvin, Philip G. Zimbardo, and Minerva Bertholt, "Shy Murderers," *Psychology Today,* November, 1977, pp. 68–78.

Frustrated and belittled past endurance, they believe there is no way out of their pain or, rather, no *other* way out.   Suddenly, they attack.

Liebgold, Howard B., "Motorcycles — The Two-Wheeled Monster," *Planning for Health, 20*(2), 1977.

Lundberg, Alan, "Poisonings, How Parents Can Prevent Accidents," *Planning for Health, 20*(4), 1977.

Lunde, Donald T., "Our Murder Boom," *Psychology Today,* July, 1975, pp. 35–42.

———, Interview with Nancy Faber of *People,* regarding "Son of Sam," Spring, 1977.

———, *Murder and Madness.*   San Francisco: SF BK Co, 1976.

Rising expectations and economic frustrations lead us to kill each other, and July is a peak month for murder.   The most likely murderer is a victim's relative, but felony murders are surging.

Mahoney, John, Diane Kyle and Gary Katz, "The Anticipation of Death by Violence: A Psychological Profile," *Life-Threatening Behavior, 5*(2), Summer, 1975.

A study of college students anticipating sudden violent death vs. those anticipating natural death shows that the former were characteristically more anxious and socially isolated.   Females in the former group are more likely to "give up" in response to stress.   Several personality factors may be associated with violent death.

Moyer, K. E., "Allergy and Aggression: The Physiology of Violence," *Psychology Today,* July, 1975, pp. 76–79.

Food allergies can produce irritability, quarrels, or murderous attacks.   Understanding the violence that follows when a sufferer eats forbidden bananas can help us decipher the causes of human aggression.

Muson, Howard, "Teenage Violence and the Telly," *Psychology Today, 11* (10):50–54.

A report of a CBS-sponsored British study that demonstrates a link between TV violence and teenage violence.

Patterson, Kathy and Margaret Pomeroy, "Nursing Care Begins After Death When the Disease is: Sudden Infant Death Syndrome," *Nursing,* May, 1974, pp. 85–88.

Pattison, E. Mansell, *The Experience of Dying.* Englewood Cliffs, New Jersey: P-H, 1977.

An excellent book dealing with interviews or accounts of dying behavior among the chronically ill, accident victims, and victims of sudden illness, from children and adolescents to adults and the elderly. Shows how death affects the family structure and explores the source of guilt feelings survivors often experience.

Schieffelin, John W., "Drowning: Common Sense Can Protect Your Family," *Planning for Health, 20*(3), 1977.

Serrill, Michael S., "A Cold New Look at the Criminal Mind," *Psychology Today, 11*(9):86–92, 106, February, 1978.

Report on a 16-year study which indicates that criminals are not the products of society; they can be spotted at an early age by their "errors of thinking."

Vollman, R. R., A. Ganzert, L. Picher, and W. V. Williams, "The Reactions of Family Systems to Sudden and Unexpected Death," *Omega,* May, 1971.

Wright, H. T., *The Matthew Tree.* New York: Random, 1975.

An excellent treatment of a stroke victim.

## SUICIDE

Allen, Nancy H., *Suicide in California, 1960–1970.* Sacramento: California State Department of Public Health, 1973.

Billings, James H., David H. Hansen, Chris Asimos, and Jerome A. Motto, "Observations on Long-term Group Therapy with Suicidal and Depressed Persons," *Life-Threatening Behavior, 4*(3), Fall, 1974.

Account of a long-term, open-ended group of 200 depressed and suicidal persons with previous attempts. Includes recommendations for starting such groups and "emphasizes that this method of therapy appears to be an effective mode of suicide prevention."

Cain, Albert, "Survivors of Suicide: Current Findings and Future Directions," *Proceedings,* 6th International Conference on Suicide Prevention, Mexico City, pp. 192–198. Ann Arbor, Michigan: Edward Brothers, Inc., 1968.

A good brief summary of what appears later in his book. Feels deeply the vulnerability of suicide survivors. Gives several kinds of reactions to suicide by their survivors that are commonly encountered.

—— (Ed.), *Survivors of Suicide.* Springfield: Thomas, 1972.

A valuable book by an author concerned with the suffering of the victims of the suicidal act. Devotes a large portion of book to the children whose parent suicides; children who suicide leaving parents; marital partners. How the intensity or degree of relationship affects the impact of grief; the data and motivation of the suicide. The best book directed toward the survivors of suicide.

Danto, Bruce L., "Firearm Suicide in the Home Setting," *Proceedings,* 6th International Conference on Suicide Prevention, Mexico City, pp. 388–92. Ann Arbor, Michigan: Edward Brothers Inc., 1968.

——, "Firearms and Their Role in Homicide and Suicide," *Life-Threatening Behavior, 1*(1), Spring, 1971.

Firearms and deaths by suicide, homicide, and/or accidental means in Detroit and Wayne County; the profile of the victims; the preference for handguns; need for more inquiry into suicidal behavior and behavior of the family by police and investigating officers.

—— (Ed.), *Jailhouse Blues.* Orchard Lake, Michigan: Epic Pubns, 1973.

An examination of the psychology of the offender and the study of suicidal behavior, the jail setting, those in the prison situation, and in the hospital for the criminally insane. Conditions in jails and in prisons, including rampant homosexuality, deterrence to crime, factors leading to suicide, the role of guards, etc. Also material on countries outside the United States. Some articles by inmates. Good, readable.

Dizmang, Larry, "Self-Destructive Behavior in Children: A Suicidal Equivalent," *Proceedings,* 4th International Conference for Suicide Prevention, Los Angeles, 1967, pp. 316–20.

An excellent paper by a NIMH doctor. Should be must reading for all physicians dealing with young children.

Dorpat, T. L., "Suicide, Loss, and Mourning," *Life-Threatening Behavior, 3*(3), Fall, 1973.

Intensive treatment of six suicidal patients is used to explore the relationships among object loss, the mourning process, and suicide. Covers how to work through arrested mourning reactions, survivor guilt, and developmental defects and their implications for treatment.

Doyle, Polly, "The Anniversary Interview in Grief Counseling for the Survivors of Suicide," *Proceedings,* 8th Annual Meeting, American Association of Suicidology, St. Louis, Missouri, pp. 27–32. Houston, Texas: American Association of Suicidology, 1976.

——, "Grief Counseling for Children," in Danto, Bruce, *Suicide and Bereavement,* New York: Arno, 1977.

Durkheim, Emile, *Suicide, A Study in Sociology.* Translated by Spaulding and Simpson. New York: Macmillan, 1951.

The major prototype of systematic attack on suicide by means of data, techniques and knowledge. Written in the last decade of the nineteenth century, but his views still cannot be disregarded.

Faigel, H., "Suicide Among Young Persons: A Review of Its Incidence and Causes and Methods of Its Prevention," *Clin Pediatr,* 5:187–90, 1966.

Recommended reading.

Farberow, N. L. and E. S. Shneidman, *Cry for Help.* New York: McGraw, 1961.

—— (Ed.), *Suicide in Different Cultures.* Baltimore: University Park Pr, 1975.

Compilation of expanded versions of papers presented at the 6th International Congress of Suicidology at Mexico City in December, 1971. Cross-cultural research; descriptions and explanations of suicide in particular cultures; etiological findings. Points out the necessity for standardizing data collection procedure and conceptual tools for further development.

Finch, Stuart and Elva O. Poznanski, *Adolescent Suicide.* Springfield: Thomas, 1972.

Written for professionals who deal with emotionally disturbed adolescents. Covers various aspects of suicidal behavior: the act, types of adolescents who are suicidal, history and family background, relationship between aggressive behavior and suicide, and special groups such as college students. Also deals with assessment and management of suicidal behavior.

Folinsbee, Marjory C., "Time Passes — A History of Two Suicidally Oriented Adolescents," Proceedings, 4th International Conference for Suicide Prevention, Los Angeles, 1967, pp. 391–95.

Two teenagers are examined in depth by the doctor who treated them. Interesting family conflicts which are often the beginning of the depression that leads to threats or attempts.

French, Alfred P. and Margaret Steward, "Family Dynamics, Childhood Depression, and Attempted Suicide in a 7-Year-Old Boy: A Case Study," *Life-Threatening Behavior,* 5(1), Spring, 1975.

Reviews the literature in areas of suicidal behavior and depression in children. Gives family dynamics of a suicidal attempt of a young boy and the course of treatment.

Haim, A., *Adolescent Suicide.* New York: Intl Univs Pr, 1974.

Recommended reading; ranks alongside Cain's book.

Hendin, Herbert, *Recognition and Treatment of Potentially Suicidal Persons.* New York: The Social Psychiatry Institute,

Available from The Social Psychiatry Institute, 150 East 69th St., New York, New York, 10021.

Herzog, Alfred and H. L. P. Resnik, "A Clinical Study of Parental Response to Adolescent Death by Suicide," *Proceedings*, 4th International Conference for Suicide Prevention, Los Angeles, 1967, pp. 381–90.

Limited number of cases does not permit any valid statistical analysis, but the paper gives excellent insights into the family problems, parental responses to loss and grief. A few cases given.

Huffine, Carol L., "Equivocal Single-Auto Traffic Fatalities," *Life-Threatening Behavior, 1*(2), Summer, 1971.

Comparison of drivers involved in equivocal traffic accidents and drivers involved in other fatal traffic accidents. While some of the findings are suggestive of suicide, there is not strong evidence in this direction. Characteristics differentiating between equivocal accident victims and other drivers involved in fatal accidents do exist.

Jacobs, Jerry, *Adolescent Suicide*. New York: Wiley, 1971.

A book written for clinicians and others whose disciplines deal with the problems of human behavior. Declares unwarranted the traditional explanations of adolescent suicide as being forms of irrational, maladaptive, or impulsive act; states firmly that these acts result from conscious, rational choice.

Klagsbrun, Francine, *Too Young to Die, Youth and Suicide*. Boston: Houghton Mifflin, 1976.

A book for both parents and young people to read. It calls attention to an important area of human experience — when we fail in our efforts to support adolescents.

Litman, Robert, "Acutely Suicidal Patients: Management in Clinical Practice," *California Med, 104*:168–74, 1966.

Required reading for professionals; interesting and helpful for others.

——, "Police Aspects of Suicide," *Police*, January-February, 1966.

Litman, Robert, Theodore Curphey, Edwin S. Shneidman, Norman L. Farberow, and Norman Tabachnick, "Investigations of Equivocal Suicides," *JAMA, 184*:924–29, June 22, 1963.

Deals with the uncertainty about the correct certification results when the victim's intention is ambivalent, when the self-destructive action is inconclusive, or when death follows the action after considerable delay.

Litman, Robert E. and Norman Tabachnick, "Fatal One Car Accidents," *The Psychoanal Q, 36*: 248, 259, 1967.

Motto, J., "The Recognition and Management of the Suicidal Patient," in Flach, F. and S. Draghi (Eds.), *The Nature and Treatment of Depression*. New York: Wiley, 1975, pp. 229–54.

A former president of the American Association of Suicidology, Dr. Motto has done extensive research in the area of depression and the suicidal person. Required reading.

——, "Treatment and Management of Suicidal Adolescents," *Psychiatric*

*Opinion, 12*:14–20, July, 1975.

Recommended reading.

———, "Suicide Prevention for High-Risk Persons Who Refuse Treatment," *Suicide and Life-Threatening Behavior, 6*(4), Winter, 1976.

A large-scale study of suicidal or depressive patients admitted for in-patient service to determine if postdischarge plan was followed. The divergence between the contact and no contact groups provides tentative evidence that a high-risk population for suicide can be identified and that a systematic approach to reducing that risk can be applied.

Motto, Jerome A., Richard M. Brooks, Charlotte Ross, and Nancy H. Allen, *Standards for Suicide Prevention and Crisis Centers.* New York: Behavioral Pubns, 1974.

A good selection of topics on standards that need to be emphasized in the daily work of a crisis center.

Motto, J. and E. Stein, "A Group Approach to Guilt in Depressive and Suicidal Patients," *J Religion and Health, 12*:378–85, 1973.

Recommended reading for persons dealing with depression and guilt in suicidal persons.

Murphy, George, "Clinical Identification of Suicide Risk, *Arch Gen Psychiatry, 27*:356–59, 1972.

Directed toward professionals but important for others as well.

Parker, A. Morgan, *Suicide Among Young Adults.* Hicksville, New York: Exposition, 1974.

Rev. Parker deals with various aspects of the subject, but much of his data is old, sometimes even inaccurate; relies too much on old information instead of more contemporary sources of information.

Patel, N.S., "Life Style of the Completed Suicide," *Proceedings,* 6th International Conference on Suicide Prevention, Mexico City, pp. 158–64. Ann Arbor, Michigan: Edward Brothers, Inc., 1968.

An English doctor looks at the configuration of factors in suicide; looks also at attempters vs. completers and their life-styles.

Peck, J. and R. Litman, *Current Trends in Youthful Suicide.* Tribuna Media, 1975.

Peck, Michael L., "Two Suicide Syndromes — Discarded Women and Adolescent Crisis." Paper presented at annual meeting of the American Psychological Association in San Francisco, California, September, 1968.

Peck, Michael L. and Richard H. Seiden, "Youth Suicide," *Exchange, 3*(2): 17–20, May/June, 1975.

Required reading for all suicide prevention centers. Brief summaries of psychodynamic factors, characteristics of suicidal youngsters, how to detect and assess suicidality.

Pikorny, Alex D., James P. Smith, and John R. Finch, "Vehicular Suicides," *Life-Threatening Behavior, 2*(2), Summer, 1972.

An intensive study of twenty-eight consecutive auto crash fatalities, 4 of which were suicides. Revealed a pattern of alcoholism, depression, impulsiveness, and acute emotional upheavals of drivers. Concludes that a discernible portion of auto accidents are suicides.

Pretzel, Paul W., "Two Suicidal Syndromes: The Malignant Masochist and the Harlequin." Paper presented at the American Psychological Association in San Francisco, California, 1968.

———, *Understanding and Counseling the Suicidal Person.* Nashville: Abingdon, 1972.

Good book.

Price, R., *Permanent Errors.* New York: Atheneum, 1970.

Reuveni, Uri, *Networking Families in Crisis.* New York: Human Sci Pr, 1978.

How to mobilize the extended system of family, relatives, friends, and neighbors for helping a family during times of emotional crisis. A description of results in constructive change in situations that had previously seemed beyond the scope of professional guidance. Especially good for workers in field of crisis intervention.

Rosen, D., "Suicide Survivors: Psychotherapeutic Implications of Egocide," *Life-Threatening Behavior, 6:*209–215, 1976.

Important reading for professionals; effective and helpful for others as well.

Rosenbaum, Milton and Joseph Richman, "Family Dynamics and Drug Overdoses," *Life-Threatening Behavior, 2*(1), Spring, 1972.

A study of 40 patients who overdosed and 18 of their relatives. The pattern of family factors that appeared relevant; author's discussion of them: expectation of the family, identification with another suicidal family member, high level of oral preoccupation, trauma in life.

Ross, Charlotte and A. Russell Lee, *Suicide in Youth and What You Can Do About It.* West Point, Pennsylvania: Am Assn Suicidology, 1977.

A small pamphlet directed toward school personnel but excellent also for all agencies and persons involved in youth counseling. Who is a risk, why, what do I do? Danger signs, how to get help, and what not to do.

Seiden, Richard H., "Campus Tragedy: A Study of Student Suicide," *J Abnorm Psychol, 71,* 1966.

———, "Current Developments in Minority Group Suicidology," *JBHP,* August/September, 1974.

A compilation of recent research in area of minority group suicides, statistical tables and graphs illustrating the current situation and trends since World War II, conclusions and recommendations based on these findings. Required reading for persons dealing with minorities.

———, "Suicide: Preventable Death," A Public Affairs Report of University of California, Berkeley: Institute of Governmental Studies, Vol. 15, no. 4, August, 1974.

This report identifies the groups at high risk, what can be done through public policy measures, the suicide prevention movement. Required reading by all suicide prevention center personnel.

———, "Suicide Prevention: A Public Health/Public Policy Approach," *Omega, 8*(3), 267–76, 1977.

An important and timely presentation of a public health/public policy model to prevent suicide through community action and legislative change in the availability of such lethal instruments as firearms, drugs, poisons and gases, and barriers to such places as high buildings and bridges.

Shneidman, Edwin S., *The Study of Lives.* New York: Atherton Pr, 1963.

——— (Ed.), *On the Nature of Suicide.* San Francisco: Jossey-Bass, 1969.

———, "Perterbation and Lethality as Precursors of Suicide in a Gifted Group," *Life-Threatening Behavior, 1*(1), Spring, 1971.

An analysis of 30 cases for whom longitudinal personality data were available from 1921-1960. 5 had suicided, 10 died natural deaths, and 15 were still living. Deals with instability, trauma and personality controls, significant others, and the "burning out" effect.

———, "Postvention and the Survivor-Victim," *Proceedings,* 6th International Conference on Suicide Prevention, Mexico City, pp. 31–39. Ann Arbor, Michigan: Edward Brothers, Inc., 1972.

The best, most brief guide for working with survivors of suicide.

———, "The Survivors of Death," in Shneidman, Edwin S. (Ed.), *Death: Current Perspectives.* Palo Alto, California: Mayfield Pub, 1976.

A section of the book has papers by Toynbee, Parkes, Shneidman, and Silverman. The book itself is a compendium of papers on cultural, societal, interpersonal, and personal aspects of death. An abundance of papers by leaders in their fields.

Shneidman, Edwin S., Norman L. Farberow, and Robert E. Litman, *The Psychology of Suicide.* New York: Science House, 1970.

A formidable volume of 44 articles. Picks up on the "dependent-dissatisfied" behavior pattern that predisposes to suicide, the psychological autopsy, and much, much more. Excellent.

Shneidman, Edwin S. and Philip Mandelkorn, *How to Prevent Suicide.* Public Affairs Pamphlet No. 406, Public Affairs Committee, Inc., August, 1967.

Stone, H. W., *Suicide and Grief.* Philadelphia: Fortress, 1972.

Sullivan, Patricia, "Suicide by Mistake," *Psychology Today,* October, 1976, pp. 90–92.

The system failed Steven Karagianis. Despite the help of a corps of professionals, he ended his short life in a Yonkers jail.

Tabachnick, Norman, "Self-Destruction in Automobile Accident: A Psychoanalytic Research Report," *Proceedings,* 6th International Conference on Suicide Prevention, Mexico City, pp. 132–35. Ann Arbor, Michigan: Edward Brothers, Inc., 1968.

A well-balanced report in which the author concludes that specific cases of self-destruction may have contributed to much distortion of previous research.

Tabachnick, Norman, John Gussen, Robert E. Litman, Michael L. Peck, Norman Tiber, and Carol I. Wold, "Accident or Suicide? Destruction by Automobile," *Life-Threatening Behavior, 5*(4), Winter, 1975.

More on the ongoing conjecture that some traffic accidents may have a suicidal aspect. This is a research report on a series of studies (NIMH). The authors reverse earlier beliefs and say they believe a very small proportion of crashes may have a self-desrtuctive component and are baffled by the result. Increased alcohol intake from two days to a few hours preceding accident but no blood alcohol data are given.

Varah, Chad (Ed.), *The Samaritans in the 70s.* (Revised ed.). London: Constable, 1977.

One part deals with the birth and phenomenal growth and spread of The Samaritans; the greater part of the book is by professionals and experienced Samaritans who relate their findings in various fields of psychiatry, drug treatment, counseling, and related areas. Excellent and readable.

Wallace, Samuel E., *After Suicide.* New York: Wiley, 1973.

An account of interviews with a group of widows of suicide. Good in spots, but arrangement of book makes keeping track of the widows a bit frustrating.

Weis, Sandra and Richard H. Seiden, "Rescuers and the Rescued: A Study of Suicide Prevention Center Volunteers and Clients by Means of a Death Questionnaire," *Life-Threatening Behavior, 4*(2), Summer, 1974.

A comparative analysis of these two groups revealed substantial differences between volunteers and clients. Volunteers were older, better educated, had greater emotional stability, almost no suicide attempts and were not inclined to consider suicide as a justifiable problem-solving option.

Weisz, Alfred E., Donald C. Straight, Peter Houts, and Michael P. Voten, "Suicide Threats, Suicide Attempts and the Emergency Psychiatrist," *Proceedings,* 4th International Conference for Suicide Prevention, Los Angeles, 1967, pp. 227–41.

First-year residents examine and compare 199 patients who were seen over a six-month period following the initial emergency. Good suggestions on coping strategy and suggested follow-up.

Welu, T. C., "Broadening the Focus of Suicide Prevention Activities Utilizing the Public Health Model," *Am J Public Health, 62*(12):1625–28, 1972.

———, "A Follow-up Program for Suicide Attempters: Evaluation of Effectiveness," *Life-Threatening Behavior, 7*(1):17–30, Spring, 1977.

## THERAPY AND COUNSELING

Billings, James, D. Rosen, C. Asioms, and J. Motto, "Observations on Long-term Group Therapy with Suicidal and Depressed Persons," *Life-Threatening Behavior, 2*:239–51, 1972.

Coleman, James C., *Abnormal Psychology and Modern Life,* 4th ed. Glenview, Illinois: Scott F, 1972.

A good textbook approach to abnormal psychology; helpful for the non-professional.

Combs, A., D. Avila, and W. Purkey, *Helping Relationships: Basic Concepts for the Helping Professions.* Boston: Allyn, 1971.

An excellent guide for the new counselor.

Eysenck, H. J. and S. Rachman, *The Causes and Cures of Neurosis.* San Diego: Knapp, 1965.

A good overview of that large catchment basin known as neurosis.

Fabry, Joseph B., *The Pursuit of Meaning.* Boston: Beacon Pr, 1968.

A readable book for anyone interested in the purpose of life. It sets out to popularize Dr. Frankl's logotherapy, to simplify its theories and to "Americanize" its practice by focusing on those aspects that speak to American readers of today. Preface by Viktor Frankl.

Farberow, Norman, "Vital Process in Suicide Prevention: Group Psychotherapy as a Community Concern," *Life-Threatening Behavior, 2,* 1972.

Glasser, William, *Reality Therapy.* New York: Har-Row, 1965.

———, The Identity Society. New York: Har-Row, 1972.

Koch, Joanne and Lew Koch, "A Consumer's Guide to Therapy for Couples," *Psychology Today,* March, 1976, pp. 33–40.

Marriage therapists treat couples with concentrated techniques that come from sex labs, behavioral research, and humanistic psychology. These authors tell what to watch out for in the coming therapy market.

Kopp, Sheldon B., *If You Meet the Buddha on the Road, Kill Him!* New York and London: Bantam, 1976.

MacKinnon, R. A. and R. Michels, *The Psychiatric Interview in Clinical Practice.* Philadelphia: Saunders, 1971.

A good overview of what the professional does.

Mayer, D., "Psychiatric Approach to the Suicidal Patient," *Br J Psychiatry, 119:*629–33, 1971.

Interprets the components of the suicidal wish, demonstrates her concern for the patient and the need for the autonomy of the patient — autonomy vs. "rescue."

Mendel, W., *The Suicidal Patient in Supportive Care.* Santa Monica, California: Mara, 1975.

Especially good reading about the chronically suicidal patient; not much on the schizophrenic patient.

Mintz, R., "Basic Considerations in the Psychotherapy of the Depressed Suicidal Patients," *J Psychotherapy, 25,* 1971.

Motto, J. and E. Stein, "A Group Approach to Guilt in Depressive and Suicidal Patients," *J Religion and Health, 12,* 1973.

Rogers, Carl, *Client-Centered Therapy.* Boston: Houghton Mifflin, 1951.

An excellent text approach, good for professionals and nonprofessionals alike.

Steinzor, Bernard, *The Healing Partnership.* New York: Har-Row, 1967.

How the client and the therapist can work together toward a healing resolution. Very good.

Szasz, T., *The Myth of Mental Illness.* Secker and Warburg, 1961.

An exciting, provocative book about mental illness which catapulted the author into vigorous debate with numerous persons of the psychiatric persuasion.

Traux, C. and R. Carkhuff, *Toward Effective Counseling and Psychotherapy: Training and Practice.* Chicago: Aldine, 1967.

Travis, L. and D. Baruch, *Personal Problems of Everyday Living.* New York: Appleton, 1941.

## TRAINING SKILLS

Danish, Steven and Allen L. Hauer, *Helping Skills, A Basic Training Program.* New York: Human Sci Pr, 1973.

A teaching tool for paraprofessional, human service, and social service personnel. Emphasis on six basic skills for enhancing their helping abilities. Includes a trainee workbook and a leader's manual.

DeMott, Benjamin, "The Day the Volunteers Didn't," *Psychology Today, 11*(10):23–24, 131–32.

A journalist looks at the social, political, and economic forces that could result in the "death by erosion" of the American tradition of "voluntarism."

Kahn, R. L. and C. F. Cannell, *The Dynamics of Interviewing.* New York: Wiley, 1957.

An older book that is quite good, if one can forgive the term "interviewing."

Kennedy, Eugene, *On Becoming a Counselor.* New York: Seabury, 1977.

An excellent basic guide for the beginning counselor.

Lester, David and Gene Brockopp, *Crisis Intervention and Counseling by Telephone*. Springfield: Thomas, 1973.

A must manual for all telephone counseling and crisis situations.

Lowen, Alexander and Leslie Alexander, *The Way to Vibrant Health, A Manual of Biogen Exercises*. New York: Har-Row, 1977.

Do-it-yourself exercises to help bring about a positive effect upon energy, mood, work. Not a substitute for needed therapy.

Parad, H. J., *Crisis Intervention: Selected Readings*. New York: Family Serv, 1965.

Rogers, Carl, *On Becoming a Person*. Boston: Houghton Mifflin, 1961.

An eminent teacher, therapist, and writer gives a good account of how to become yourself.

Satir, Virginia, *Conjoint Family Therapy*. Palo Alto, California: Science & Behavior, 1967.

An excellent book for counselors.

Snyder, W. U. et al., *Casebook of Non-Directive Counseling*. Boston: Houghton Mifflin, 1947.

Vriend, John and Wayne Dyer, "Counseling the Reluctant Client," *J Counseling Psychology, 20*(3), 240–46, 1973.

What to do, what not to do, and how to bring out the client.

# INDEX